JEWISH PHILOSOPHY AND PSYCHOANALYSIS

JEWISH PHILOSOPHY AND PSYCHOANALYSIS

Narrating the Interhuman

Michael Oppenheim

LEXINGTON BOOKS

A division of
ROWMAN & LITTLEFIELD PUBLISHERS, INC.
Lanham • Boulder • New York • Toronto • Oxford

LEXINGTON BOOKS

A division of Rowman & Littlefield Publishers, Inc.
A wholly owned subsidiary of The Rowman & Littlefield Publishing Group, Inc.
4501 Forbes Boulevard, Suite 200
Lanham, MD 20706

PO Box 317
Oxford
OX2 9RU, UK

British Library Cataloguing in Publication Information Available

Library of Congress Cataloging-in-Publication Data

Oppenheim, Michael.
Jewish philosophy and psychoanalysis : narrating the interhuman / Michael Oppenheim.
p. cm.
Includes bibliographical references and index.
ISBN-13: 978-0-7391-1697-5 (cloth : alk. paper)
ISBN-10: 0-7391-1697-5 (cloth : alk. paper)
1. Philosophy, Jewish. 2. Judaism and psychoanalysis. 3. Psychoanalysis and philosophy. I. Title.
B5802.P75 O67 2006
181'.06—dc22 2006010210

Printed in the United States of America

∞™ The paper used in this publication meets the minimum requirements of American National Standard for Information Sciences—Permanence of Paper for Printed Library Materials, ANSI/NISO Z39.48-1992.

In memory of my parents
Maxine Roth Oppenheim and Cecil Oppenheim

Contents

Foreword

THIS WORK HAS HAD A LONG LABOR and is a product of two loves: modern Jewish philosophy and post-Freudian psychoanalysis. Throughout my academic career I have been exploring the ways that the self is fashioned through interaction with and indebtedness to the other. In examining subjectivity through intersubjectivity, two disciplines or discourses have fascinated me. What Jewish philosophers term the domain of the interhuman and what post-Freudian psychoanalysts label the field of the interpersonal identify engaging and fruitful approaches to the complex, partially hidden and partially revealed, life of persons with other persons.

Jewish Philosophy and Psychoanalysis represents the first major effort to examine and compare selected streams within these two disciplines in terms of this focus. It does not presuppose that the reader has familiarity with either, not to mention both, discourses. In light of the wide scope, including the introduction, examination, and comparison of nine individual thinkers, the level of analysis must be limited. There are certainly interesting and important dimensions of these theorists that are not delineated, in terms of both primary and secondary sources, in a way that books of narrower range would achieve.

Initiating a dialogue between modern Jewish philosophy and post-Freudian psychoanalysis presents fundamental challenges to both disciplines, despite the common theme of the life with others. Contemporary scholars in the two disciplines may be wary of such a dialogue. For modern Jewish philosophers, there is the presupposition that psychoanalysts cannot speak of human meaning or the nature of the human in a sophisticated way. They see psychoanalysts as possibly introducing interesting empirical descriptions of various types of interactions, but believe they cannot contribute to the philosophical discussions of the questions, values, and goals that delineate what it means to be a person. For the psychoanalysts, the possible contribution of modern Jewish philosophy is also circumscribed. Even if they respect some of their insights about the interhuman, the religious language of these Jewish philosophers is often ignored or dismissed. Psychoanalysts can recognize philosophic ideas that are compatible with their theories, but the term "God" will not compute. This book tries to meet these obstacles to dialogue. It attempts to demonstrate that the psychoanalysts present a tremendously fertile array of ideas and insights about the interhuman that directly address issues of meaning and the human enterprise overall. It also hopes to show that the use of the term "God" is integral to the Jewish philosophers and that the term opens up special dimensions of the human—the transcendent possibilities of the interhuman—that are unavailable to other languages. Only by surveying and comparing the two discourses can these features become visible. The discussion of Martin Buber's notion of the human as "fettered surprise" is one of the ways that the strengths and weaknesses of each discipline is explored. The assessment of the significance of the project and the success of the dialogue, I happily entrust to my readers.

I want to thank Mercer University Press for permission to reprint some material in chapter one that earlier appeared in the chapter, "Four Narratives of the Interhuman: Kierkegaard, Buber, Rosenzweig, and Levinas," in *International Kierkegaard Commentary: Works of Love*, vol. 16, edited by Robert L. Perkins.

In a book about what one receives from the other, the feature of the author's acknowledgments must always be an understatement. I have been graced with innumerable meetings and discussions with colleagues, students, friends, and family that have deeply enriched me and affected this project in both calculable and incalculable ways. I would like to specifically note a few names. Barbara Galli's scholarship on Franz Rosenzweig and enduring friendship has taught, inspired, and supported me for many decades. Intricate exchanges about Jewish philosophy and contemporary theology with Marc Lalonde never failed to be stimulating. Norma Joseph's deep commitments to Judaism and to feminism have left enduring impressions on all my work. I have studied psychoanalytic and philosophic material with three graduate students, Patricia Saxton, Gordon Aronoff, and Heather MacDow, and have always come away with more than I was able to give. James DiCenso of the University of Toronto, as well as Patricia Saxton, Gordon Aronoff, and David Oppenheim have read through various versions of this book and offered important corrections and insights. Discussions concerning Freud and Lacan with a good friend, Moshe Peled, never ceased to stimulate and challenge. Of course, nothing would be the same without the unfaltering support of my wife, Sarah Uriash, and children, David and Aaron.

Michael Oppenheim
Montreal, 2005

Introduction

An Apology

> Apology, in which the I at the same time asserts itself and inclines before the transcendent, belongs to the essence of conversation. (Levinas 1969, 40)

WHAT DOES IT MEAN TO BE HUMAN? What roles do others play in the coming to be of the self? What types of narratives can best present the stories of the self with others? How might complementary sets of narratives reveal the complexity of that dynamic between human and interhuman?

This book sets the stage and then puts into place a dialogue. The dialogue is between modern Jewish philosophy and post-Freudian psychoanalysis. The book explores the models of human development, or better, the clusters of narratives about what it means to be a person with other persons that emerge in the discourses of these two disciplines. Through vivid narrative accounts a stream of modern Jewish philosophy and prominent post-Freudian psychoanalytic theorists detail relationships between the human and the interhuman.

The narratives of three twentieth-century Jewish philosophers—Franz Rosenzweig, Martin Buber, and Emmanuel Levinas—are the foci for the presentation of the discourse of modern Jewish philosophy. The second discourse brings together models of the self and others that have an important place in contemporary psychoanalytic discussions. These include the narratives of development of Erik Erikson, and the British object relations theorists Melanie Klein, W. R. D. Fairbairn, and D. W. Winnicott. The psychoanalytic account will begin with a presentation of the narrative of Sigmund Freud. The work of the French feminist thinker Luce Irigaray is also examined. She challenges both disciplines in their appreciation for the other, through her insistence that every other is ultimately subverted unless gender or sexual difference is acknowledged.

The comparison or dialogue follows the presentations of the narratives of the Jewish philosophers and the psychoanalysts. The dialogue will allow each to speak out of its integrity and strength, while exploring similarities and differences, overlaps and divergences, as well as the critical possibilities within these contemporary discourses. The dialogue will uncover the basic structures, important models and concepts, and key terms and metaphors in each discourse. Often these elements have been left unexamined or regarded as incontestable, but they represent choices that delineate specific understandings and rule out other ones. One distinguishing characteristic in the two discourses is that the one constructed by the three modern Jewish philosophers utilizes religious language, that is, gives prominence to the relationship to God in portraying the nature of the human. A featured objective thus concerns the consequences or affects on the story of the self with others that follow upon the insistence that the relationship to God be an essential element in one's narrative.

Philosophers, psychologists, and other theorists have disagreed about the place of human relations in understanding the nature of the person. In the modern West, the autonomous individual is often the starting point, and essential human activities, such as the quest for truth, and qualities, such as maturity, authenticity, and liberty, are often defined in terms of the lack of constricting ties with and interference from others. For example, Descartes began his pursuit of truth with a radical doubt that cut all ties with other persons. Following this, it was essentially in terms of the individual on his or her own that Kant—and, later, Freud—defined maturity; many philosophers, including Heidegger and Sartre, examined authenticity; and the English tradition of political philosophers described liberty. This dominant portrait of the human is contested by the narratives in the two intellectual streams that we will examine: modern Jewish philosophy and post-Freudian psychoanalysis. Their accounts provide a distinct portrait of the human, of a relational self, one that is built upon the gifts of the interhuman. For the Jewish philosophers and the psychoanalysts, the interhuman is at the heart of the development and meaning of what we all are as persons.

A few words are needed here regarding the choice of the term "interhuman." It is used as an inclusive concept to bring together all the different types of relationships or interactions among persons that are detailed by both the philosophers and the psychoanalysts studied here. Psychoanalysts have utilized the terms "intrapsychic," "interpersonal," and "intersubjective" to delineate particular types of relations. The intrapsychic realm refers to the internal psychic economy of an individual. Post-Freudian psychoanalysts emphasize the importance of different unconscious processes—including identification, introjection, and projection—by which relationships with other persons are internalized, constructing an internal object world. The interpersonal dimension includes both the intrapsychic and the unconscious effects of this on relationships with others and interactions with persons in the world. Stephen Mitchell speaks of the relationship between the two as a cycle: "Intrapsychic becomes interpersonal; interpersonal transforms intrapsychic, in a perpetual cycle of expansions and enrichments" (1993, 119). The intersubjective can mean a number of things, but I find it most useful to restrict its sense to those relations between persons where each recognizes the other as a full subject.[1] Martin Buber has written that he created the term "interhuman" (*das Zwischenmenschliche*) to refer to the relationship between persons where the mutuality of partnership emerges (1965a, 72, 79). I do not intend that the interhuman only covers such ideal relationships, but use it to include all the types of relations discussed by the psychoanalysts as well as referring to the personal, communal, and wider social dimensions of relationships that are often part of the discussions of the Jewish philosophers.

The theories and methods that this treatment enlists reflect developments in multiple academic disciplines and areas. The focus upon and analysis of language, for example, the way theorists in the two disciplines construct and express their positions, draws upon a number of insights in modern philosophy. The use of dialogue as a method of exploration is featured in contemporary discussions in a wide range of areas. The examination of notions of the self and others, in addition to the contexts above, is a dominant interest in the works of post-modern and feminist thinkers. Finally, the discussion of the role of religion or religious language in examining the ways people develop, live out their lives, and see themselves also has a place in current studies in psychology of religion. The purpose of this introductory "Apology" is to briefly reflect upon the diverse intellectual currents that are the backdrop for this study. Alternately, it is to make the case for the focus, scope, theories, and methods employed here.

For all that, I want to insist that this presentation is partial and inconclusive. It is partial in at least two ways. While I will argue that there are crucial developments in the disciplines that frame this work, it is also important to note that each of these areas is complex and that there are other very significant trends and figures that are not discussed. Additionally, this study is partial in the sense of being engaged. As I work through the materials, I will give my best effort in providing a balanced presentation, but it will also obviously reflect my views, interests, and concerns. Thus, every selection, description, and interpretation I present is, happily, contestable. Finally, this project is inconclusive—in the spirit of Johannes Climacus' (Søren Kierkegaard's) *Concluding Unscientific Postscript*—in offering a voice that opens the way for other voices. Following this commitment, the book employs a two-step approach. The positions of the various thinkers are presented and then the processes of analysis and comparison follow. By first offering and illuminating the material, I hope that the reader is encouraged to follow with her or his own analysis and comparison. Success is measured by whether this account convinces others to join in—to read, question, add to, and critique—the examination of multiple ways of narrating the interhuman.

Philosophy and Jewish Philosophy

Major developments in much of contemporary philosophy, and twentieth-century philosophy more widely, are echoed in the approach of this work, particularly the interest in how language gives birth to and shapes understanding. From the beginning of the twentieth century, and many would look earlier, at least to Friedrich Nietzsche, there has been a deep interest in language, in the ways that all forms of human life are contoured by our linguistic endowment. This insight is concisely formulated by Hans-Georg Gadamer: "Human experience is essentially linguistic" (cited in Rorty 1987, 34). Although there are many important differences between analytic philosophers, continental philosophers, and post-modern philosophers, the focus on language is held in common. Two prominent thinkers in the mid-twentieth century were J. L. Austin and Ludwig Wittgenstein. Wittgenstein's attack on private language and his discussions of the relationships between meaning, types of discourse or language games, and forms of social life have proved pivotal for many later thinkers

Actually, what has been termed the "linguistic turn" overflows the discipline of philosophy. The nature and dimensions of this revolutionary concern have been well described by Terry Eagleton, who wrote:

> The hallmark of the "linguistic revolution" of the twentieth century, from Saussure and Wittgenstein to contemporary literary theory, is the recognition that meaning is not simply something "expressed" or "reflected" in language: it is actually *produced* by it. It is not as though we have meanings, or experiences, which we then proceed to cloak with words; we can only have the meanings and experiences in the first place because we have a language to have them in. What this suggests, moreover, is that our experience as individuals is social to its roots; for there can be no such thing as a private language, and to imagine a language is to imagine a whole form of social life. (cited in Mitchell 1988, 18)

Another way to look at this is in terms of the critique of objectivism. Objectivism is the view that what makes our statements true is that they correspond to an "objective" reality outside of language, and thus, as humans, we have access to the world unmediated by language and our wider social nexus. The critique of objectivism has been a central feature in philosophy in the last century.[2] Suzanne Kirschner finds that this critique is "shared by theorists associated with a variety of philosophical and theoretical movements, including ordinary language philosophy, postempiricist philosophy of science, ontological hermeneutics, social constructionism, poststructuralism, postmodernism, and neopragmatism" (1996, 7–8).[3] For Kirschner, all these movements place an "emphasis on language, social life, culture and history as generative sources of our knowledge, particularly our social knowledge" (1996, 8).

Thus, the study of language, or better, our lives within language, has been a major activity cultivated by philosophy. Among its diverse and important representatives are the post-modernist Jean-Francois Lyotard, the deconstructionist Jacques Derrida, and the pragmatist Richard Rorty. Reflecting the acknowledgment of the significance of language, Rorty's much cited essay "Pragmatism and Philosophy" describes a shift in how philosophy itself is seen. He distinguishes between "Philosophy" and "philosophy." Thinkers who practice "Philosophy" search for ultimate truths that transcend cultures, languages, and particular discourses. Adherents of "philosophy," "compare and contrast cultural traditions" and find that "in the process of playing vocabularies and cultures off against each other, we produce new and better ways of talking and acting" (1987, 54). These post-Philosophical philosophers study "the comparative advantages and disadvantages of the various ways of talking that our race has invented" (1987, 58).[4]

In harmony with the linguistic turn and its associated developments in philosophy, I am exploring the ways that the relationships between the self and others—one aspect of the social dimension of the human—is expressed in Jewish philosophy and post-Freudian psychoanalysis. These expressions are in the form of stories or narratives.[5] (Alternately, as we will see, one can say that these narrative forms create the ways that the interhuman is understood.) The project is comparative, attempting to assess "advantages and disadvantages" of these "various ways of talking" about the self and others. The goal of the comparison is not to determine which narrative is "true," or corresponds to some unmediated, empirical reality. Rather, the overriding interest is to access how each of these ways of narrating the interhuman provide resources for helping us think about the complex configurations, contours, tensions, and possibilities that punctuate the life with others.

This approach to the Jewish philosophers and to the post-Freudian psychoanalysts escapes the Scylla of reductionism as well as the Charybdis of apologetics. It is not reductive, that is, it does not endeavor to argue that psychoanalytic narratives provide a scientific account of what, for example, the Jewish philosophers can only hint at through religious myth. Neither is it apologetic, seeking to demonstrate the "truth" of religious narratives or of "religion." In addition, this approach to the two disciplines demonstrates how each can supplement the other in thinking about the interhuman. The Jewish narratives are sensitive to issues and concerns that dominate modern philosophy and also indicate philosophic and ethical implications of recognizing the significant place that others have in every human life. The psychoanalytic narratives provide a refined vocabulary of subjectivity and the interpersonal as well as highlighting the attractions and tensions that punctuate all relationships. They also are connected and respond to data generated by psychoanalytic analysis, that is, the therapeutic situation, and psychological research.

It is often suggested that the discipline of modern Jewish philosophy begins with the philosopher Moses Mendelssohn's *Jerusalem: Or on Religious Power and Judaism* of 1783. While there is a consensus about the evolving philosophical influences (Kantian, Hegelian, existential, etc.) that have impacted modern Jewish philosophers, critics have disagreed about the more elemental question regarding the nature of modern Jewish philosophy as a discipline.[6] Many have portrayed it in terms of the philosophical investigation of Judaism, and others as a way of doing philosophy that emphasizes distinctive Jewish points of departure or categories. I view it in terms of the latter: that is, as a way of looking at perennial issues of philosophy from perspectives that emerge from Jewish experience and literature. In these terms, Jewish philosophy can be seen to parallel Islamic philosophy, Hindu philosophy, or Buddhist philosophy. Each of these long-standing philosophic traditions explores questions about metaphysics, epistemology, ethics, and religion from the points of view of their own history and experience. For the present study, I am suggesting that some modern Jewish philosophers who attempt to ground their work on various aspects of Jewish literature, history, and experience provide insightful and fertile ways of describing our lives with others.

While modern Jewish philosophers have examined a great variety of issues concerning the Jewish tradition, the nature of modernity, and the challenges that beset Judaism, one of the most creative and influential circles has explored the dynamics of the relationships between persons. The focal point of this group of Jewish philosophers has been variously described as the "interhuman," the "life of dialogue," or the "sphere of the between." Franz Rosenzweig, Martin Buber, and Emmanuel Levinas are widely recognized as its central figures.

Since his death, the German-Jewish thinker Franz Rosenzweig (1886–1929) has often been acknowledged as the outstanding Jewish philosopher of the modern period. He, along with Buber, took part in that effluence of dialogical thought that appeared at the time of and following World War I.[7] In his major work, *The Star of Redemption* of 1918, and his later essays, Rosenzweig described an absolute empiricist "New Thinking" or "Speech Thinking" that built upon the centrality of time and speech for human experience (1999). He believed that these two pivots were deeply related, since to take time seriously meant to recognize "the need of an other" or that we are "dependent on the other for what is ours" (1999, 87). Rosenzweig detailed major elements of the relationship between persons through evocative analyses of such features as the dynamics of speech, the giving and calling of a name, and the hearing of and responding to God's call.

The subject of dialogue and the name of Martin Buber (1878–1965) have almost become synonymous. His famous book of 1923, *I and Thou*, is perhaps the quintessential philosophic portrayal of and argument for the meaningfulness of the dialogical life. Its early clarion call, "There is no I as such, but only the I of the basic word I-Thou and the basic-word I-It" (1970, 54),[8] richly profiles the two basic human attitudes toward the world through the grammar of language. Buber contrasts the I-It way of living that objectifies every relation, to the I-Thou relation, in which mutuality and reciprocity reign. It is through the latter, Buber believes, that the fully human is achieved and the call of responsibility is concretely heard and answered. The religious dimension that hovers over the interhuman is emphatically affirmed in the formulaic statement: "Extended, the lines of relationships intersect in the eternal Thou" (1970, 123).

The philosophic stature of Emmanuel Levinas (1906–1995) is based primarily upon two major works that were written rather late in his life, *Totality and Infinity*, in 1961, and *Otherwise Than Being or Beyond Essence*, in 1974. They have called for a revolution in philosophy, and, in essence, the ways of thinking that have dominated the modern West. The insistence on seeing "Ethics as First Philosophy" (1989) places the ethical demand of responsibility to the other prior to the individual's self-regard. In dazzling phenomenological analyses of concrete facets of everyday life, Levinas suggests that closer to the self than self-consciousness and more dear than freedom is the rupturing, ravishing call of the other. While Levinas assiduously avoids turning God into a theme within his work, the welcome that one gives to the proximity of the other testifies also to the trace of an Other.

The history of the scholarly acknowledgment of these contributions of Rosenzweig, Buber, and Levinas has been varied and complex. Due in part, perhaps, to his early death, Rosenzweig's work was largely ignored by scholars for a considerable time. It was not until the first English translations of his work appeared in the 1960s and 1970s that his views began to be seriously queried. At first this was limited to the context of "Jewish" scholarship, but in the last two decades, writers in North America, Europe, and Israel have begun to plumb more widely his difficult but exciting insights. The power and expanse of Martin Buber's thought, as well as his longevity, insured that his writings were read and respected throughout the twentieth century. Buber's influence has always been more pronounced than that of Rosenzweig, his younger friend and colleague. However, as with Rosenzweig, Buber's philosophic legacy is treasured primarily within Jewish circles. From the time of *Totality and Infinity*, Emmanuel Levinas' influence has not been restricted to Jewish philosophy. He has had a great impact on contemporary continental philosophy, and is seen as a crucial figure in studies of post-modern thought. The book *Altarity*, Mark C. Taylor's important examination of post-modern thinkers, devotes a chapter to him, along with such post-modern luminaries as Lacan, Bataille, Kristeva, Blanchot, and Derrida.[9] Levinas has graciously acknowledged the pervasive influence that Rosenzweig's thought has had on him, and this may bring more Western philosophers, who have up to now ignored Jewish philosophy, to turn to Levinas' intellectual mentor.

The examinations of these Jewish philosophers, particularly in the last decade, both separately and in combination with each other, have concentrated on their relation to other modern Jewish philosophers, some pivotal Western philosophers, and to post-modern concerns, such as language, ethics, hermeneutics, and translation.[10] Much less has been done in the broad context of psychology. A recent book on Rosenzweig and Freud, Eric L. Santner's *On the Psychotheology of Everyday Life*, marks the beginning of the fruitful examination of the correlations between the former's philosophic deliberations and psychoanalysis. However, it is in the context of post-Freudian developments that the ideas of Rosenzweig should find their real complement. Buber's thought has been examined in the context of psychology for many decades.[11] Essays on dialogical psychology and the book *Martin Buber and the Human Sciences* (Friedman, ed., 1996), are examples of such treatments. Nevertheless, these efforts do not carefully compare Buber's thought with the leading psychoanalytic theorists, particularly those with the most influence on post-modern thought. Instead, they discuss his manifest or possible influence on other psychological models or types of analysis. Finally, the literature concerning Levinas and psychoanalysis is quickly developing, which is not at all surprising, since there seems to be a new work produced on Levinas each month, if not each week! The focus is usually on Jacques Lacan, as in the edited book, *Levinas and Lacan: The Missed Encounter* (Harasym, ed., 1998). Yet, the choice of Lacan as Levinas' dialogical partner is somewhat problematic, since Lacan did not see relationships to others as the foundation for authenticity, which is Levinas' preeminent message.

One of the major aims of the present work is to expand the reception and appreciation of the work of Rosenzweig, Buber, and Levinas. I hope to demonstrate that their powerful narratives of the interhuman are not just some idle "philosophical" or "religious" musings. Rather, we will see that a fertile, mutually illuminating, and surprising conversation can be initiated among their distinctive accounts of the nature and dynamics of the interhuman and those of post-Freudian psychoanalytic theorists. The possibilities that the latter can bring to the exchange are richly previewed in a statement by Jane Flax. She wrote: "For all of its shortcomings psychoanalysis presents the best and most promising theories of how a self that is simultaneously embodied, social, 'fictional,' and real comes to be, changes, and persists over time" (1990, 16).

Finally, the present book is integrally connected to my earlier research. In the last decade, I have published two books in the area of modern Jewish philosophy that have probed the thought of Rosenzweig, Buber, and Levinas. The latest, *Speaking/Writing of God: Jewish Philosophical Reflections on the Life with Others* (1997), was an examination of religious language in Rosenzweig and Levinas. It also explored the critique and challenge of Jewish philosophy offered by feminist Jewish thinkers. *Jewish Philosophy and Psychoanalysis*, thus, extends the examination of a central stream of modern Jewish philosophy, continuing the exploration of religious language and the challenge of feminism, by introducing another discourse and variety of narratives about the interhuman.

Freudian and Post-Freudian Psychoanalysis

Fundamental developments in psychoanalysis since Freud open the way to the approach toward psychoanalytic narratives, and more broadly, the dialogue between psychoanalysis and modern Jewish philosophy brought forward here. The post-Freudian narratives coalesce around two general transformations: seeing the subject of psychoanalysis within the matrix of the interpersonal and understanding the methods of psychoanalysis within the context of hermeneutics. These reorientations are well known within the discipline of psychoanalysis, but quite unfamiliar to most well-educated persons outside of that discipline. Four specific shifts in psychoanalytic theory can be delineated: from drive theory to object relations and the interpersonal; from the Oedipal to the mother-infant dyad; from analysis as objective and neutral to analysis as an interpersonal meeting—in terms of participant observation and countertransference; and from psychoanalysis as a scientific discipline to psychoanalysis as a hermeneutical activity that offers a variety of narratives.[12] It should also be noted that many, if not all, of these features of contemporary psychoanalytic theory and practice were presaged in the complex, fluctuating currents of Freud's work itself. In recent decades, the post-modern critique and contextualization of Western thought and science, as well as the emergence of new models and paradigms in the social sciences and humanities, have allowed these unexplored features of Freud to blossom.

First, Freud's formulation of the dynamics of the unconscious was expressed through a mechanistic model and seen in terms of the instincts that drove the self. He spoke of forces, such as libido and aggression, with their accumulations, shifts, and expenditures of energy. The forces themselves were portrayed as primitive animal instincts, following Darwin. For Freud, the key to understanding the intrusions of the unconscious into consciousness and behavior lay with the pulsating drives, while the "objects," that is, persons and parts of persons, of the expenditures of energies were of secondary interest.

After Freud, human interaction began to be taken as central to the formation and health of the psyche. Persons were seen as being programmed to need and relate to others, to be "object-seeking," in the vocabulary of W. R. D. Fairbairn (1994, 162). One critic described this alteration as the shift to "the psychical relations *between* human beings rather than the inner world of the individual subject alone" (Elliott 1994, 18).[13] Object relations theorists highlighted this departure. They regarded the emergence of the psyche as the outcome of "interpersonal activity, reciprocity, and emotional exchange," giving primary attention to the self's need for connection and recognition (Elliott 1994, 22). Thus, the concentration on instincts or drives within the individual psyche was replaced by a focus on human connectedness.

Second, the Oedipal complex was certainly one of the greatest creative leaps in all of Freud's groundbreaking work. He saw the son's desire for the mother in the context of the rivalry with the father as the central organizing myth/principle of psychic life. Of course, the prominence given to this myth underscored the phallocentricism of his construction of psychoanalysis. During the last years of Freud's life, the attention of some psychoanalysts turned to an earlier scene of interaction, the mother-infant dyad. The notion of the infant's emotion-laden merger with and emergence from the mother came to be regarded as the fundamental process(es) that structured the psyche as well as the template for all later interactions.[14] These processes are highlighted by theorists of the object relations and feminist schools. In an address appropriately titled, "The Waning of the Oedipus Complex," the theorist Hans Loewald gave witness to "the contemporary decline of psychoanalytic interest in the oedipal phase and oedipal conflicts and the predominance of interest and research in pre-oedipal development, in the mother-infant dyad and in issues of separation-individuation and of the self and narcissism (2000, 386).[15]

The change in orientation from the Oedipal to the mother-infant dyad is best illustrated in an almost passing remark made by one of the key figures of this study, Fairbairn. Freud's emphasis on the Oedipal scene reinforces a number of his notions, one of which is the definition of women in terms of lacking a penis—with their corresponding "envy." However, for Fairbairn, since the relationship to the mother in the first few months of life dominates the infant's perception and development, the father is now left a secondary and derivative role. This demotion is colorfully described in terms of the first impression that the father makes on the infant. Fairbairn writes: "It is chiefly as a parent without breasts that the child would appear to regard his father in the first instance" (1994, 174). In light of the view of many object relations theorists that the relationship to the mother is universally repressed in later life, one may see this depiction of the breastless father as a return, if not revenge, of the repressed.

Third, Freud offered a model of the interaction between analyst and analysand, or patient, that was derived from Newtonian physics. The analyst was an objective, impersonal observer, who interpreted the raw data that was supplied by the analysand, particularly through free association and dreams. He also thought that any gratification or support given by the analyst would retard the progress of the treatment by reinforcing resistance. Still, Freud formulated a consensual form of interaction that converged on words, rather than one that relied on either medical intervention, that is, surgery, or that undermined the patient's motives and choices, as in hypnosis. He also saw transference: that is, the process through which the patient projects residues of his or her earliest experiences upon the analyst, as the engine that drove change in the analytic situation.

Later psychoanalytic theorists accentuated the interpersonal and dialogical nature of the exchange between analyst and analysand. Not only was the transference of the patient's early experience and patterns of relationship onto the analyst meaningful, but also the counter-transference of the analyst's unconscious patterns upon the patient. The interaction between the two sides has become increasingly important for understanding the nature of the patient's past and, once again, for providing the dynamics for change, especially in the object relations and self psychoanalytic schools.[16] For some theorists, such as Margaret Mahler, it was fundamentally the human engagement itself that healed or overcame the patient's past wounds and limitations (Mitchell and Black 1995, 59). Again, as Loewald put it: "To discover truth about the patient is always discovering it with him and for him as well as for ourselves and about ourselves. And it is discovering truth between each other, as the truth of human beings in their interrelatedness" (2000, 297–98). A complementary way of speaking of analysis in a contemporary mode suggests that the patient provides a story or text and the analyst helps with interpretation. Together the two construct a more adequate—insightful, empowering—story of the self (Shafer 1992, 177).

Fourth, Freud had sought to legitimize his pioneering, albeit extremely controversial, theories and discoveries by insisting that they were in harmony with the contemporary scientific models of his time. As we have seen, he utilized such frameworks as those provided by Newton, in terms of objective, scientific observation, and Darwin: that is, the biological framework. In addition, it appears that a major goal of psychoanalysis was to "scientifically" chart psychological processes, what is called today metapsychology.

Hermeneutical strategies, certainly part of Freud's work, as in dream interpretation, have become even more important for some later theorists and philosophical commentators.[17] In this vein, the psychoanalyst molds memories and self-images into an insightful story of the self: the different psychoanalytic schools offering an array of choices on the ways that the life of the self can be told or narrated. The particular choice of "storylines" (Schafer 1992, 29–35), or constellation of themes, depends upon the analyst's training and experience and the patient's memories and present self-understanding. The efficacy of a narrative choice can be judged by such things as the coherence, insight, behavioral opportunities, and the agency for the patient that it provides.

The two most prominent writers who take this approach to the world of analysis are Donald Spence, especially *Narrative Truth and Historical Truth* (1982), and Roy Schafer, *Retelling a Life* (1992). Spence's basic view is that the construction of a narrative of the patient's past by the analyst and analysand not only structures how the past is seen, but creates or constructs that past. He argues that "narrative truth has a special significance in its own right and that making contact with the actual past may be of far less significance than creating a coherent and consistent account of a particular set of events" (1982, 28). In his examination of the nature of narrative, Spence highlights a number of elements. Narrative is a particular literary structure or "kind of artistic product" that provides a convincing sense of continuity, coherence, and comprehensiveness. It features a construction or reconstruction of events, put into a consistent and coherent account, accompanied by a sense of closure at the end. Both sequence and transformation are important ingredients (1982, 21–37). Schafer also emphasizes the heuristic and literary aspects of analytic interpretation. He has written: "so-called self-concepts, self-images, self-representations, or more generally the so-called self may be considered to be a set of narrative strategies or storylines each person follows in trying to develop an emotionally coherent account of his or her life among people" (1992, 34).

These four fundamental changes in theory are captured and woven together in Stephen A. Mitchell's *Relational Concepts in Psychoanalysis* (1988) and *Relationality* (2000). Following his co-authored earlier work (Greenberg and Mitchell 1983), Mitchell divides the history of the discipline of psychoanalysis into two roughly equal periods, with the watershed around 1950. The first was governed by Freud's drive model, in which the autonomous individual was the basic unit of inquiry. The mind was understood to be wired in a particular way, more or less independent of outside factors, and its driving forces or energies, particularly libidinal, were focused around a succession of erotogenic zones (mouth, anus, etc.). In Mitchell's words:

> We are portrayed as a conglomeration of asocial, physical tensions represented in the mind by urgent sexual and aggressive wishes pushing for expression. We live in the clash between these wishes and the secondary, more superficial claims of social reality; our very thought itself is derivative of, a transformation of, these primitive, bestial energies. (1988, 2)

The second psychoanalytic model followed upon, among other things, more directed research on infants, as well as clinical insights that emerged from soldiers traumatized in World War II. Mitchell sees the schools of British object relations, interpersonal, and self psychoanalysts as laying the basis for an "integrated relational model." Their outlook consistently places the individual within a social field. The interhuman is the basic unit, as it were, and persons are seen to be tied to one another in various ways. For some analysts, humans are physiologically "wired" to connect with others. Fairbairn's notion of object-seeking expresses a different view of the interpersonal bond, the idea that people have powerful desires for relationship. Finally, self psychoanalysts describe how negotiations with others figure in the individual's quest for identity and authenticity.

The selection of the specific psychoanalytic theorists examined in this work follows upon a number of considerations. The choice of the first person to be treated is not contentious, even if the same could not be said of the figure himself. Sigmund Freud (1856–1939) obviously stands at the beginning of the discipline of psychoanalysis. He is more than its originator: he is its creator. Freud's voluminous work left a legacy of theories about development, the structure of the psyche, and the dynamism of analysis, as well as of psychological models, narratives, and metaphors. His formulations and presuppositions constitute the point of departure for all later theorists. Even those who part from his basic positions find that there are hints of or sanctions for their digressions in his opus. Our primary interest will be in his foundational narrative of development, which features elemental instincts and the succession of erotogenic zones.

The group of psychoanalysts that can be identified as post-Freudian is extensive and diverse. For example, in *Freud and Beyond,* Stephen Mitchell and

Margaret Black detail thirty-nine individual treatments of theorists. Even if the field is narrowed to object relations psychoanalysts, over a dozen significant thinkers can be justifiably included. Further, these counts do not take into consideration many of the most recent developments, particularly the emergence of the school of "Relational Psychoanalysis."[18] The present book will limit its focus to some of the central figures who stand within what might be called the first generation of post-Freudian psychoanalysts. The crucial insights of these psychoanalysts often emerged while Freud was still alive, and most of their basic writings were published by the end of the 1960s or the early 1970s.

Erik Erikson (1902–1994) is included for a number of reasons. He is often depicted in terms of either the "self" or "ego" schools of psychoanalysis, with various other important thinkers such as Kohut, Mahler, and Loewald.[19] Erikson's work features a well-developed psychoanalytic narrative built upon the axes of self and identity. The scope of this narrative, from infancy to old age, and its fulcrum, the psychosocial crisis, are particularly impressive. Overall, the treatment of Erikson adds not only the concern with how interaction with others (the social side of the psychosocial) helps to bring the self to fruition, but also illuminates post-Oedipal stages or crises, from identity to ego integrity. In terms of this study, Erikson represents one of a range of possible mid-positions between Freud and the object relations school.[20]

Melaine Klein (1882–1960) will be the next thinker to be examined. Her work is powerful in its own right as well as being tremendously influential. She is usually regarded as head of her own school of "Kleinians," and at times loosely included as the first of the object relations theorists.[21] Klein's narrative about pre-Oedipal formation in terms of the famous paranoid-schizoid and depressive positions is an explosive portrayal of hate, anger, and attempted reconciliation. In addition, her approach toward psychoanalysis primarily in terms of "inner objects" or imagoes cultivates one of the most fertile roots of post-Freudian development.

W. R. D. Fairbairn (1899–1964) and D. W. Winnicott (1896–1971) are recognized as the most important representatives of the British object relations school. They offer particularly interesting accounts of the dynamic between internal and external objects. While not rejecting Klein's emphasis on fantasy and internal figures, Fairbairn and Winnicott accent somewhat more tangible elements in the relationship between mother and infant as the key to both psychological health and illness. Fairbairn is probably the most consistent relational theorist. His developmental narrative, from infantile dependence to mature dependence, clearly demonstrates that persons are always in one or another type of relationship with others. Winnicott's description of the emergence of the infant from the holding environment of the mother, this re-imagining the intricacy of the synthesis of self and m/other/object, is profoundly suggestive. In addition, many critics have been fascinated by his discussions of the transitional stage between merger and autonomy, which he ties to such wider human enterprises as play, art, and religion.[22]

Post-Modernism, Feminism, and the Psychology of Religion

The project of investigating narratives of the interhuman featured in modern Jewish philosophy and post-Freudian psychoanalysis also takes up strands of arguments in—and hopefully makes contributions to—other related fields: post-modernism, feminism, and the psychology of religion. While the definition and scope of post-modernism is deeply contested, if it is seen as a range of perspectives within the humanities and social sciences, certain features can be identified. In this light, post-modern reflections seem to parallel some of the developments in post-Freudian psychoanalysis charted above. Post-modern discourses feature interests in the social matrix—including the interhuman or interpersonal, language, and hermeneutics. They frequently reveal what may be termed an "obsession with the other," especially when this other is conceived as the irrational, threatening, foreign, lost, hidden, or missing.

There is a mutual indebtedness between psychoanalysis and post-modernism. From one side, the wide-ranging post-modern critique of prominent social, humanistic, and scientific discourses has influenced the discipline of psychoanalysis. Some critics now hold the view that Freud presented a master narrative in the guise of science—itself a particular type of narrative. Such characteristic post-modern strategies as the overturning of hierarchies and dualisms and the uncovering of rhetorical strategies have been trained upon psychoanalytic discourse. From the other side, it cannot be forgotten that the post-modern notion of the self as flawed, fractured, and de-centered grew out of the Freudian legacy. Freud's vibrant portrait of the power of the unconscious id undermined that "modern" notion of the person that saw the self in terms of the rational, centered, self-directive, and self-conscious. As one treatment noted, the post-Freudian "understanding of self as decentered, multiple, and contextualized is central to the ways subjectivity and experience have been explored in many areas of contemporary philosophy, literature, and social criticism" (Mitchell and Black 1995, 84).

The juxtaposition of Jewish philosophical narratives of the interhuman with post-Freudian narratives places this project within the post-modern framework. The comparison or "dialogue" will help to unearth some of the reigning presuppositions and strategies within the literature of psychoanalysis. It will add one more perspective to the multi-disciplinary endeavor—often with a post-modern stance—that has so significantly affected psychoanalysis. Referring to the importance of a critique that comes from beyond the boundaries of psychoanalysis, it has been observed that:

> Psychoanalytic criticism today is pursued less by psychoanalysts than by cultural and literary critics, feminists, media and communication analysts, and social and political theorists. This tradition of analysis and critique has led to some of the most important innovations and developments in psychoanalytic theory in this century. (Elliott 1994, 2)

The above observation by Anthony Elliott is one of the key pieces of evidence in this presentation of the case, in the argument for, the logic and relevance of this study. It proposes that the analysis and critique of psychoanalytic theory is not confined to those who stand within one of the schools or institutions of the discipline. Psychoanalytic writings, both theoretical and clinical, can be analyzed philosophically, as well as explored as particular forms of literature emerging out of a bounded historic time and place. While psychoanalysis is certainly nourished by the observations of behavior and therapeutic interchanges between analyst and patient, its theories and narratives are open to investigation and critique from the academic perspectives of some of the outsiders Elliott features.

Further, by utilizing one set of religious narratives, the deep bias against religion that often pervades post-modern discourses can also be examined.[23] For many critics, religion is synonymous with domination, totalization, exclusion, and illusion. The post-modern critique of Enlightenment presuppositions and prejudices, which brings so many contemporary thinkers together, comes to a halt in terms of the Enlightenment's naive rejection of religion. Many philosophers, post-modernists, psychoanalysts, feminists, and others need to become acquainted with the ways religious thinkers bring out critical and pluralist strands within their traditions. For the three Jewish philosophers, it is precisely a sense—Levinas' trace—of the transcendent that nurtures a radical critique of concrete forms of domination, totalization, exclusion, and illusion, as well as expresses a persisting hope in their overcoming.[24]

Looking at the lives of countless individuals, across huge expanses of time and space, great numbers of different cultures, societies, and languages, it seems absurd that "religion" needs to be justified before the court of its intellectual "despisers."[25] If there is a way to speak of the truth of religion, perhaps it is best put forward, in my view, by Rosenzweig through his "messianic theory of knowledge," that "evaluates truths according to the price for its verification and to the bond that they establish among human beings" (1999, 99).[26] This presents a view of religion in terms of the meaning it provides for a life, for lives, for people together in communities.[27] It understands religion's contribution in terms of the intensity, purity, constancy of passion, direction, orientation, or what Kierkegaard spoke of as "subjectivity."

Another crucial relationship—for psychoanalysis, post-modernism, and this project— is with feminist theory. Feminist thinkers have made significant contributions to the critique of psychoanalysis, particularly influencing the turn from the Oedipal to the mother-infant dyad, the interest in object relations or the interpersonal, and the rethinking of psychoanalytic practice. They have powerfully uncovered and undermined the patriarchal bias in psychoanalysis: particularly in the Freudian classics as well as in Lacan's significant revisions.[28] The extent of the impact of feminism has been summarized by one commentator in the following way: "the encounter between feminism and psychoanalysis has proved to be of crucial importance in transformations of gender power, sexual identities and practices, and the restructuring of emotional intimacy in modern societies" (Elliott 1994, 114).[29] In this light, the book introduces a consideration of the work of the French feminist Luce Irigaray (b. 1930). As a feminist, philosopher, and psychoanalyst, Irigaray contests many of the disciplines we have reviewed, finding that they eclipse women's subjectivity. She is also important because of her new and creative visions of social, cultural, and interpersonal life, especially gender relations.

Finally, in addition to the developments in modern Jewish philosophy and post-Freudian psychoanalysis, post-modernism, and feminism, something needs to be added concerning recent works in psychology of religion as a setting for this study. This field, like many others, seems to be divided into two basic streams. On the one hand, there is the "scientific," technical or experimental side, and the other side is seen as "humanistic." The first studies the impact of religious beliefs on individual development and behavior, as well as the phenomenon of religion in its social manifestations. In this context, psychological research is conducted under such headings as god-image, conversion, integration of the personality, prejudice, the relation of religious cognition to moral judgment, and the development of personal religious identity. Scholars in this stream use the scientific method—theory, hypothesis, experiment, results, analysis—and value observation and the ability of experiments to be reproduced.[30] The second stream, which is more germane to the present work, explores religious feelings, experiences, and viewpoints. It has an interest in issues of meaning, that is, how religion provides direction or orientation to a life. Here the data may be taken from a wider group of sources: religious classics, literary documents, historical texts, dream materials, autobiographical writings, case-study methods, myths and folklore, and various philosophical works. In this vein, some current works that look at religion and contemporary currents in psychoanalysis have, for the most part, noted the four major developments in psychoanalysis. This is true despite the fact that the recognition of the contribution of feminist theorists is, as usual, missing.

Works in the humanistic side of the psychology of religion customarily examine "religion" as a whole category. For example, Stanley Leavy's *In the Image of God* (1988) and James Jones' *Contemporary Psychoanalysis and Religion* (1991) explore the origin, place, and meaning of religion in terms of some of the developments in psychoanalysis noted above. A major feature of both is the argument that there is no longer a need for psychoanalysis to delegitimize religion. Jones' recent works further discuss the possibilities for a more positive view of religion that emerges out of post-Freudian perspectives. James DiCenso, in *The Other Freud* (1999), presents a sophisticated treatment of relationships between Freudian and post-Freudian psychoanalysis, and religion. He finds room for an appreciation of religion's impact on subjectivity and culture within a re-reading of Freud. DiCenso's primary concern is to suggest how religion can be seen to foster critical reflection and ethical capacities.

Suzanne Kirschner's *The Religious and Romantic Origins of Psychoanalysis* (1996) stands even closer to the present work. It explores the developments in psychoanalytic theory, especially the understanding of the metaphorical character of psychological knowledge (1996, 15–16), which is one way of understanding the psychoanalytic narrative. She traces the origin, as well as endemic presuppositions, of narratives in British and American psychoanalytic schools to romantic developmental narratives about the self and, ultimately, to basic biblical storylines. This contextualizes psychoanalytic narratives, indicating that they are not neutral and universal, but have very specific cultural origins. Significantly, she also suggests the importance of the study of other narrative frameworks in order to widen understandings of the self.

Method and Contents

The use of the method of dialogue between a number of discourses concerning subjectivity and intersubjectivity is best illustrated in the work of the philosopher and analyst Jane Flax, especially in her *Thinking Fragments* (1990). In that work, she formulates a dialogue between psychoanalysis, "postmodern philosophies," and feminism, which shows the strengths of these fields and opens each to the needed interrogations by the others. She states that her book will "represent, interrogate, juxtapose, and construct conversations between three important modes of contemporary Western thought: psychoanalysis, feminist theories, and postmodern philosophies" (1990, 3). Another example of dialogue or conversation can be found in my *Speaking/Writing of God* (1997). One of its chapters features a dialogue between Franz

Rosenzweig and Emmanuel Levinas, on one side, and such feminist Jewish thinkers as Judith Plaskow, Sylvia Fishman, Rita Gross, and Marcia Falk. The method confirmed common assumptions and opened the way for new challenges to be directed to each side. In the end, both groups were pushed to encounter unexplored possibilities, sometimes ending with shades of agreement and sometimes with a principled "No!"

Beyond the use of dialogue, Jane Flax's *Thinking Fragments* and *Disputed Subjects* (1993) inspire the present book in a number of ways. She treats the variety of notions of the human in terms of narratives, writing: "Conceptions of subjectivity should be read as narratives whose construction and motives are provisional and subject to doubt" (1993, 117). Further, Flax insists that the complexity and heterogeneity of the human requires a plurality of perspectives or stories. In her words: "Each [the psychoanalytic and the postmodern] discourse tries to order the heterogenous components of subjectivity within one master narrative or category. . . . We will need multiple stories in a variety of styles to appreciate its complexity" (1993, 98). I hope that her pluralist attitude and the sense of the incompleteness of every project can also be seen in this present work.

Five chapters, with an introduction and conclusion, comprise *Jewish Philosophy and Psychoanalysis.* This introduction, "An Apology," discusses the object, context, and methodology of the book. The first chapter, "Jewish Philosophical Narratives of the Interhuman," compares the narratives of the self and others in the Jewish philosophers Franz Rosenzweig, Martin Buber, and Emmanuel Levinas. It surveys three crucial segments within their stories: the "natural state" of relations between persons, the dynamics of the individual's God-relationship, and the character of the transformed interhuman that follows in the wake of the divine-human relationship. At the end of the chapter, the three portraits of what it means to be human are reviewed by examining four features: the understanding of the social nature of the self, the depiction of the types of alienation from others, the view of how the transcendent opens the way for overcoming alienation, and the role of the metaphor of God as person.

The second chapter, "Psychoanalytic Narratives of Development," isolates and presents some early narratives or storylines that are important for current theoretical work within psychoanalysis. The psychoanalysts examined include Sigmund Freud, Erik Erikson, Melanie Klein, W. R. D. Fairbairn, and D. W. Winnicott. Each treatment examines the basic terms and categories within the discourses, the narrative stages, and some of the philosophical implications about subjectivity that follow upon the treatments. The chapter concludes with a panorama of the views concerning self and other, portraits of some of the symptomatic scenes of human interaction, and the important contribution each theorist makes to the overall project.

The third chapter, "Of Gifts," follows upon the two presentations with a comparison between the Jewish philosophical narratives of the interhuman and the psychoanalytic narratives of development. It explores the similarities in these understandings of how the self is made through the other. It features common views about the overall significance of the interhuman, how the self's openness to the other is expressed, and what features of the individual's life emerge from the interaction with others. The multi-disciplinary rubric of "the gift" is used to provide the major metaphor for this discussion of the similarities between the two narratives. The overriding question: What are the gifts that one receives from the other?

The fourth chapter, "Transference and Transcendence," probes the distinctive and the different in the discourses of the Jewish philosophers and the psychoanalysts. It begins by comparing the narrative patterns and rubrics that the Jewish philosophers use for discussing a life, with the particular structure of the narrative of development that characterizes psychoanalytic writing. Three themes that each of the discourses treat in characteristic ways are taken up next: illness/alienation, transformation (transference/transcendence), and health/fullness. The comparison concludes by sketching the strengths and lacunae of each stream in their descriptions of the human and the interhuman. Two considerations guide this treatment. The first is the contrast between the relationship to the transcendent continually utilized by the philosophers and the immanent frame of reference of the psychoanalysts. The second is the insight that once the complexity of narrating the personal and interpersonal is brought to the fore, the differences between the two discourses emerge not as liabilities but as profound virtues

The attention to the work of the French feminist Luce Irigaray adds a unique and important element to the examination of the sets of narratives. She is a philosopher and a psychoanalyst whose work weaves together these two strands to challenge both disciplines in the name of that sex/gender woman. The fifth chapter, "Luce Irigaray: An/Other Fling with the Philosophers," takes its point of departure from two of Irigaray's essays on Levinas. It explores her contention that Levinas' presentation reinforces the dereliction or abandonment of women, a situation that she finds pervades Western philosophy and culture. It also examines her vision of the almost utopian potentialities of love, its "fecundity." The two viewpoints are tied together by her argument that unless woman is given her specificity (of desire, body, subjectivity) the powers of the erotic are subverted by men's love of themselves. Irigaray's questions to Levinas haunt, interrogate, persecute, and liberate in ways reminiscent of both Levinas' other and the unconscious in psychoanalytic discourse. At the end there is a dialogue between Irigaray and the three Jewish philosophers in terms of the place of gender, the erotic, and the ethical in narrating the interhuman.

The conclusion, "Narrating Life and Death," explores the question of whether these accounts of the interhuman contain original ways of addressing issues concerning society, history, and the individual's encounter with death. It is found, for example, that despite some important differences, the Jewish philosophers provide a surprisingly harmonious, and somber, vision of history. While the psychoanalysts do not consistently address all of the abovementioned issues, they offer important, and sometimes startling, insights. Many of the thinkers in both streams see a relationship between inauthentic ways of facing death and destructive forms of individual and communal life. The book concludes with a brief discussion, in the context of facing death, of the meaning of the Jewish philosophers' allusions to messianism, that "awaiting, where nothing is awaited."

Notes

1. Jessica Benjamin's work has focused on intersubjectivity. See her *Shadow of the Other.*
2. See Richard Rorty's "Pragmatism and Philosophy" (1987), especially 31–36.
3. Kirschner provides helpful bibliographic notes on each of these theoretical streams (1996, 7–8).
4. The psychoanalyst Charles Spezzano extends this approach to the notion of truth. He has written:

> Truth emerges out of our conversations and confrontations, remains the truth for a time because no one can talk about the matter at hand in a more useful and compelling way, and then becomes not true or an irrelevant truth because someone does find another way to talk about the same matter that now seems more useful and more compelling. (in Mitchell and Aron, eds., *Relational Psychoanalysis,* 429)

5. The distinction between story and narrative is somewhat elusive within the diverse literature on narrative. For the purposes of this work, I have used the term "story" to refer to the ways that a person thinks about her or his self and its history, while "narrative" refers to the general models or patterns that philosophers or schools of theorists construct to give shape to individuals' lives.
6. See my discussion of some of the different views of the nature of Jewish philosophy in "Feminism, Jewish Philosophy, and Religious Pluralism" (1996, 147–48).
7. See Buber's "The History of the Dialogical Principle" in *Between Man and Man* (1965), and also Harold Stahmer's *"Speak that I may see Thee!"* (1968).
8. Throughout the present book, I have replaced the word "You" with the word "Thou," in Kaufmann's translation of *I and Thou.* I find that there is a long history of speaking of the I-Thou relationship, and I want to continue this.
9. Derrida also has a very important essay on Levinas in his *Writing and Difference* (1978). There are essays on Levinas by such formative figures within post-modernism as Blanchot, Lyotard, and Irigaray in *Face to Face with Levinas* (Richard Cohen, ed., 1987).

10. See, for example, Robert Gibbs' treatment of Rosenzweig and Levinas in *Correlations* (1992) and Richard Cohen's book on the same figures, *Elevations* (1994). Also important is Barbara Galli's examination of Rosenzweig's views on language and translation in *Franz Rosenzweig and Jehuda Halevi* (1995) and Steven Kepnes' discussion of Buber's dialogical hermeneutics and narrative theology in *The Text as Thou* (1992).

11. See, for example, the two collections of essays on Buber, *The Philosophy of Martin Buber* (Schilpp and Friedman, eds., 1967) and *Martin Buber: A Centenary Volume* (Gordon and Bloch, eds., 1984) as well as such journals as *The Journal of Humanistic Psychology.*

12. See also Stephen Mitchell's enumeration of the shifts in psychoanalysis (1993, 175).

13. Also see, for example, James Jones (6).

14. This model of early merger has itself come under some critique. Luce Irigaray is suggestive here, as always. She looks again at the *in utero* relationship between mother and fetus in *Je, Tu, Nous* (1993, 37–44). Daniel Stern in *The Interpersonal World of the Infant* also disputes the notion of an initial merger and charts types of interaction beginning the first few weeks after birth.

15. In Loewald's essay, waning refers to the developmental transformation of the Oedipal complex and to the shift of focus of later psychoanalysts. Lacan, with his "law of the father," has certainly not given up the Oedipal complex as a key to understanding psychic development.

16. Some of the most revolutionary views of the dynamic between patient and analyst are found in articles by Irwin Hoffman, Lewis Aron, Owen Renik, and Thomas Ogden in the book *Relational Psychoanalysis* (Mitchell and Aron, eds).

17. See, for example, Paul Ricoeur's *Freud and Philosophy* (1970).

18. The book *Relational Psychoanalysis: The Emergence of a Tradition* (Mitchell and Aron, eds.), includes a preface that details the beginnings in the 1990s of this new school, as well as some of the essays during that decade that helped define its evolution.

19. There is no uniformity in how the different schools of psychoanalysis are identified or in which theorists belong with which school. Elliott characterizes ego psychology as being "generally concerned with the genesis, development, and adaptive capacities of the ego," and includes here Anna Freud, Heinz Hartmann, Ernest Kris, R. M. Lowenstein, Erik H. Erikson, and David Rapaport (1994, 19). Mitchell and Black put Erik Erikson and Heinz Kohut together under the heading of "psychologies of identity and self" (1995). While Morris Eagle identifies Kohut, Sullivan, Erikson, Jacobson, G. S. Klein, and Gedo, as theorists with a concern for the importance of "a concept of self and of self-organization" in understanding human behavior (1987, 71).

20. As the previous footnote indicated, there are many other theorists who could represent this "mid-position." These might include Kohut, Mahler, and the early "interpersonal psychoanalyst" Harry Stack Sullivan.

21. Judith Hughes offers an insightful analysis that places Klein with Fairbairn and Winnicott in the context of the overall developments of the "British psychoanalytic community" (1989). Mitchell and Black have separate treatments of Klein and her

contemporary followers, and the British object relations school of Fairbairn and Winnicott (1995).

22. Winnicott has become a very valuable resource for the relational psychoanalysts. There are a host of essays with references to him in *Relational Psychoanalysis: The Emergence of a Tradition* (Mitchell and Aron, eds.).

23. One illustration of this bias against religion is found in Jane Flax's *Disputed Subjects.* As is true of her earlier book, this work is a model of openness to various intellectual standpoints, and also offers an impassioned argument against many forms of oppression. However, she directly and indirectly refers to religion as a dangerous illusion that leads to totalistic views and violent actions (1993, xiii, 114, 146, 170). Rorty, as another example, sees it as a positive step when the Enlightenment found religious intuitions not to be "among the intellectually respectable candidates for Philosophical articulation" (1987, 55). The present book contests both views. In particular, it sets up a pragmatic test of religious narratives to see what might be gained from their perspective on the interhuman. I will take up this question again at the end of the book.

24. David Tracy's *Plurality and Ambiguity: Hermeneutics, Religion, Hope* explores the resources within religion for critique and for hope (82–114). I discuss the ways Jewish thinkers have responded to the challenge of religious pluralism in *Speaking/Writing of God,* "Faith and Mystery" (115–54).

25. This is, of course, a reference to the book of the nineteenth-century German theorist Friedrich Schleiermacher, *On Religion: Speeches to Its Cultured Despisers.*

26. See the author's *Speaking/Writing of God* for an analysis of Rosenzweig's definition of this "messianic" conception of truth (1997, 127–28).

27. I believe that this view of language, community, and belief fits in well with Richard Rorty's overall position of pragmatism. See, for example, his essays in *Philosophy and Social Hope.*

28. This might be an appropriate place to briefly note why I do not discuss Lacan's psychoanalytic thought in this book. His narrative of the mirror stage and the Oedipal complex is fascinating and influential. However, it does not add to this discussion of the fruits of the interhuman. On the whole, I agree with Flax's assessment that he presents a view of desire that is "non-object related" (1990, 91). I believe that her examination of his work, under the provocative subtitle of "The Ontology of Narcissism," is accurate (1990, 91–96). See, also, the books by Jane Gallop, *Reading Lacan* (1985), and Elizabeth Grosz, *Jacques Lacan: A Feminist Introduction* (1990).

29. See, also, Flax's *Thinking Fragments* and *Disputed Subjects.*

30. See James Byrnes, *The Psychology of Religion,* or Spilka and McIntosh, eds., *The Psychology of Religion: Theoretical Approaches.*

1

Jewish Philosophical Narratives of the Interhuman

THERE IS NO MORE COMPELLING WAY to begin an examination of the nature of the human and the interhuman than with the works of Franz Rosenzweig, Martin Buber, and Emmanuel Levinas. At the heart of their writings are powerful and incisive narratives about the interhuman, that is, the importance, possibilities, and limits of relationships between humans. They also stand as preeminent examples of those who argue that religious language has a legitimate place in philosophy. These three Jewish philosophers testify to the superabundance that is religious language, which may both complement and interrogate contemporary philosophic narratives. Their apology, without being apologetic—as in either dogmatic or contrite—begins with the question: Can one narrate the exceptional possibilities of the human and the fullness of the interhuman without reference to that transcendent trace which is the divine?

The project of examining three philosophers in one chapter, especially three as complex as these, is more than a little overwhelming. However, I believe that it is manageable and fruitful if the proper parameters are respected. First, the analysis will be restricted to a text or a few central texts in the case of each thinker.[1] For Buber it is *I and Thou*, with Rosenzweig it is *The Star of Redemption*, and with Levinas, *Totality and Infinity* and *Otherwise Than Being or Beyond Essence*.[2] Second, this comparative effort will confine itself to the narratives of the interhuman that the three provide. Third, this is only an initial inquiry. It will diagram important and distinctive elements in each portrayal, while some areas will be addressed in later chapters.

In this chapter, I will explore these philosophers' discussions of the relationships between humans and the role that the God-relationship plays in these by lifting, reworking, and constructing three narratives/midrashim from the texts. I have broken the narratives into three segments, each with a particular focus. The first part will explore the ways in which the authors characterize the "natural state" of relations between persons. Each author provides an explicit portrait of the individual and a detailed discussion of what relationships to others in the everyday world are like. The second segment looks at the individual's God-relationship. It will examine the way that this relationship emerges, the basic dynamics or moments that constitute this interaction, and the nature of the transformation that the individual has undergone. The third section examines the character of the transformed interhuman that follows in the wake of the relationship to God.

The first and third sections will also include a discussion of the lives of persons in *community*. Since the interhuman is more than just about dyadic relations, this is a crucial dimension of the work of all three thinkers. For Rosenzweig and Levinas, the "natural" state of human community exhibits an alienation that is only overcome through a transformed communal life that has been reoriented by the divine. Finally, an explicit comparative discussion will come at both the beginning and conclusion of this chapter. At the beginning I will present three views that tie together their presentations. At the end, I will briefly explore some of the major themes that dominate the narratives and also suggest that the relevance of this analysis of the interhuman might extend beyond the confines of the discipline of philosophy.

For the Sake of Comparison

In order for this comparison to be more than a mere juxtaposition of positions, the objects of analysis must share a common core of views. This shared foundation allows the differences to have significance as competing or complementary options concerning a particular subject. In such a case, differences may be subtle, but they chart meaningful alternatives. The narratives of the interhuman offered by Buber, Rosenzweig, and Levinas diagram meaningful alternatives because they reveal three common, underlying themes in their storylines. These are: that relationships to other persons are the sine qua non of human living; that the quest for authenticity ultimately points to a relationship to the divine; that the relationship to God requires the individual to turn to the neighbor.

The first view testifies to the absolute importance of relationships between persons in any examination of the nature and meaning of human existence. All of these philosophers reject the model of the self that has been preeminent at least since the time of Descartes, one that gives primacy to autonomy and autarchy, that is, to self-consciousness, self-reliance, and self-direction.[3] The second theme underscores their shared understanding that human life points beyond itself and is grounded in a relationship to the transcendent. The last position unequivocally finds that the God-relationship is expressed and verified through the approach to the neighbor. Together, these themes fuse together narratives of the relationship to other persons with the discourse about the relationship to God.

Buber phrases in dramatic fashion the matter of the pivotal place that others have in the narrative of a life. In *I and Thou* he is insistent that it is impossible to speak of a person in isolation. Early in the text he writes that "there is no I as such" (1970, 54). Further, he affirms that to become an authentic self, an "I" or "person," one must enter into significant relations to others. In his words: "Man becomes an I through a Thou"[4] (1970, 80), and "Persons appear by entering into relation to other persons" (1970, 112).

In poetic language Rosenzweig indicates that the quintessential relationship to another is the love for the neighbor that both brings the development of the self to fruition and directs it in the world. *The Star* relates that with the commandment to "love the neighbor," the "soul is declared of age . . . and sets forth into the world" (1972, 205).

It is diagnostic of Levinas that the relationship to the other that Buber portrays as the relationship to a Thou, and Rosenzweig sees by way of the religious commandment to love the neighbor, he describes in terms of ethics. For him, one comes to be, one is born, through "serving" the other. In *Totality and Infinity* he writes: "The accomplishing of the I qua I and morality constitute one sole and same process in being . . . [coming] to birth . . . [in] serving the poor, the stranger, the widow, and the orphan" (1969, 245).

A second proposition that lies at the foundation of each of the three narratives is the idea that the God-relationship is essential to the development of a self. However, this statement, this presupposition, is more implicit than explicit in the narratives. A major goal of all three authors is to demonstrate that the God-relationship is not an end in itself or something that can be vital if lived in seclusion. As a consequence of this paramount interest, the discussion of the importance of the God-relationship itself is usually somewhat subdued. The following examples will illuminate both this presupposition and its de-centered place.

One way that Buber discusses the essential nature of the God-relationship for the individual is by suggesting that it fulfills or completes all other truly defining relationships—that is, the realm of the I-Thou. He writes that the inner power in each person to turn toward another, that is, "the innate Thou," "attains perfection solely in the immediate relationship to the Thou [God] that in accordance with its nature cannot become an It" (1970, 123). Elliptically Buber also expresses the notion that the relationship to the divine sustains and provides meaning. In his words: "You need God in order to be, and God needs you—for that which is the meaning of your life" (1970, 130).

Rosenzweig affirms that to be able to move beyond oneself, and thus to become fully human, God must first transform the self. He writes that it is "only by virtue of the fact that he [God] loves us and awakens our dead Self" that the person emerges to that status of "beloved and requiting soul" (1972, 381).

There are many ways in which Levinas expresses the integral role of the God-relationship in the constitution of the self. In the following citation he holds that the self is upheld or confirmed by standing before God's judgment in the context of the relation of the self to the other. In his terms: "To place oneself under the judgment of God is to exalt the [one's] subjectivity. . . . The judgment of God that judges me at the same time confirms me" (1969, 246).

A third theme that pervades the three narratives is the connection between the God-relationship and the neighbor. Unlike the second theme just discussed, there are a plethora of explicit examples that illustrate this message. Buber underscored the tie between the interhuman and the relationship to God in his afterword to *I and Thou*. The afterword contains comments on the main text that he had written three and a half decades earlier. Buber stated: "the close association of the relation to God with the relation to one's fellow men . . . is my most essential concern" (1970, 171).

In *The Star*, Rosenzweig virtually seals the two relationships. His condensed statement is: "The love for God is to express itself in love for one's neighbor" (1972, 214). Levinas again utilizes the vocabulary of ethics to discuss the juncture of the self's relationship to the divine and to other humans. The austerity of the terminology does not eclipse the depth of expression, as he writes: "God rises to his supreme and ultimate presence as correlate to the justice rendered unto men" (1969, 78).

The Self as Obstacle

The point of departure for the three narratives is the portrait of life of the self with others, a life that has not yet established what one might call a personal relationship to the divine. This first stage will profoundly color all the succeeding characterizations and have important ramifications particularly in terms of what the God-relationship provides to the interhuman. The key question here is whether persons are so constituted that they have it in their own power to form meaningful human relationships or whether the self is its own obstacle to establishing and maintaining these. Put in another way, in beginning the narrative of the self, is the interhuman an arena of authenticity or of alienation? We will see that while there are distinctive elements in each position, there are also a number of overlapping features.

Martin Buber's *I and Thou* presents a complex portrait of what it means to be human. For him, the interhuman is characterized by *two* types of relationships or modes of interaction. There is "the I of the basic word I-Thou and the I of the basic word I-It" (1970, 54). Buber is saying that persons have two potential ways of relating—to other persons, nature, and things—and that these ways indicate and express the two-fold character of the I. His use of the terminology "basic word" suggests that language is a key to both understanding this dual feature and to its living expression.

The basic word "I-It" refers to an approach or attitude of experiencing something or someone as a static thing. It is an instrumental or functional way of attending to a world "of nothing but objects" (1970, 64). In this realm the I or self determines what is important in the relationship to the other. Relationships are ruled by "goal directed verbs" (1970, 54), that is, by the self's feelings, needs, and goals. The other person is just an extension of the self and the relationship follows from what the subject wishes to do "with the things that he experiences and uses" (1970, 63). At one point Buber speaks of the I-It in terms of the "false drive for self-affirmation" with its correlate of "the having of things" (1970, 126). Overall, Buber maintains that the I-It attitude is not bad, it only becomes evil when it dominates and overwhelms the possibility of a second type of relation (1970, 97).

The "I-Thou" attitude that Buber portrays has no precise parallel in the presentations of Rosenzweig or Levinas. The I-Thou attitude is one of standing in a true or "direct" relation (1970, 62). The self speaks as "a deed of my whole being . . . my essential deed" (1970, 62), and the other is affirmed on its own terms or in its entirety (1970, 58). Correspondingly, the self's preoccupation with itself is lost as the other takes hold of it in what Buber describes as the "power of exclusiveness" (1970, 58). The relationship is also characterized by an authentic reciprocity and mutuality of the one side of the relation for the other (1970, 67). He writes: "One should not try to dilute the meaning of the [I-Thou] relation: relation is reciprocity" (1970, 58).

According to Buber, since the other is not an object and cannot be sought, the I-Thou relation emerges out of "sacrifice and grace" (1970, 110). He means by this that the self and its interests must be put aside or sacrificed and, even beyond this, that the relationship requires more than just a willingness of the self. The other, it seems, must also be open to a meeting that is beyond his or her designs. Buber also describes this relationship in terms of love. However, this is obviously not the love that arises out of desire or need but a love that is "responsibility of an I for a Thou" (1970, 66).

Although Buber holds that both relations are integral to being a full person, the priority of one to the other is essential to his presentation. The I-Thou relation is in some sense both ontogenetically and phylogenetically, that is pertaining to the development of the individual and the species, anterior to the I-It relation. He writes: "In the beginning is the relation—as the category of being, as readiness, as a form that reaches out to be filled, as a model of the soul; the *a-priori* of relation; *the innate Thou*" (1970, 78).

In *I and Thou*, Buber unravels the meaning of "the innate Thou" or Thou of relation. For him, there is a deep interaction between fetus and mother in the womb. Even the prenatal human, the fetus, exhibits the urge toward relation, or "a pure natural association" with its carrier (1970, 76). After birth, in the earliest stages, the innate "longing for relation" is clear and dominates the infant's life. Buber writes about the infant's "drive to turn everything into a Thou" (1970, 78), that is, a partner in relationship, and sees it as *independent* of other drives and requirements, such as that of nourishment (1970, 77). The natural attitude of the infant, who does not know the distinction between animate and inanimate objects, will even bring her or him to respond to any sound as if to a "conversation" (1970, 78).[5]

It is from the basis of this desire for relation that all else in the development of the infant unfolds. An independent sense of the self as something separate from the relationship with the other slowly crystallizes through the activities of the infant encountering persons and things. In Buber's words: "it comes closer and closer to the bursting point until one day the bonds are broken and the I confronts its detached self for a moment like a Thou—and then it takes possession of itself and henceforth enters into relations in full consciousness" (1970, 80).

Both the fully developed I-Thou relation and the I-It relation follow upon the first moment of self-consciousness of the I. In terms of the latter, only now can the object be isolated from its tie to the self, examined, and compared with other objects. Among other features of the I-It relationship, the ability to put things into a "spatio-temporal-causal context" develops (1970, 81).

Buber notes a parallel between the life of the individual and that of human history in terms of the "progressive increase of the It-world" (1970, 88). Thus, while the I-Thou relation is the first relation and also that which makes the individual a human in the fullest sense, the I-It relation—with its tendency toward alienation—has become the norm or customary mode of the everyday.

Individuals living together in communities and societies reflect the impact of the expanding I-It world. According to Buber, a prevalent sense of doom haunts the communal life of modern persons. They feel caught in institutions over which they have no control. Here "one works, negotiates, influences, undertakes, competes, organizes, administers, officiates, preaches" (1970, 93).

The sense of helplessness is deepened by a myriad of academic theories—biological, psychological, sociological, cultural—concluding that this state of affairs is inevitable (1970, 105). In an attempt to find some comfort from this situation, modern persons separate their lives into two distinct arenas. It is hoped that by investing in a personal life where "feelings" hold sway, one can partially escape the estrangement of public life and the world "out there" (1970, 92–93). For Buber, this path of separation does not lead to liberation. Another answer, as we will see, is required.

It is important to note that Buber finds that there are three spheres or areas of relations that are addressed by the two basic types of attitude, as well as an additional sphere for the I-Thou. The three are the relations to the natural world, humans and the cultural products of humans, and the realm of art (1970, 56–57). Despite these three areas of possible relations, the model for the I-Thou attitude is the life with persons (1970, 112). It is primarily with persons that this relation is fulfilled. Finally, the relation to God or what Buber calls the "eternal Thou" is only possible in terms of the dialogue between "I" and "Thou." God is hidden from every approach that attempts to treat Him or Her as an object.

Rosenzweig's portrayal of the natural state of humans in *The Star of Redemption* is very much in narrative form, for he insists that real life can only be narrated (1999, 81). There are phylogenetic and ontogenetic dimensions to his narrative of the self. Rosenzweig holds that the individual is not born a self. One is born as just another member of the human species, a creature or "piece of the world" (1972, 71). At this stage, the personality distinguishes one from others, but this is no fundamental marking off. The full distinctiveness of what one means by a self erupts. At a certain point in its maturation, the self wills itself in its particularity, out of the combination of "defiance and character," or, alternately, of "hubris and *daimon*" (1972, 167). With this emergence, the individual is an utterly self-contained entity: one who is "solitary man in the hardest sense of the word" (1972, 71). Formed in this way, it is not surprising that relationship, speech, trust, and love are foreign to the self. The life of solitariness, one's being alone facing death, fully characterizes the cage of life for the self. This cage will only be opened by God's approach.

The Star contains some enigmatic statements about the place of sexual difference in the development of persons (1972, 156). Rosenzweig suggests that the encounter with eros has something to do with the timing of the emergence of the self. For a man, the self crystallizes through the meeting with eros (which I assume means with woman at this point), and its final form only comes by facing thanatos. For a woman there is no "two-fold encounter," just one. For her: "Thanatos can approach . . . in the sweet guise of Eros" (1972, 156), which seems to mean that through facing her (male) lover, the self of a woman is fully formed. Her character is finalized, her life course is fulfilled, and she is now prepared for death in the same way that a man is only in old age.[6]

Rosenzweig looks to the tragic hero of Greek drama to illustrate the basic nature of the human untouched by the divine. This is a tale of fundamental alienation from the other. The hero of tragedy lives a life of isolation and self-containment, which culminates in his or her self-destruction. This figure, driven by a distinctive character, remains unrelated in any significant way to anyone else. Living essentially speechless, the hero is able to trust only in him-self or herself. The central and defining event of that life is the encounter with death. Rosenzweig writes: "Death, his own death, has become the sovereign event of his life" (1972, 76–77).

There is a significant political dimension to Rosenzweig's treatment of death that is often overlooked. For him, the attempt to evade death, to escape fleeting time by holding onto something that cannot die, is a persistent feature of human life. Philosophy offers its false elixir of a "soul" disengaged from the corruptible body, but most persons place faith in their state or nation. They believe that the state will provide an immortality that is out of reach of single individuals. According to Rosenzweig, the rise of the modern state is tied to this promise of eternity. Through "holy war," law, and coercion, states assert their claims to eternity over both those outside and those within. For Rosenzweig "war and revolution"—in terms of the latter he means instituting new law through coercion—are the only realities known to the state (1972, 328–35).[7] His understanding of communities that in truth introduce eternity into time points toward later discussions of Judaism and Christianity.

Emmanuel Levinas presents a complex narrative about the nature of the human that has two layers. One layer can be fairly easily narrated, while the other, the transcendent or metaphysical aspect, follows no systematic time or history (1981, 155). Levinas characterizes the I as being fundamentally turned back upon itself or being self-absorbed. He writes in *Totality and Infinity* that "To be an I is . . . to have identity as one's content" (1969, 36). This is also expressed as interiority. The term points to the elemental fact that the self or ego stands at first separate from all systems and totalizations. From this point of departure, the human is a "being whose existing consists in identifying itself, in recovering its identity throughout all that happens to it" (1969, 36). Some features of this identification are explored by the author in terms of the body, labor, possession, and economy (1969, 38).

The separation of the individual, its integrity and independence, is concretized in the experience of enjoyment. In Levinas' words, separation is produced "in the psychism of enjoyment, in egoism, in happiness, where the I identifies itself" (1969, 62). The individual, thus, first stands in its freedom enjoying life through pleasures of sensing, acting and taking. Life is tasted, it is not just lived. Again, in his words: "Life is *love of life*, a relation with contents that are not my being but more dear than my being: thinking, eating, sleeping, reading, working, warming oneself in the sun" (1969, 112).[8] Levinas calls this state the "concreteness of egoism" (1969, 38), and depicts its freedom as "egoist spontaneity" (1969, 43).

However, this mode of existence is not innocent! Other persons are encountered, but only as objects, subject to my power and freedom (1969, 84). The other is something to be dominated, possessed, or discarded; to be incorporated, surmounted, enveloped by my world—the same—or to be wiped out. Here freedom is arbitrary and unjustified, and beneath it lurks a self murderous and violent (1969, 84). This is the "I" of egoism, which Levinas does not hesitate to characterize from the point of view of ethics as "detestable" (1969, 88).

Still, Levinas sees the constitution of the self as more complex than this basic egoism. The self is not a single whole. While it is ruled by its own egoism, enjoyment, and happiness, it also is pulled or inspired by a metaphysical desire for what is beyond the self (1969, 34). This desire is metaphysical in the sense that it transcends all of one's ability to incorporate or even account for it. As a desire, it is in a totally different register than drives or needs, which emerge from oneself. In *Otherwise Than Being* this dimension is discussed in terms of the way that subjectivity is an openness to the other: "Subjectivity . . . obligated with regard to the neighbor, is the breaking point where essence is exceeded by the infinite" (1981, 12). While this is initiated by that other, it is structured by the very skin of one's body and the breath taken into one's lungs, in terms of the self's passivity and vulnerability to the outside.

Thus, existing as a self entails both the ego and its enjoyment, and subjectivity, that is, being assigned and compelled by the other (1981, 101). The encounter with the other is discussed in terms of the face in *Totality and Infinity* and as proximity in *Otherwise Than Being*. Thus he writes:

> Infinity presents itself as a face in the ethical resistance that paralyses my powers and from the depths of defenseless eyes rises firm and absolute in its nudity and destitution. (1969, 199–200)

> Proximity, difference which is non-indifference, is responsibility. It is a response without a question, the immediacy of peace that is incumbent on me. . . . Proximity is fraternity before essence and before death. (1981, 139)

Although Levinas' treatment is somewhat reminiscent of Buber's depiction of humans' two-fold attitude, there are significant differences.[9] Most importantly,

Buber sees the I-Thou relationship as being a primary ingredient or expression of living as a person, while Levinas insists that what is dominant is the egoism that entraps the individual: an egoism that must be ruptured by something from the outside, something transcendent, that is, the Other.[10]

Finally, the scope of Levinas' analysis of the natural state of things, as it were, sees a direct relation between the personal/interpersonal and the political. *Totality and Infinity* begins with a discussion of war and its opposite, not that violent peace enforced between wars, but an "eschatology of messianic peace" (1969, 22).[11] Levinas connects war with ontology, that is with totalities, totalitarianisms of the same. States express the egoism of humans, who wish to aggrandize the self infinitely by either incorporating that which is outside or expelling/crushing the unalterably alien. They are also heir to that notion of freedom built upon rights, one's "place in the sun,"[12] rather than responsibilities. We will soon inquire into the meaning of a transformed, an eschatological, politics.

The Relationship to God

The next stage in the three narratives examines the initiation and genesis of the relationship to God. This relationship eventually either overcomes the alienation of the interhuman in the cases of Rosenzweig and Levinas, or fulfills the integrity of the interhuman, as in the instance of Buber's narrative. There are three foci for this examination of the divine-human relationship, and these bring to the fore issues of sequence, of dynamics, and of the nature of the transformed individual. As will become apparent in the following, while I have noted these three different dimensions of the relationship to God, they are actually blended together in distinctive ways by each of the three philosophers.

First, there is the question of sequence, that is, whether an authentic relationship with other persons precedes or follows the divine-human relationship. The relationship to the divine must take precedence, if humans are inextricably entangled in solitude or egoism. Alternately, if the capacity for healthy relationships is innate, a rescue from the outside is unnecessary and the God-relationship can follow upon the establishment of the interhuman.

Second, the nature, various steps, or dynamics of the relationship with God need to be described. We will look at the way that the relation is initiated and also at the expression of its evolution or unfolding. Third, the manner in which the individual is transformed by the encounter with God will be explored. How has an incursion from the transcendent changed the character of being human? What is the nature of the new powers bestowed upon persons?

For Buber the I-Thou relationship between persons precedes or has priority over the divine-human encounter. As we saw earlier, humans have the power to actualize two types of relationships, and one of these, the I-Thou relationship, is the highest human expression. Buber does not hesitate to designate this relationship as one of "love" in terms of the interhuman realm. For him, life with other persons, that mutuality and reciprocity of the I-Thou realm, is the necessary training or preparation for the later relationship to God. In his words: "When one has achieved steadfastness in this state [of relating to the world], one is able to venture forth toward the supreme encounter" with God (1970, 125).

There are two additional, and somewhat mitigating, aspects of the priority of the human over the God-relationship in Buber's presentation. First, the I-Thou turning toward the world and others is not seen as fully autonomous or separate from the meeting with God. Buber holds that the relationship to God is the natural, the inevitable, step occurring at the same time, as it were, as the full meeting with others. He writes: "Through every single Thou the basic word addresses the eternal Thou" (1970, 123). Buber's view that the God-relationship is a dimension of every true encounter in the world is an alternative way of expressing the virtual simultaneity of the two relationships. In this connection we find: "In every sphere, through everything that becomes present to us, we gaze toward the train of the eternal Thou" (1970, 57).

Second, it is in some sense accurate to say that a prior relationship to God grounds the I-Thou relationship to others. This point is not a major one in Buber's text, but it is implied. A prior relationship to God, at least in terms of the human as created, is what provides the initial potentiality of humans to turn towards others and address them as "Thou." He puts this as: "The mediatorship of the Thou of all beings accounts for the fullness of our relationships to them" (1970, 123). However, since being a creature or created being is what characterizes the natural condition of persons, it is still proper to declare that for Buber humans are so constituted that they can relate meaningfully to others and that these relationships must precede the specific turning toward God.

In an extremely important section of *I and Thou* (1970, 157–60), in some sense its highlight, Buber provides a careful description of the dynamics or essential features that make up the relationship to God, at least to the extent that this can be put into words. He labels this "the primal phenomenon, present in the here and now, of what we call revelation" (1970, 157). Buber divides revelation into three interrelated movements. The recipient of revelation, first, has a sense that there has been a real encounter, that there has been a "reciprocity" between two who were present. Second, the individual finds "an inexpressible confirmation of meaning" (1970, 158). One now knows or has learned something that was not known before. This is not a knowledge with a concrete content, but a confidence about meaning.[13] As Buber puts it: "the inexpressible confirmation of meaning. It is guaranteed. Nothing, nothing can henceforth be meaningless. The question about the meaning of life has vanished" (1970, 158–59). From this it appears that one steps out of the encounter with a sense or feeling—as against a knowing with a specific content—that one's life and all of life have meaning. For Buber, the two would be inseparable. How could one's life have meaning, divorced from all of one's Thous?

The third aspect of the encounter is that the individual is thrust back into the world. The God-relationship requires that one puts its truth "to the proof in action" in the world with others (1970, 160). According to Buber, in fulfilling God's word or mission as it is given, one "always has God before him" (1970, 164). We will look at this again a little later on.

Although Buber unhesitatingly affirms the importance of the relationship to God, the nature of the transformation that the God-relationship brings to the self is rather discrete. As we saw, the relationship to other humans and the world is a training of the self and the God-relationship is a supplement to as well as a deepening of that meaning. In Buber's words, the "innate Thou," that is, the individual's innate power to call upon others, achieves "perfection solely in the immediate relationship to" the eternal Thou (1970, 123). It is clear that following revelation the self sees the world in a new way: "the world becomes wholly present to him for the first time in the fullness of the presence, illuminated by eternity" (1970, 157). In addition, I have noted that the person now recognizes the meaningfulness of her or his life and life overall. While the insecurity, challenge, and openness of the realm of the I-Thou must always remain (1970, 83, 126), following the encounter with God the self has a firmer direction. Again, the everyday is illuminated, but neither it nor the self are made more secure.

Rosenzweig's position concerning the question of sequence follows upon his view of humans' original situation. Since humans on their own are closed in upon themselves and fixated by the threat of death, they require an outside catalyst to overcome this predicament. Consequently, the God-relationship necessarily precedes authentic human meetings. He writes: "It is only . . . in the love of God that the flower of the soul begins to grow out of the rock of the self. Previously man had been a senseless and speechless introvert; only now is he—beloved soul" (1972, 169).

The intricate dynamics of the relationship to God is depicted by Rosenzweig in *The Star* as a love scene between two lovers (1972, 156–204). God is the initiating lover and the individual or soul is the beloved. In this scenario Rosenzweig has God play the male/active/lover part and the soul play the female/reactive/beloved role. However, he indicates that for men and women, whose love mirrors the relationship between God and the soul, "the roles of giver and receiver of love pass back and forth" (1972, 169). This statement is one of many indications that these dynamics are applicable to relationships between humans.

God initiates the relationship with the soul by commanding that the beloved love in return. Rosenzweig insists that the love of the lover is so momentary that nothing beyond a first person commandment would reflect its immediacy. In making a command/demand the lover actually is the first to be transformed. God turns out of isolation and self-sufficiency in entering into a relation to the other. Rosenzweig describes this turning as a "continually renewed self-sacrifice," and a "momentary self transformation, his self-denial" (1972, 162–63). Later, from the response of the soul, God will receive back "affirmation and constancy" (1972, 171), which is God's renewal or recreation. With an ear for something beyond the dynamics of divine revelation, Rosenzweig concludes: "Only in the discovery of a Thou is it possible to hear an actual I" (1972, 175).

There is a powerful effect upon the soul, "the other pole in revelation" (1972, 167). Its isolating defiance is transformed into the quiet, confident, secure pride of humility. In a more expansive way, Rosenzweig describes the love of the beloved as "an awe compounded of humility and pride, together with a feeling of dependence and of being securely sheltered" (1972, 168). However, the first actual response of the beloved is shame, for not having loved before. Shame is expressed in the beloved's confession that it has sinned. For Rosenzweig, "the acknowledgment of belief originates in the acknowledgment of sin" (1972, 181). Eventually the soul accepts God's love in trust, faithfulness, and peace (1972, 170–71). Here the authentic I emerges in response to God's presence as an I.

The exchange between the two partners necessitates another step. God's momentary revelation must be both made everlasting and expressed in the world. For Rosenzweig, this cannot be achieved in the isolation of the "I" and "Thou" between God and the soul. Only in the world, through the individual's turning in love to the neighbor, is permanence or redemption achieved. Rosenzweig writes about this as: "He whom God's love has chosen hears God's command . . . and sets out for the land that God will show him . . . the realm of redemption" (1972, 251).

How does the God-relationship transform the individual in Rosenzweig's narrative? As we have seen, *The Star* outlines the becoming of a person as the movement from being an enclosed self to a speaking and loving soul. The fear of death that was the sole concern, a concern that prevented a real life with others, is no longer allowed to be the capstone of life. It has been replaced by trust: trust in the Creator and patience and hope to wait for the Redeemer (1972, 382).

Revelation, which is God's liberating love, elicits in return both speech and love from the individual. For Rosenzweig, the two are synonymous. Both require that the self be opened up to the other. Both are the currencies in the mutuality of relationship. The other can be of concern, because the individual's fear of death has been lifted. Rosenzweig writes: "The living soul, loved by God, triumphs over all that is mortal, and that is all that can be objectively stated about it" (1972, 202).

Another way of describing what is given to the individual is to examine Rosenzweig's concept of orientation. Revelation teaches that neither the individual's life nor the world are ruled by blind fate. There is providence, that is, purpose. The world has been created and is pointed toward redemption. The transformed individual feels that she or he has been assigned a particular time and place to answer with her or his "Truly in midst of the Truth" (1972, 392). Thus, as does Buber, Rosenzweig transmits a very powerful conviction of the way that the individual's everyday life is permeated by a sense of mission and a need to verify God's command in the world (1972, 392–93).

With Levinas, the narrative of the development of the self does not include a statement about the precedence or priority of one relationship, either the divine-human or the authentic interhuman, over the other. Since the two relationships are so intimately bound together, there is no real priority. He rules out the priority of the God-relationship, because he contends that there is no direct relationship to God. The relationship to God is always mediated by ethics, that is, the relationship to one's neighbor. Levinas is insistent that "Ethics is spiritual optics," and that "The Other is the very locus of metaphysical truth, and is indispensable for my relation with God" (1969, 78).

Still, there is a trace of the presence of the divine in the authentic relationship to the neighbor. More concretely, a trace of God is revealed when one looks into the face of the other. As Levinas states it: "The Other is not the incarnation of God, but precisely by his face, in which he is disincarnate, is the manifestation of the height in which God is revealed" (1969, 73).[14]

However, before commencing on this part of the narrative, I would like to point out two central issues. First, for Levinas it is the other person, the neighbor, stranger, widow, and orphan, that transforms, not God. Second, this is no actual event. It cannot be accounted in history or biography, and it affects that transformation into subjectivity as "an anachronous birth, prior to its own present, a non-beginning, an anarchy" (1981, 139). Levinas means by this that the seizure by the other is structured into human existence, as was suggested earlier. In the very "corporeality" of the human, even in its passivity of fatigue and aging, is uncovered one's being for another (1981, 55).

Levinas displays great austerity in speaking of God or the God-relationship. His primary allusion to this is through the command not to kill. In the encounter with the other the first impression upon the self is the forcefulness of a command that "Thou shall not kill!" This is correlative with the potential murderousness of one's power and freedom and also the nakedness and vulnerability of the other's face. Levinas expresses this as: "This infinity, stronger than murder, already resists us in his face; in his face is the primordial *expression*, is the first word: 'you shall not commit murder'" (1969, 199). While a divine voice is not heard here, the command certainly represents a "clandestine dimension of the judgment of God," which has called the self to justify itself (1969, 247). The movement from purely ethical to ethical-religious terminology in one's "election" by and response of "Here I am!" for the neighbor are a few of the other indirect references to the divine encounter behind the human one.

In the case of Levinas, the focus on the other person is inescapable even in our discussion of the dynamics of the relationship to God. The other, or the neighbor, or, in biblical language, the poor, widow, orphan, and stranger, overturns my being-for-myself. He or she is experienced as both commanding and vulnerable, or in Levinas' vocabulary, in both the other's "Height" and "destitution" (1969, 200).

A suggestive breach to the austerity of Levinas' references to the divine appears in the final footnote to *Otherwise Than Being*. He alludes to the rabbinic commentary about Moses' expiry with the kiss of God (*Deut.* 34:5), and ties this mysterious closeness to God with the "passivity and obedience, in the inspiration by the other for the other" (1981, 200).

In terms of Levinas' depiction of the transformed individual, since the egoism of the self is so entrenched, the shattering of the individual's natural attitude must be radical. The language utilized by Levinas to speak of this shattering is nothing less than violent. In order to achieve authentic subjectivity the individual must become hollowed out, inverted, extroverted, denucleated, even persecuted. In his words: "The subjectivity of the subject is persecution and martyrdom" (1981, 146). The individual is made nothing less than a "substitute" or "hostage" to the other (1981, 146).

Again, it is the face of the poor and the stranger that overturns the individual, that overcomes every defense that the person might erect (1969, 213). The other forces the individual to justify herself or himself, recognizing that the other has a right over the self (1969, 40). Alternatively, the spontaneity of egoism is brought into question through ethics (1969, 40). Ultimately, standing face-to-face before another person causes shame, "where, qua I, I am not innocent spontaneity but usurper and murderer" (1969, 84).

Levinas has a more positive way of seeing the results of this rupture of the self, an issue that will also be taken up in the next section. At the highest stage, language is derived from the encounter with the other. Language is the essential expression of the social situation of persons being (ethically, responsibly) with other persons, or what Levinas sometimes describes as "saying." Thus, for him, language is not some mere "act, as a gesture of behavior" (1969, 67), as seen by some psychologists. It is not secondary to that inner thought or reason to which some philosophers give primacy, nor is it that independent system or medium that many post-modernists posit. As Levinas puts it: "Meaning is the face of the Other, and all recourse to words takes place already within the primordial face-to-face of language" (1969, 206).

Following upon a theme of Rosenzweig's, Levinas sees the face-to-face relation as answering even the threat of one's death. The other does not eliminate death, but allows a "forgetting of death" (1981, 141), or provides a meaning that even death cannot wipe away. In the encounter with the other, the subject's fear of death is forgotten, because it has been turned into an overriding concern for the other's death, especially at my hands (1969, 244). Levinas writes: "No one is so hypocritical as to claim that he has taken from death its sting. . . . But we can have responsibilities and attachments through which death takes on a meaning" (1981, 129).

The Transformed Interhuman

The last stage that will be explored in the three narratives is the exposition concerning the way that the interhuman has been healed by the encounter with the divine. This includes a description of both what has changed in terms of the relationship to others and how the new interhuman is lived-out. Since all of the philosophers insist that the fruits (in the terminology used by Søren Kierkegaard)[15] of the God-relationship must be expressed among others, this is a necessary part, in fact, the climax, of their overall narratives.

The first stage of the examination of Buber's narrative in *I and Thou* indicated that humans have the ability to authentically turn to one another, in some sense prior to and outside of the God-relation. In light of this, it is not easy to see what the encounter with the divine directly adds to this realm of the "between." The change will be a matter of degree rather than of some dramatic transformation.

One possible way of eliciting what might be changed is to explore the third feature of Buber's description of the nature of (all) revelation. We saw that the meeting with the eternal Thou must be verified or put "to the proof in action" in the world (1970, 159). In this way there might be an additional depth to all human relations, because they are not just a matter of persons either singly or in communities entering into I-Thou relations. Such relations are verifications or extensions of the encounter with the divine.

Thus, God's presence and direction continually accompany I-Thou relations. Again, what might be meant by this? One expression in the afterword to *I and Thou* that elaborates the notion of how God's presence is felt is: "God's address to man penetrates the events in all our lives and all the events in the world around us . . . and turns it into instruction, into demands for you and me" (1970, 182). This statement is clearly tied to Buber's view, which we have seen before, that each person has a unique place in the world or a mission given by God.

It is interesting that the impact of the relationship to God may be more apparent in the realm of the communal and political. In response to the hollow I-It experiences of living in modern society, Buber insists again upon the remedy of true relationship. However, this, in turn, rests upon contact with the divine. Fulfilling community life requires that individuals maintain two axes: "a living, reciprocal relationship to a single living [divine or transcendent] center, and . . . a living, reciprocal relationship to one another" (1970, 94). Here the exchange of I and Thou is not limited to two in dialogue, but permeates all aspects of political life.

With Rosenzweig, the change in the possibilities of human relationships, except for the domain of the religious community, is expressed in poetic language and only through clues. Still, some elaboration is possible. This will be based upon Rosenzweig's discussion of revelation, which he saw as a model for the exchange of "I" and "Thou" between persons (1972, 199), and redemption.

If the command to love God signals the commencement of the personal experience of God's presence, the way leads out of the personal and private experience of God by the second command, to love the neighbor (1972, 214). The individual's life in the world is henceforth guided by this obligation. Who is the neighbor, according to Rosenzweig? The neighbor is everyone and concretely, the one who stands closest to one, the nighest (*das Nebenmensch*) (1972, 218). This means that one consequence of the encounter with God is that the individual has an obligation to every person she or he meets in the unfolding of the hourly and daily rhythms of their life.

Loving the neighbor adds a new dynamic to the interhuman and even to the divine processes of creation, revelation, and redemption. Turning to the other begins again that process—for the neighbor—of hearing of the divine word, feeling the divine presence, and then turning to the next one. Through love of the neighbor, the other ceases to be an "it," simply another part of creation. She or he becomes a soul, as did the original beloved of God. As Rosenzweig put it: "Rather he [the neighbor] is like You, like your You, a You like You, an

I—a soul" (1972, 240). This ensouling of the other and eventually of the world constitutes the course of redemption.

Rosenzweig indicates that a trace of the divine animates and remains present throughout the transformed interhuman. In fact, turning toward other persons is portrayed in *The Star* as walking in the presence of God (1972, 422–24). The human face reflects God's truth; the face of the neighbor radiates God's countenance. Rosenzweig writes that God's truth has "become a countenance which glances at me and out of which I glance" (1972, 423).

Perhaps it is in speech between persons—and, once again, for Rosenzweig the dynamics of love and speech are similar—that the results of the divine encounter are clearest. Just as God's love brought the individual out of her or his isolating fear of death and mute existence, the love of neighbor opens up the neighbor to the possibilities of the I and Thou of speech for the first time. In turning to the neighbor the other is acknowledged as something separate from the self, as something "independent and freely confronting" (1972, 175). Speech exhibits a mutuality, where the acknowledgment of the other can be exchanged between the partners.

Thus, although the details of the new relation to others are not fully worked out in *The Star*, there is no doubt of a significant difference between human existence before and after God's revelation. The self is not limited to its initial isolation and muteness. For Rosenzweig, radical transformation of the self through the love of God and love of neighbor is a reality. In his words: "love [and thus also speech] is man's momentary self-transformation, his self-denial" (1972, 163).

Finally, Rosenzweig holds that there is a significant communal dimension to the new possibilities of human relationships. The end of isolation allows persons to form together into a "we." This "we" grows out of the dual of I and Thou and continually increases. Although limited and recognizing that there are others that stand outside, its goal is to eventually include everyone (1972, 236–37). Starting with the nighest the "we" builds to an "all." In Rosenzweig's words: "The effect of the love of 'neighbor' is that 'Anyone' and 'all the world' thus belong together" (1972, 236).

This political dimension of Rosenzweig's transformed interhuman is intriguing. We saw that Rosenzweig characterized modern states as coercive institutions in which the violence of "war and revolution" form people together and promise them some "eternal" meaning to their lives. In opposition to these states, Rosenzweig held that the Jewish and Christian communities actually provided contact with eternity in the midst of time. While they differed in the ways through which they achieved this, Rosenzweig held that both provided meaningful experiences of the divine with which one could confront the hard, worldly reality of death. For him, these were transformed communities, truly non-coercive assemblies, of those seeking a divine kingdom that would include everyone.[16]

For Levinas, the face-to-face relation, with the concomitant divine command not to kill, fundamentally transforms the possibilities of human interaction. The other is no longer just an object for the self, something to be mastered, usurped, or even murdered. The other stands in its height above the self and through this the egoism of the self is crushed. As Levinas expresses it: "To recognize the Other is to give. But it is to give to the master, to the lord, to him whom one approaches as 'You' in a dimension of height" (1969, 75). In other words, the face-to-face establishes for the first time an authentic, if unsymmetrical, interhuman, the realm of ethics.

Perhaps the most pervasive characteristic of the altered interhuman is responsibility. The self which is turned upon itself and is de-legitimated in its own eyes becomes subsequently a responsible self. The individual comes to recognize—to be obsessed with—an unrelenting responsibility, where one must answer with a "*here I am* . . . for everything and for everyone" (1981, 114). More importantly, not only is the self made responsible, but it is granted the powers to fulfill that which it is called upon to give (1969, 215).

Many of the features of the authentic interhuman, of a fraternity of equality and command (1969, 214), are discussed by Levinas in terms of language. Language unveils the separation of the partners, the dependence of the self on the other, and even the priority of the other (1969, 73). The communication between persons reveals a discourse where welcoming is possible (1969, 178). Such communication is more than a repeat of the same: it is creative. The new is allowed to appear, because the other represents something outside of mere being, something of transcendence (1981, 182). Further, through communication meaning is created (1969, 66), and truth can be legitimately sought. Finally, language or discourse is even tied to love. In Levinas' words: "The metaphysical event of transcendence—the welcome of the Other, hospitality—Desire and language—is not accomplished as love. But the transcendence of discourse is bound to love" (1969, 254).

Large expanses of the books *Totality and Infinity* and *Otherwise Than Being* are devoted to detailed arguments outlining the ways that major features of the human are born from the interhuman, informed by the face of the other. Language is the first feature, which we have taken up many times before. Language is built upon an openness of one for another: upon a feeling of being obligated to respond (1981, 119). Levinas puts this in terms of "saying": "Saying is communication, to be sure, but as a condition for all communication, as exposure" (1981, 48). Thus, saying, the essence of language, is derived from exposure, or the ethical dimension of the human. Reason follows from language. In *Totality and Infinity*, Levinas writes: "reason lives in language . . . the first rationality gleams forth in the opposition of the face to face" (1969, 208). In addition to reason, that book lists, among other features, rationality, intelligibility, signification, universality, justice, objectivity, fraternity, and time flowing from the ethical encounter (1969, 204–24). In terms of time, for example, Levinas finds that facing the other is expressly what is meant by living in time. He writes: "Time is precisely the fact that the whole of existence of the mortal being—exposed to violence—is not being for death, but the 'not yet' which is a way of being against death" (1969, 224). His summary statement is:

> The establishing of this primacy of the ethical, that is, of the relationship of man to man—signification, teaching, and justice—a primacy of an irreducible structure upon which *all the other structures rest* . . . is one of the objectives of the present work. (1969, 79; my emphasis)

In *Otherwise Than Being* the argument about the ramifications of the ethical, or the nature of the interhuman, is pursued somewhat differently. Here, justice is pivotal. For Levinas, while justice is distinguished from the ethical, it is derived from it. Once the subject is exposed to the infinite responsibility for the other, the issues of the subject's responsibility for other neighbors, and of those neighbors for still others arise. These responsibilities, that constitute "justice," are a matter of equality and deciding what each is due. They must be determined through reason, calculation, and the careful observation of the particular problems that beset others (1981, 157–63). Only now does the actual face of another person become significant, with its specific, concrete problems (1981, 157). Levinas writes about the consequences of this more calculable responsibility: "The fact that the other, my neighbor, is also a third party with respect to another, who is also a neighbor, is the birth of thought, consciousness, justice and philosophy" (1981, 128). Justice and the third party are the womb for correction, weighing, science, philosophy, and even the state in this text (1981, 157–60).

How is the state connected to justice? For Levinas, the state is not the mediator which enforces peace in the face of Hobbes' "war of all against all." It appears that the "egalitarian and just state" provides an impartial forum for deciding what is owed to the third parties, as well as the means for fulfilling these responsibilities which each person has for others. However, the state often ignores its foundations for the other/s in proximity and justice, and turns into a totalizing institution with itself as its own raison d'etre. The response to this must be a prophetic eschatology that never forgets that the infinity of the face is the real inspiration and only justification behind every form of social life (1981, 158–60).

Conclusion: Of the Self, the Interpersonal, and Transcendence

The narratives of Buber, Rosenzweig, and Levinas present distinct yet overlapping portraits of what it means to be a human with others. In this conclusion I want to recapitulate and extend the treatment by examining the understanding of the fundamental social nature of the self, the depiction of the types of alienation from others, the view that a transcendent opening from this alienation is both possible and necessary, and finally, the role of the metaphor of God as person in the narratives. While these are only a few of the areas that appear in the above presentation, I believe that they are some of the more diagnostic ones. These foci will illuminate what the narratives share rather than what separates or clearly differentiates them.

All of these portrayals are built upon the insight that, in Buber's words: "There is no I as such." Individuals cannot be understood or examined in isolation from others. These philosophers' expositions of the nature of the human converge on the social character of existence. Thus, such features as love, speaking, and being responsible are taken as quintessential. More pointedly, it is only in relation to other persons and to God that life gains direction and meaning. Meaning is not self-engendered. Life becomes meaningful when the self is put aside and a concern for the other takes precedence. Put in another way, alienation is the result of living for oneself, of living in isolation. The other and language do not alienate the self from itself—as, for example, Lacan suggests—they are instruments of redemption.

Yet, these treatments of the social character of human life do not conclude with some view that, ultimately, the individual self is not real or that (ethical) agency is an illusion. The discourse about authenticity does not abandon the vocabulary of the individual self by arguing that the highest is a losing of the self or a merging of the self with either other persons or the divine. The uniqueness of each life is upheld through relationship, in fact, exclusively through relationship.

For Buber, Rosenzweig, and Levinas, the individuality of the self or the uniqueness of one's life results from accepting the call in the midst of the interaction with the particular persons one comes up against. Buber expresses this as: "The meaning we receive [from revelation] can be put to the proof in action only by each person in the uniqueness of his being and in the uniqueness of his life" (1970, 159). Rosenzweig explores the unique place each person is given in God's plan in terms of "mission": "The personal is verified as eternal truth: birth and rebirth, station and mission, located Here and decisive Now of life" (1972, 394). Finally, Levinas extends this view of the way that relationship to the other establishes distinctiveness or individuality. He affirms something that, I believe, is an element in the other thinkers as well, which is that specific others draw out the self one is to be. He writes: "Exposedness ['exposure to the other'] is the one-in-responsibility [the self], and thus the one in its uniqueness" (1981, 56).

The three narratives probe in an intense, unrelenting manner the types of alienation or sickness that haunt relationships between persons. Buber's portrayal of the dynamics of the interhuman is filled with hope about the possibilities for authentic mutuality, but it is by no means a naive narrative. The I-Thou encounter momentarily and, at best, briefly, sporadically punctuates the everyday. It must redeem those other relations that are the customary ones. These, of the I-It realm, always tie the other to the self's desires and plans. The other is objectified, a passive piece, moved not by concern for but by the self's designs upon. Further, because the objectifying modus vivendi of the I-It is set by the self before the other is encountered, no word or protest can be heard in the midst of the relationship. In the I-It realm there is no present; there is no speech or listening, no real interchange.

Rosenzweig's natural self is also blind to the other. However, rather than self-interest, Rosenzweig finds fear prevents true relation. Limited by his or her own powers, the individual sees no meaning in life and finds himself or herself hurled upon the road to death. Haunted by this, there is no speech, no love. The self is closed upon itself, not by choice, but through, as it were, fate. This conclusion is embodied in the figure of the tragic hero.

For Levinas, egoism does not allow the other to be seen, to be faced. The other, once more, is an object. At best "it" is used, abused, moved for the sake of the individual's enjoyment or happiness. More ominously, the self seeks to either incorporate or eradicate. It wants to build up more of the self-same, and is violent toward that which cannot be made over into its image.

Each of these portraits of sickness add perspectives upon the customary failures of the interhuman realm. They also indicate that the ramifications of the alienation of the interhuman extend all the way to interaction at the level of community and society. Equally important, the narratives indicate that sickness has a remedy. While the overcoming of the self's predicament cannot be accomplished by the self alone, there is the possibility of the individual transcending her or his usual condition. Freedom, spontaneity in relationships, and, more importantly, love and responsibility are not apparitions. These features of human experience may not be easy to achieve and may not be dominant in the normal run of things, but they are not totally outside of human existence.

The divine teaches of the category of the neighbor, that one is responsible to each of one's others. In addition, relationship to the divine provides the powers to realize this responsibility. Transcendence of one's normal condition is reached through a relationship to the divine, or to human relationships that witness the divine, and this transcendence is the basis for further relationships. The narratives' constant refrain is that the transformed self must be put to the "proof in action" in terms of the neighbor.

A final area of inquiry concerns the place and role of the metaphor of God as person in the narratives. Buber's use of the metaphor of God as person is transparent. God is a Thou, in fact, the only Thou that cannot be transformed into an it. The I-Thou relationship, of mutuality, reciprocity, love, and responsibility, becomes in Buber's discourse equally as true in terms of the encounter with the divine as it does in the interhuman realm. He writes: "the relation to a human being is the proper metaphor for relation to God" (1970, 151). In the afterword he adds that for him: "The designation of God as a person is indispensable" (1970, 180), and "It is as *absolute person* that God enters into direct relationship to us" (1970, 181–82).

For Rosenzweig, the relation between lovers, which he draws from the Bible's erotic poem the "Song of Songs," drives the entirety of *The Star*. For the book's centerpiece is the relationship between God/the lover and the soul/the beloved, which explores the nature of revelation. The power and poetry of this section are dazzling. Rosenzweig expresses the response of the individual to God's command to love God with all one's heart and soul as: "The beloved's admission of love responds to the lover's demand of love" (1972, 178). His depiction of faithfulness becomes: "And because the soul holds on to him, therefore God allows himself to be held by it" (1972, 170). Finally, of the peace that characterizes the relationship to God: "The soul is at peace in the love of God, like a child in the arms of its mother" (1972, 171).

While Levinas is more austere than the other philosophers, anthropomorphic metaphors are vitally important for his narrative.[17] For it is that "invisible but personal God" who is approached through "human presence" (1969, 78). There is no direct relationship to God, but in the face-to-face relation God appears to call, command, and judge. One, in turn, bears witness to God by being accountable for the other. In Levinas' words: "the 'here I am' signifies me in the name of God, at the service of men" (1981, 149).

Why is the metaphor of God as person featured so significantly in each of the three narratives of the interhuman? The importance of the interhuman is reinforced through the understanding that God is to be experienced not as void, principle, or inner power, but in the same manner as persons, as the neighbor. If God were nothingness or void, the ultimate parallel notion for the other would be void or nothingness, and the notion of responsibility to the other would be left vacant. If a vocabulary of God as principle dominated, then the realm of thought might overcome the importance of what can be done and experienced in the everyday. Finally, if the divine were an inner power, then the narrative about the self as obstacle would not be possible.

When the divine is narrated as person, and the encounter as a dialogue or love relationship, then the ultimate value of the neighbor as separate but also as one who is met in the everyday is confirmed.

Still, the discourse that Buber, Rosenzweig, and Levinas utilize to portray the divine in relationship to the human is not one that they identify as theological. Each of these philosophers finds that theological discourse is too literal, systematic, secure, and isolated to convey that transcendent break into the everyday which they regard as so important. Buber is suspicious of theological formulae and the ways that the term "God" is often used (1970, 160–61). Rosenzweig calls for a new language that is neither strictly philosophical nor theological (1999, 89). Levinas sees theological discourse as remaining within the confines of the grammar of being and totality, and thus he finds that "theological language destroys the religious situation of transcendence" (1981, 197).

All of them insist that the strictly theological or religious, as a separate realm, must be transcribed into the language of the interhuman. For Buber revelation provides a meaning that can only be uncovered by "actualizing God in the world . . . daily" (1970, 163). Rosenzweig sees his new discourse, "the new thinking," as a translation: "theological problems are to be translated into the human, and the human driven forward until they reach the theological" (1972, 89). With Levinas: "language about God . . . can never be taken literally" (1981, 197). He summarizes his position as: "It is our relations with men, which describe a field of research hardly glimpsed . . . that give to theological concepts the sole signification they admit of" (1969, 79). Perhaps it is by reason of this translation that the psychological reverberations of their descriptions of the interhuman appear so vibrant.

Buber, Rosenzweig, and Levinas are not the only philosophers who provide narratives of the interhuman.[18] However, it is a major contention of this book that the importance of their work can best be appreciated and more valuably drawn upon by turning to another discipline: psychoanalysis. As the introduction to this book argued, the interest in the self in relation has been prominent in psychoanalytic theory from its beginnings with Freud. Yet, in contemporary streams of post-Freudian psychoanalysis this interest has been greatly magnified. In such streams or schools as object relations and feminist psychoanalysis, there is a deep concern with the way that the self comes to be through relation to the other. Further, some interpreters of psychoanalytic theory have moved away from Freud's insistence on the scientific basis for or model of psychoanalysis to focus on its fundamental narrative features. In seeing psychoanalysis in terms of narrative instead of a scientific metaphysics of the self, a path is opened toward a mutual interaction between the narratives of the three Jewish philosophers we have just examined and post-Freudian narratives of development.

Notes

1. Although I will not discuss it here, there is a primary literature of commentary and critique by some of these thinkers of one another. There is Rosenzweig's famous critique of Buber's *I and Thou* (in Casper, ed., 1984) and Levinas' discussions of Rosenzweig (Levinas 1983; 1990). Levinas' criticism of Buber's thought is discussed in Bernasconi's article "'Failure of Communication' as a Surplus: Dialogue and Lack of Dialogue Between Buber and Levinas" (in Bernasconi and Wood, eds., 1988). As well, there is a limited secondary literature of comparison, especially in terms of Rosenzweig and Levinas, including books by Cohen (1994), Gibbs (1992), and myself (1997).

2. There are important differences between these two works of Levinas, which will not be apparent from this treatment. See Alphonso Lingis' "Translator's Introduction" (Levinas 1981, xv–xvi).

3. The importance of this model for Western thought is explored in Suzanne Kirschner's *The Religious and Romantic Origins of Psychoanalysis*, especially 33–62.

4. I want to reiterate what was noted in the introduction, that I have replaced the word "You" in Kaufmann's translation of *I and Thou* with the word "Thou."

5. Buber's explicit portrayal of what object relations thinkers will describe as the drive for an object is dramatic. *I and Thou* is written, between 1918 and 1922, just as psychoanalysis is turning to studying children and the British Psycho-Analytical Society is being founded (1919). This common view of development will be explored in later chapters.

6. We will examine the issue of sexual difference and the relation to eros and thanatos in chapter 5.

7. The "political" side of *The Star* is well brought out in Eric Santner's *On the Psychotheology of Everyday Life.*

8. Also see, Levinas (1981, 73).

9. Levinas has written many articles that critique Buber's presentation. On the whole, he is deeply suspicious of the mutuality of I and Thou as just another expression of egoism. See footnote 1, above.

10. Levinas often capitalizes the term "Other." This signifies the transcendence of the other beyond the self. This Other may be either a person or the divine. Alphonso Lingis, the translator of many of Levinas' works, briefiy discusses the capitalization of this term in a note (Levinas 1969, 24–25).

11. The dedication of *Otherwise Than Being* to all victims of the "hatred of the other man," which he sees symbolized in the anti-Semitism of National Socialism, demonstrates that it addresses the same concern (1981, v).

12. This phrase from Pascal is quoted at the beginning of *Otherwise Than Being* (1981, vii).

13. Buber's paradoxical characterization of revelation as providing a deep sense of meaning despite this meaning being inexpressible is in harmony with William James' depiction of the mystical experience in his famous *The Varieties of Religious Experience.* The first two features of James' description are "ineffability" and "noetic quality."

He writes: "They [mystical states] are states of insight into depths of truth unplumbed by the discursive intellect. They are illuminations, revelations, full of significance and importance, all inarticulate though they remain; and as a rule they carry with them a curious sense of authority for aftertime" (319).

14. Although it might appear that the face has priority over the relationship to the divine, again, this is not the way that Levinas presents the matter. As one commentator summed up this point: "For Levinas there is no gap between the encounter with the other and the self-sanctification before God; the two moments are entwined in the experience of the face of the other" (Gibbs 1992, 187).

15. The insistence that love must have real consequences or fruits in the world is a major theme in Kierkegaard's *Works of Love* (1995).

16. See Robert Gibbs' illuminating treatment of this in his *Why Ethics?* (2000, 200–209). The nature of these communities will again be taken up in the conclusion of this book.

17. This austerity is discussed, as well as compared with Rosenzweig's vibrant use of religious language, in my *Speaking/Writing of God* (1997, 28–52).

18. For example, Søren Kierkegaard's *Works of Love* (1995) presents a detailed and fascinating narrative. See also Oppenheim (1999). Much of the present chapter has been adapted from that 1999 book chapter.

2

Psychoanalytic Narratives of Development

AMONG THE MOST IMPORTANT developments in psychoanalytic theory and practice are changes in the ways that its diverse accounts of the self's development and interaction with others have come to be understood. The scientific model championed by Freud, in which theories of the self's development could be linked with empirical data and, ultimately, to other scientific disciplines, has given way to envisioning psychoanalysis as a hermeneutical activity that offers a variety of narratives. The developments behind this transformation were presented in the introduction and need not be fully recounted here. This chapter will begin with a brief explanation of the ways that psychoanalytic theories are to be treated. This will be followed by a presentation and analysis of some of the more important developmental narratives. A comparative overview of the distinctive features of the different narratives will comprise the conclusion. The two chapters that follow will compare and contrast the psychoanalytic stories with the Jewish philosophical ones delineated in the first chapter.

A number of contemporary theorists explicitly use the term "narrative" to discuss the ways that psychoanalysts organize and contextualize the information they receive, uncover, or alternatively, jointly discover/create with their patients. The following are some examples.

Donald Spence:

> Freud made us aware of the persuasive power of a coherent narrative—in particular, of the way in which an aptly chosen reconstruction can fill the gap between two apparently unrelated events and, in the process, make sense out of non-sense. (1982, 21)

Roy Schafer:

> Selves are told through dialogue, in words, images, and enactments, and they are retold by observers whose narrative preferences and strategies express specific aims, values, and competencies. (1992, xvi)

Jane Flax:

> Psychoanalysts from Freud on have seemed to feel the need to develop teleological narratives of subjectivity. These narratives begin with the premise that there is a unitary substance (or potential) present from the beginning. Given "good enough" environmental conditions, this substance will unfold in definite, innate stages toward its "natural" end or purpose (adult maturity/health). (1993, 99)

Suzanne Kirschner:

> The relatively close ancestor of psychoanalytic developmental theory is a generic narrative pattern that can be found in Romantic and post-Romantic literature and philosophy. Its more distant ancestor is the Christian mystical narrative of the history and destiny of mankind in the individual soul. (1996, 66)

Stephen Mitchell:

> We are our stories, our accounts of what has happened to us. . . . To have a self, we need a protagonist, someone who does things and to whom things happen. The past needs to be organized into a narrative, or several alternative narratives. *No stories, no self.* (2003, 145; emphasis added)

There are somewhat different conceptions of narrative among the authors who use the term, from those who would define it more widely "as a telling or . . . presenting of a version of an action" (Schafer 1992, xiv) to those who have an elaborate framework (Kirschner 1996, 63–94), but there is also a shared understanding. Psychoanalytic narratives are complex accounts of psychic development, of the unconscious and the conscious mind, in terms of instincts or innate forces, passions, anxieties, fantasies, conflicts, and experiences. One may suggest, as do Schafer and Mitchell in the above quotations, that the notion of an individual self is not only a major feature of the account, but a creation of the form of the narrative itself. Experiences are organized, continuity is introduced, and "gaps" can be filled in by utilizing the "self" as a pivot for events. In other words, these are accounts of "subjectivity." Still, we have seen that object relations theorists have turned the emphasis from the presentation of the inner forces that constitute the self, to the interaction of the self with others—both internal images of others and real others.

Developmental narratives are accounts that unfold in a linear and chronological arrangement. The range and primary focus of the stories vary. It may start with birth, or even with intra-uterine existence. The process of the coming to be of the self may focus on the first years of life as it does with Freud, or it may extend through sexual maturity to old age, as exemplified in the works of Erik Erikson. Detailing particular stages or phases is a major ingredient of the narrative. These stages are usually depicted in terms of developmental challenges or obstacles—Erikson's "crises," that must, to some extent, be met, overcome, or resolved. There is usually an understanding that the earlier stages are determinative, or have a powerful influence on all that follows. This determinism is somewhat mitigated by another idea, which is that later experiences, or at least psychoanalytic intervention, can change the way that earlier resolutions have formed the individual. Further, as Jane Flax alludes to by the term "teleological," the psychoanalytic accounts incorporate the idea that there is a drive toward health or maturity that pushes the narrative along.

Schafer's terminology of "master narratives" and "storylines" illuminates some of the features of the stories that analysts utilize. The most influential theorists or schools, such as Freud, Klein, self or ego theorists, and object relations psychoanalysts, have formulated master narratives. Each master narrative, in turn, utilizes a variety of storylines, which establish "guidelines and constraints" for telling the story of the self (Schafer 1992, 29). Storylines consist of "one or more symbols, metaphors, similes, images, themes, or dramatic scenes" (Schafer 1992, 29). The Oedipus complex—the triangular relationship of child, mother, and father—is one example of a storyline that is employed in different master narratives. Still, the valence and even definition of the Oedipal storyline may vary among the master narratives of the psychoanalytic schools. The analyst's choice of master narrative is influenced by, among other factors, her or his training, dispositions, and sense of coherence, as well as the patient's memories and overall condition. Through the master narrative and storyline, the stories and fragments that the patient tells can be recast in a more inclusive narrative and given new meaning.

Discussing psychoanalytic theories in terms of narrative introduces them to literary and philosophical analysis. The elements—stages, images, metaphors, and dramatic scenes—can be studied independently of any recourse to outside data. For example, Steven Mitchell has examined the implications of two different metaphors of the "baby" in the narratives of Freud and the object relations theorists (1988, 127–50). The extraordinary significance and richness of these narratives are opened up when psychoanalytic narratives are seen to address central philosophical and religious questions about the nature of being human. In fact, Kirschner considered them to be modern, secularized versions of basic religious stories about alienation and redemption. She wrote that these "embody attempts to delineate and address the deepest and most difficult existential issues that human beings face: suffering, loss, frustration, and various forms of moral 'evil'" (1996, 6).

Psychoanalytic narratives of development may be seen to confront some of the perennial philosophic issues, such as what can be known, the nature of the good, and what one may hope for in the future. In psychoanalytic terms, these might be questions about the relation between the unconscious and the conscious mind—and the access the latter has to the former, the conflict between eros and thanatos or between love and hate, the goal or telos of development, the definition of health or maturity, and the possibilities for cure through therapy. Of course, they are not typical forms of philosophical theory. As quoted earlier, Flax underscored some of the differences, especially in terms of psychoanalysis' emphasis on the body, emotions, and conflict. In her words: "Unlike many philosophers Freud conceptualizes the mind as fully embodied, inherently conflictual, dynamic, nonunitary, and constituted in and through processes that are intrinsically different and cannot be synthesized or organized into a permanent, hierarchical organization of functions or control" (1990, 60).

Additionally, the different master narratives, and the particular narratives of development formulated by theorists within each of the psychoanalytic "schools," provide competing and conflicting answers to fundamental questions about what it means to be human and how persons relate to other persons. Life is seen very differently according to whether one holds that humans are fundamentally pleasure-seeking or are primarily motivated to establish relationships to other persons; that the first stages of development (and thus the basis for all that follows) can be characterized in terms of narcissism or by a mixture of hate and remorse turned toward the mother; that the goal of development is procreation or separation and individuation.

As discussed earlier, there are a number of concerns that affected the choice of the specific narratives to be explored in this chapter. Representatives of some of the basic schools have been included: Freud, Klein, ego or self psychology (Erikson), and object relations psychoanalysis (Fairbairn and Winnicott). This selection illustrates a range of views about the importance and dynamics of the relationship between the self and others. Freud's narrative represents one pole, where the account of development focuses on basic drives and libidinal or psychosexual stages. Erikson modifies Freud's account, exploring the social context of development through his psychosocial stages. With Klein, the various relationships to the m/other define her two stages, the paranoid-schizoid and depressive positions. Finally, with Fairbairn and Winnicott the other pole is delineated. For them, the mother's crucial role in the infant's development is explored through the movement from infantile dependence to mature dependence, or from extreme dependence to independence.

Each of the following individual treatments will highlight the theorist's developmental narrative. The presentation of the narrative will be preceded by a brief introduction that illuminates the primary orientation of the theorist and defines the basic terms that he or she uses. Following each narrative there will be an exploration of some of the philosophical implications of the position. While the psychoanalysts' descriptions of psychopathology, that is, the genesis of psychological illness, and therapy are often closely related to the developmental narrative, these areas will only be considered later in the book. At the end of the chapter, there will be an overview and comparison of these psychoanalytic narratives.

Freudian Narratives: A Brief Sketch

It is very difficult to reduce Freud's work to a single narrative, and every presentation, especially a more compressed one, distorts in one way or another. Freud's oeuvre is extremely large and covers a period of over forty years. If just the major books are listed, this creative period begins with the *Interpretation of Dreams* (1899) and concludes with *An Outline of Psychoanalysis* (1938). Freud readily admits that this body of thought was marked by radical changes and lacunae, and that much remained incomplete.[1] Despite his great abilities as a theorist and writer, this production was punctuated by conflicts, inconsistencies, and ambiguities–mirroring, as it were, the unconscious itself—as well as being open to the widest range of interpretations.[2] The post-Freudian developments in psychoanalytic theory reflect these diverse elements in Freud's multifaceted portrayal. Yet, despite the difficulties just cited in arriving at a single narrative, in the mature writings there is a deeply compelling and complex account of human life woven out of the barest—but most explosive—of chords: the instincts of eros and thanatos.

The treatment of Freud will begin with a discussion of the basic elements that constituted his understanding of psychoanalysis. This will be followed by a presentation of his developmental narrative and an examination of the philosophical implications of his work. Much of the material will be taken from his *A General Introduction to Psychoanalysis* (lectures from 1915 to 1917), which provides a very clear and popular-oriented exposition, and *An Outline of Psychoanalysis* (1938), which was the last book-length overview of psychoanalysis that Freud wrote. Many of Freud's classic smaller studies provide a much more complex and nuanced understanding than the presentation here, drawn primarily from his more panoramic overviews. However, since

Freud's work is only the background and not the foreground for this study, I believe that this will suffice.[3]

Freud was trained as a neurologist and started out as a researcher in neurophysiology. He turned from an interest in the physiology of nerves and the brain to work as a clinician with patients. The first paper that he wrote was with Josef Breuer, "A Preliminary Communication" in 1893, which presented their discoveries with hysterics, that is, with those who suffered from physical or behavioral ills but showed no neurological damage. Through hypnosis the two doctors discovered that the cause of their patients' suffering was unacceptable trapped memories and their associated feelings. Freud soon found that hypnosis provided only short-lived recovery, and developed methods of free association and dream analysis to uncover these repressed memories and feelings.

The notion that dominates Freud's narrative is that of drive or instinct. The basic drives, at least as he first saw them, were self-preservation, including hunger and thirst, and that of sex. He wrote in *A General Introduction*: "In every way analogous to *hunger*, libido is the force by means of which the instinct, in this case the sexual instinct . . . achieves expression" (1969, 274). Freud came to see the sexual instinct or libido as the central stimulus within the mind. Libido was conceived in a very wide way, as pleasure tied to different zones of the body. The biological sexual instinct or libido, as transformed into wishes and desires, was the major subject matter of his work.

While Freud had earlier written about the instinct for self-preservation, it was after World War I that he codified, as it were, the death instinct. This part, along with libido, of the dual instinct theory arose as his response to a number of phenomena that could not fully be accounted for through the one central sexual drive. Among these were phenomena of sadism and masochism and the repetition compulsion, that is, the puzzling compulsion to re-experience very painful traumatic events. With the addition of the death drive, human life is now narrated in terms of two primary, two conflicting instincts (1949, 21). One seeks preservation and continuation, and the other is the root of aggression and even the destruction of the organism. Freud wrote: "The aim of the first of these basic instincts is to establish ever greater unities and to preserve them thus—in short, to bind together; the aim of the second, on the contrary, is to undo connections and so to destroy things . . . to reduce living things to an inorganic state" (1949, 20).

There are two corollaries to the instinct theory, the constancy and pleasure principles. The first is the notion that the human organism seeks a quiet stasis but is continually interrupted by needs and drives. The psychic system seeks for release of the tension or energy that the drive/s bring to the system.[4] For example, the goal of dreams is to discharge the unconscious, latent wish so that sleep will continue undisturbed (1969, 115). Pleasure, and the pleasure principle, is equated with drive discharge (1969, 311). Freud viewed conflict within the psyche as the cause of much behavior, such as dreams, but also neurotic symptoms. Conflict arises when the expression of the drive is blocked, because the wishes and desires are experienced as unacceptable. The wishes and desires that the person refuses to acknowledge, finds uncivilized or immoral, are repressed, that is, defended against by the ego and refused entry into consciousness. However, the drive cannot be completely denied: there is a "return of the repressed." Freud writes, for example:

> The removal of the symptoms of hysterical patients by psycho-analysis proceeds on the supposition that those symptoms are substitutes—transcriptions as it were—for a number of emotionally cathected mental processes, wishes and desires, which, by the operation of a special psychical procedure (repression), have been prevented from obtaining discharge in psychical activity that is admissible to consciousness. (1986a, 31)

Jay Greenberg and Stephen Mitchell categorize Freud's narrative as the "drive/structure model" (20–49). The designation of Freud's position in terms of providing a structural model refers to one of the central shifts in his overall work. Freud first spoke of the mind in terms of what has been called the topographical model of unconscious, preconscious, and conscious. In this tripartite system the point of origin as well as the dynamic forces were deeply set in the mind, in the unconscious. The unconscious, which is inaccessible to normal experience, contains the repressed wishes, impulses, and memories. The preconscious contains all that can be made available, at any one time, to consciousness. Unacceptable sexual and aggressive material must be transformed, that is, disguised, for it to have the possibility of being conscious.

The structural model replaced the notion of a topographical one. Here are the familiar id, ego, and super-ego, which Freud presented in *New Introductory Lectures on Psychoanalysis* thus:

> We approach the id with analogies: we call it a chaos, a cauldron full of seething excitations . . . a striving to bring about the satisfaction of instinctual needs subject to the observance of the pleasure principle (1965, 73). . . . This system [the ego] is turned towards the external world, it is the medium for the perceptions arising thence, and during its functioning the phenomenon of consciousness arises in it . . . it has [also] taken on the task of representing the external world to the id (75). . . . On the other hand it [the ego] is observed at every step it takes by the strict super-ego, which lays down definite standards for its conduct . . . and which, if those standards are not obeyed, punishes it with tense feelings of inferiority and of guilt (78).

The id is the true foundation, "the core of our being" (Freud 1949, 108), the primary basis for mental life. The other dimensions of the psyche grow out of it. The id lies in the unconscious and continually seeks for expression. The ego appears as an outgrowth of the id (Freud 1965, 75). It is the check on that completely free-flowing id, which knows nothing of outside reality, logic or contradiction—"it might be called the Kingdom of the Illogical" (Freud 1949, 53). To accentuate the powerlessness and secondary character of the ego, Freud, in a famous allusion, suggested: "The ego's relation to the id might be compared with that of a rider to his horse" (1965, 77). The ego accommodates the whole system to the demands of outside reality—the reality principle (Freud 1969, 312), vainly trying to guide the galloping steed. The super-ego is composed of the moralistic restrictions that are taken into the mind from parents and society. The super-ego is often portrayed as a harsh, unrelenting force: another irrational and unconscious force that must be placated by the beleaguered ego.

The change from the topographical to the structural model did not bring a change in Freud's view of the dominance, or again, the importance of the unconscious in terms of the total mental or psychic operations, under which he included feeling, thinking, and wishing. He wrote that "mental processes are essentially unconscious, and that those which are conscious are merely isolated acts and parts of the whole psychic entity" (1969, 22).

Freud's developmental narrative focuses on the infant's, and later child's, libidinal or psychosexual stages. He saw the earliest years as having the most profound impact upon later life, and noted many mechanisms through which a subject regresses to the earliest sexual fixations. The stages or phases enumerate the bodily (erotogenic) zones that are the earliest organizing features of the sexual instinct or libido. Emphasizing the first three years of development, Freud differentiated the "pregenital" phases as oral, anal, and phallic. The Oedipal crisis brings the phallic phase to a conclusion, which is then followed by a period of sexual latency until puberty and the genital phase. During the oral phase, which identifies the first few months, the infant concentrates on nourishment, which is taken through the mouth. Still, there is an important sexual feature of the oral stage that goes beyond mere feeding. The anal phase, which Freud sometimes called the "sadistic-anal phase," referred to the infant's quest for satisfaction which is "sought in aggression and in the excretory function" (1949, 28). It is the first example of the complexity and ambiguity of mental life, where both passions (sex and aggression) are intertwined. The phallic phase is represented by another erogenous zone in which the child's sexual energy is concentrated. During this phase the aim of the child's desires becomes genital intercourse with the parent of the opposite sex, launching the Oedipal crisis. Although these stages thus are put in terms of a movement or progression from one bodily zone to another, in adult life there is a continual flow of oral, anal, and phallic impulses that seek gratification.

The dynamic of the Oedipal scene is the core event of development. Its resolution brings to an end the central themes of childhood sexuality and sets the underlying structure for the rest of life, according to Freud. He wrote that the Oedipal stage, with the concomitant "threat of castration," "may no doubt be regarded as the central experience of the years of childhood, the greatest problem of early life and the most important source of later inadequacy" (1949, 94–95). The desire for the mother by the male child is overwhelmed by the threat of castration that the child believes comes from his rival, the father.[5] The boy had wanted to remove the competition of the father for his mother, and assumes that the much more powerful father has the same thing in mind. In order to deter this threat, ultimately of castration, the male child renounces his interest in intercourse with the mother. For the little girl, the story is more complex. The girl "comes to notice her lack of a penis" (1949, 30) in the phallic stage, and both envies those who have it and holds it against her mother that she is disadvantaged (1949, 97–98). She eventually comes to terms with her "inferiority" (1949, 30), and instead of desiring a penis, desires a baby.

The emergence of the super-ego appears in the wake of the resolution of the Oedipal crisis. Accommodation with the father has come through the internalization of parental values and societal pressures. In Freud's words, the super-ego, which is partially experienced as conscience, "observes the ego, gives it orders, corrects it and threatens it with punishment, exactly like the parents whose place it has taken" (1949, 121).

The movement through the stages also shows a development from pleasure derived from auto-erotic to heterosexual activity. The infant turns to or becomes involved with the outside world and other persons only because the drives cannot be satisfied within the organism itself. Freud writes:

> For a child loves himself first and only later learns to love others and to sacrifice something of his own ego to them. Even the people whom he seems to love from the outset are loved in the first instance because he needs them and cannot do without them—again therefore, from motives of egoism. Only later does the impulse of love detach itself from egoism: it is a literal fact that the child learns how to love through his own egoism. (1969, 181)

Contexts and Meanings of the Freudian Narrative

The presentation above only hints at the vision, scope, meaning, and even drama of Freud's narrative. He fashions a huge variety of disciplines or discourses into an overall narrative or myth: the myth of man (in both a generic and gendered sense). Freud's weaving of threads from different disciplines and intellectual arenas is impressive. For example, in one of his overviews, *A General Introduction to Psychoanalysis*, there are references to medicine, biology, psychology, psychiatry, history, anthropology, philosophy, philology, literature, mythology, folklore, and religion. Key terms and metaphors come from biology (drive; oral, anal, phallic erotogenic zones), hydraulics (force and blockage), physics (stasis), sociology (societal morality), psychology (unconscious, conscious), Darwinian evolution (procreation and continuation of the species as the goal), and literature/myth (Oedipus, eros and thanatos). Freud is suggesting that all of these discourses or approaches are required to interpret/narrate the complex and fascinating account of the human mind.

Still, Freud is very insistent that this telling be recognized as within the basic parameters of science. It is a scientific theory, a new science, or alternately, "a method of medical treatment" (1969, 17). Psychoanalysis was seen by him as extending the reach of neurophysiology, which was his background, as well as the discipline of psychiatry. From another vantage point, the affirmation of its scientific character was one way that Freud legitimated psychoanalysis. For Freud, and many others of his time, the aura of science was extremely powerful. As a science, psychoanalysis was part of the forward march of knowledge.

Freud acknowledged that this new science was not exactly like other sciences. It looked at a variety of phenomena, including dreams, jokes, errors—such as slips of the tongue, infantile sexuality, and sexual "perversions"—that many regarded as unimportant, or even illegitimate, subjects for a knowledge of humans. Freud demonstrated that the same processes tied together the common and normal, for example, dreams and slips of the tongue, with the "freak," "mad," or "hysteric," that is, the abnormal. In addition, while he saw psychoanalysis as a general method that looked at the individual's psyche, it could be applied to all the areas where the unconscious was expressed, including religion and history (1969, 338). Of course, the controversial nature of psychoanalysis' subject matter reinforced the need for insisting on its objective and scientific status.

Further, as a new science, psychoanalysis was not in any way finished. Freud's recognition of its newness gave him the freedom to implement basic changes in theory and to acknowledge the detours as well as the progress in his work. It also brought him to examine the nature of scientific knowledge itself. In *An Outline of Psychoanalysis*, for example, he speaks of what scientific hypotheses really do. They are constructions that try to account for the unseen through reference to the seen. In the case of psychoanalysis, the unseen would be the structures of the mind—especially those that are unconscious, and the seen would be what is available to consciousness and is observable in behavior. Ultimately, for him, reality itself "will always remain 'unknowable'" (1949, 106). In another context, Freud reflected on the limits of all sciences by conceding that science "has but few apodictic precepts" and that the "scientific habit of mind" learns to be content with "approximations to certainty" (1969, 47).

Needless to say, there was great hostility to Freud's science. The combat with psychoanalysis' doubters and critics required much of his energy and deeply colored his presentations of psychoanalysis. In *A General Introduction*, for example, the theme of hostility, which Freud psychoanalytically regarded as defensive resistance, is literally present from the first page to the last. On the other hand, Freud portrayed psychoanalysis' practitioners as brave heroes, misunderstood, attacked, and lonely.

The key concept or hypothesis for Freud's investigation concerned the unconscious (1949, 105). He claimed that the psyche included conscious perceptions, feelings, thoughts, and volition, as well as unconscious memories, feelings and desires. Psychoanalysis explores the nature and workings of the psyche, in particular, the unconscious and its link(s) to consciousness. Again, what allowed the unconscious to be known was that the hints of the unconscious in conscious life, that is, errors, dreams, and neurotic symptoms, were not random or accidental. They were meaningful. As he wrote: "the 'meaning' of a mental process . . . is nothing else but the intention which it serves and its place in a mental sequence" (1969, 38). There is a structure, a kind of linguistic structure, so that our usual notions of volition, desire, goal, and object could be legitimately applied to the hidden workings of the unconscious. One could decipher or interpret the hints, in conjunction with a knowledge of the dynamics of the psyche and the particular life of the person, and suggest what unconscious intention was being expressed as well as what was affecting or obstructing that expression (1969, 34, 58, 228).

The notion of the drive is dominant in both the topographical model of unconscious, preconscious, and conscious, and the structural model of id, ego, and super-ego. It is meant to bridge the boundary between the body and mind. However, it is a mixed metaphor, having both inanimate and animate allusions. Freud portrayed drives as quantitative forces that had no qualitative dimension. The dynamic of the drive is about force and stasis. The human is a system that seeks stasis, but is continually jolted by the drives before it can return to quietude. This view of tension and release alludes to the sexual act, but utilizes the "scientific" language of hydraulics and electricity.

The drive metaphor also points to biology, where drives, as instincts, are the motivating forces of all life. In this way, Freud tied the deepest reaches of the life of humans to the animal world. Humans are just a certain type of animal, ruled by the same forces of reproduction and aggression. All of human activity can be reduced or defined by these instincts, either in rather straightforward expressions or as variations/sublimations. Even such activities as art, science, and literature were included within the purview of psychoanalysis in terms of sublimations of basic instincts, particularly the sexual instinct. Freud writes: "sexual impulses have contributed invaluably to the highest cultural, artistic, and social achievements of the human mind" (1969, 23). In fact, Freud regarded psychoanalysis as another Copernican revolution, following Kant and Darwin, which dethroned the human from the center of the cosmos or at least as being something separate, special, and unique in the universe. Psychoanalysis thus partook in modern science's noble, if not welcomed, "great outrages upon its [humanity's] naive self-love" (1969, 252).

The movement from topographical model to the narrative of id, ego, and super-ego has many ramifications. This is the basis for Freud's metapsychology, his attempt to delineate the actual structures of the mind. However, the words in German are less pretentious than they seem in English translation. Expressed in German this is simply the "it" (*das Es*), the "I" (*das Ich*), and the "above-I" (*das Über-Ich*). The id/it's domain is the unconscious, where instinctual forces become transformed into desires as eros and thanatos. At least as desires (words and images) they can be told. The id is the link with the world of animals, a foreign thing/it hidden, crouching at the core of the mind. The id forces itself through disguises into our conscious life. Freud suggests that patients, such as those who suffer from obsessional neurosis, may experience the eruption of the impulses of the id as something alien. Their symptoms seemingly intrude as "all-powerful visitants from another world, immortal beings mingling in the whirlpool of mortal things" (1969, 246).[6]

The ego directs and redirects the forces in line with the understanding of the possibilities within the real world, a world that, for Freud, is basically hostile to the demands of the drives. The ego also mediates the repressive norms and demands of the super-ego. Only part of the ego mechanism is conscious, for its defenses are not recognized. As the center of conscious willing and thinking, humans mistakenly grant much, too much, to its powers: for thinking does not take place as an "objective," independent force outside of the instincts (1969, 258). In the face of all of this, Freud concluded, from his own analysis, that the natural belief in our "psychic freedom" was an "illusion" (1969, 45).

The progression of stages—oral, anal, phallic, and genital—reinforce the meanings already discussed. These are psychosexual stages, with the telos of procreation guiding the whole process. The emphasis is on the Oedipal complex and the early stages are needed to provide background. The Oedipal is where the proper sexual orientation (heterosexual), organ (phallic), object (other than the family), and goal (procreation) are finalized. Despite the teleology built into the progression of stages, the narrative is fundamentally a lonely account, or better, a solitary one.

Freud's narrative of the powers, vicissitudes, and conflicts of life is from one perspective simple, from another complex, and in either case fascinating. It is a narrative with two elemental powers that are given at birth. These powers are inescapable and thus, in keeping with the terminology of the defining stage (Oedipal), almost a repeat of Greek drama. The drama consists of the conflict between life (eros) and death (thanatos), as well as the multiple ways—primarily unconscious—these forces or instincts are expressed. The complexity emerges in describing the latter, that is, the ways that the drives finally surface. This is most clearly seen in dreams through the ego processes of censorship, which are metaphor—condensation, and metonym—substitution. In the end, all features of the individual's existence, from simple, automatic reflexive movement to the most complex thought-out activities, as well as the breadth of human culture, are included in this eros/thanatos narrative.

In complementary ways, Freud mitigated the psychological significance of human interaction. For example, the dynamic of the drive was its force and aim and not its object/person. The psychosexual stages were defined in terms of the way the drive was expressed. The infant's first "sexual excitation" was seen by Freud to be a derivative of its seeking nourishment, not an effort to connect with a person outside. The infant focused on the breast and not the mother. As the first event of sexual fulfillment, Freud saw it as conditioning all that followed. In his words: "Sucking for nourishment becomes the point of departure from which the whole sexual life develops, the unattainable prototype of every later sexual satisfaction" (1969, 275). Further, Freud portrays the infant as born alone into a hostile world, and escape from that world is once again into solitariness. As he writes: "Our relationship with the world which we entered so unwillingly seems to be endurable only with intermission; hence we withdraw again periodically into the condition prior to our entrance into the world: that is to say, into intra-uterine existence" (1969, 79).

In fact, the first and thus definitive love object is the self, and auto-eroticism is the first type of sexual activity (1969, 361). This stage of "basic" or "primary" narcissism, following a pattern in Freud's narrative which by now should be very familiar, deeply influences all later stages. Love of the other is a development from, but not really a transformation of, narcissism (1969, 361), and in sleep the individual returns to this foundation of self-love.

In *A General Introduction to Psychoanalysis* Freud progresses from an analysis of narcissism to a wider consideration about human evil (1969, 187). This provides a good example to illustrate the philosophical views that found and permeate Freudian psychoanalysis. The specific context is Freud's examination of the "boundless and ruthless egoism" (1969, 127) in the form of wishes that drive dreams. He felt compelled to defend psychoanalysis against those critics who charge that it only sees the evil in human life, and rhetorically queries:

> but have you met with so much goodwill in your superiors and rivals, so much chivalry in your enemies and so little envy amongst your acquaintances, that you

feel it incumbent on you to protest against the idea of the part played by egoistic baseness in human nature. . . . And now look away from individuals to the great war [World War I] still devastating Europe: think of the colossal brutality, cruelty and mendacity which is now allowed to spread itself over the civilized world. . . . We dwell upon the evil in human beings with the greater emphasis only because others deny it. . . . If we give up the one-sided ethical valuation then, we are sure to find the truer formula for the relation of evil to good in human nature. (1969, 130–31)

Two critical reflections conclude this treatment of Freud. First, Freud's devaluation of the role of objects/persons in terms of the important events and processes of the mind is in tension with his understanding of some essential features of psychoanalysis. The super-ego, which is one of the basic structures of the mind, cannot be described simply in terms of impulses and defenses. The super-ego comes about through identification with the father or parents and their moral values. It is an image of the parents that is taken into the mind, and, thus, it is an internal object, a piece of another in the self. Further, Freud made transference, that is, the repetition of the earliest patterns of interaction with significant others, the catalytic event in therapy. The necessity for transference in the patient's psychoanalytic transformation certainly points to the importance of the analyst as an external object/person, as well as to the continuing power of the infant's/child's first human encounters. For many psychoanalysts after Freud, these features led to a reassessment of the impact of other persons upon the psyche and to a fundamental revisioning of the nature of psychoanalysis itself.

Second, many critics have remarked that the singular protagonist of Freud's developmental narrative is the male. Luce Irigaray, in her *Speculum of the Other Woman*, carefully and decisively puts forward this argument. Often quoted are Freud's statements that he never understood women and that the little girl is to be treated as a little man.[7] Freud held that the consciousness of sexual difference comes to the little girl by realizing that she lacks something. This absence makes the girl feel "heavily handicapped" (1969, 278), and Freud adds: "the wish to be a man is frequently met with in women, whether they are conscious of it or not" (1969, 138). Additionally, the lack of attention to the first few days and months of the infant's life in Freud's stages means that the time of dependence on the mother is forgotten. Some suggest this repression is due to fear of a return to dependence on an omnipotent female. As Jane Flax writes:

Freud deals with this material [earliest infant experiences] primarily by displacement and denial. He displaces and lessens preoedipal fears of annihilation of the self by transforming them into oedipal ones (castration). He evades the

> centrality of the preoedipal mother-child relationship by insisting that the oedipal struggle is the crucial event in the life history of an individual and culture as a whole. (1990, 18)

Even more basic, since Freud continually turned to the earlier to understand the later, one wonders why possible continuities between the pre-natal and post-natal are not explored. As we saw, however, the first stages are not highlighted in themselves, but labeled as pre-Oedipal.

The Oedipal narrative is clearly a male account of the renunciation of the mother and the fear (castration complex) and ultimate reconciliation with the father. The young girl does not fit well into this storyline, and the mature woman is only mother to the son and property of the father. The Oedipal crisis is where the bonds with the mother are irretrievably cut and the individual enters into the rationality and relationships of men. Passing through this stage constitutes the initiation into culture. The patriarchal coloring of this storyline, if not the developmental narrative as a whole, is impossible to ignore. Lacan was a true reader of Freud when designating this stage in terms of the Law of the Father.

Erik Erikson

The next psychoanalytic narrative to be explored is presented by Erik Erikson. Erikson studied in Vienna with Freud's daughter, Anna, while her father was still writing some of his most important works. As was true with Anna Freud, Erikson was very interested in children's experience and development: his early classic was titled *Childhood and Society* (1950). The title also provides confirmation of another fundamental feature of Erikson's concern, the relation between individual psychological development and the makeup, that is, the child-rearing practices, ideologies, institutions, and overall culture, of particular societies. Erikson still placed himself firmly within the stream of Freudian psychoanalysis (1964, 50), although, as we saw, critics place him in the context of various schools, ranging from "American object relations" to ego or self psychoanalysis.

Erikson's contributions and impact are not usually acknowledged as being as significant as those other theorists who are treated in this chapter, such as Klein, Fairbairn, and Winnicott, not to mention Freud. His role here, however, is based on the significant place he occupies in terms of the panorama of psychoanalytic narratives. Erikson keeps the drive model, but looks at the way that society, starting with the mother and the family, "meets," that is, responds to as well as contours the individual's bodily and psychic impulses. His account is thus bipolar: instincts and conflicts on the one hand, along with the interpersonal and social on the other. It also extends the psychoanalytic interest beyond isolated "others" to look at the "others" as they are embedded in the social and cultural matrix. Erikson speaks of psychosocial development, in order to indicate the intersection of the two perspectives:

> for we deal with a process "located" *in the core of the individual* and yet also *in the core of his communal culture*, a process which establishes, in fact, the identity of those two identities. . . . The whole interplay between the psychological and the social, the developmental and the historical . . . could be conceptualized only as a kind of *psychosocial relativity*. (1968, 22–23)

Erikson is also important because he goes beyond the focus on early stages by both Freud and Klein, providing an eight-stage cycle that includes maturity and old age.

Erikson's narrative thus takes the form of an eight-stage model of psychosocial development that looks at instincts, tensions, and conflicts, as well as care-givers and the wider social context. Before examining this narrative, a few controlling ideas need to be emphasized, as they were by Erikson. First, Erikson characterized the narrative as epigenetic, a term which he took from biology. He meant by this that the stages are structured around a chronology of developmental crises or tensions. In his words: "psychosocial development proceeds by critical steps—'critical' being a characteristic of turning points, of moments of decision between progress and regression, integration and retardation" (1963, 270–71). Further, each resolution of a crisis or developmental challenge becomes the platform upon which the next crisis is met. The resolutions thus affect and, more widely, fluidly interact with later stages. Second, the resolutions are not "once and for all" events. Later developments bring up the earlier tensions and may cause further work or reworking. For example, Erikson has spoken of the way that having children and taking care of them brings one to live through all of the earlier stages once again. Third, the somewhat successful working through a crisis brings an accrued sense to the individual. There are three dimensions that contribute to this sense: the individual's conscious feeling, the unconscious inner state, and the recognition by the outside world. Fourth, with each stage comes a widening of the circle of those others who are met and are needed to interact, co-operate, comfort, and confirm. Thus, while the initial stage focuses upon the infant and mother, the last encompasses persons of even distant locations and eras.

Erikson's Psychosocial Stages

The first stage is characterized in terms of the tension between trust and mistrust, which corresponds to Freud's oral stage, but adds the feature of a clear social dimension. At this time the infant is continually overcome by intense urges and needs, such as hunger and those emanating from the bowels. With proper care and concern from the mother, the infant experiences that these acute needs can be satisfied. The infant requires that there be a regularity or pattern of response from the mother, of its need being met by the caregiver. Through the interaction of infant and mother, in her giving care, the infant eventually develops "a sense of being 'all right,' of being oneself, and of becoming what other people trust one will become" (1963, 249). For Erikson, thus, the general sense of trust "implies not only that one has learned to rely on the sameness and continuity of the outer providers, but also that one may trust oneself and the capacity of one's own organs to cope with urges" (1963, 248). Trust is ultimately the basis for all later development. Not only does it refer to the self and other, but the world as a whole. Mistrust signals that the outside world cannot be trusted to take care, that there is no pattern or regularity, no basis for the expectation of needs being met. While the issue of trust is never fully over or successfully solved in a final way, it is the general sense of trust that leads to further positive developments.

Erikson designates the "virtue" or outcome of this first crisis as "hope." At one place he suggests the way this virtue is engendered through the mutuality of interaction of infant and mother. The dynamic of mutuality brought forward in this description, written in 1950, shows great resemblance to the views of object relations theorists, who were working with children during the same time. Erikson writes:

> The infant's smile inspires hope in the adult and, in making him smile, makes him wish to give hope; but this is, of course, only one physiognomic detail which indicates that the infant by his trustful search for experience and assurance, awakens in the giver a strength which he, in turn, is ready and needful to have awakened and to have consolidated by the experience of mutuality. (1964, 116)

The second crisis revolves around autonomy versus shame and doubt, which is an expansion of Freud's anal stage. Through the infant's experience of, among other things, being able to choose to withhold or release his or her feces, a new turning point appears. Feedback from the outside must give the infant some assurance of the appropriateness of decisions whether to retain or expel, of an assurance about the self's autonomy. A one-sided willfulness by the infant or an environment that continually overrides the infant's will can lead to shame and doubt. Erikson summarizes this as: "From a sense of self-control without loss of self-esteem comes a lasting sense of good will and pride; from a sense of loss of self-control and of foreign overcontrol comes a lasting propensity for doubt and shame" (1963, 254). This stage thus also plays upon an interaction between the infant and others, where experiences lead to either an appreciation for cooperation or a lack of faith in others and in the self.

The corresponding virtue of the second stage is will. It is defined as: "the unbroken determination to exercise free choice as well as self-restraint, in spite of the unavoidable experience of shame and doubt in infancy" (1964, 119). There is a pervasive ambivalence here, both in terms of the sense of self and the perception of others. For the self, some shame and doubt is "unavoidable," while the other or others are probably seen as both controlling, and thus as negative and alien, as well as supportive.

Initiative versus guilt is the crisis which corresponds to the phallic stage in Freud. It emerges especially with the child's ability to move herself or himself, ultimately to walk—hence, the virtue is purpose. This new freedom also is a test, and Erikson often refers to play as the way the budding person explores boundaries. The child expresses initiative, an energy of "undertaking, planning and 'attacking' a task for the sake of being active and on the move" (1963, 255). However, too much exuberance or aggression can lead to guilt. Erikson points out that this stage is also tied to Freud's Oedipal complex, where the sexual initiative of the infant comes into conflict with parents and society. To navigate this stage the child must come to be able to regulate itself, as he or she takes in the moral demands from the outside. A successful outcome means that the child is able to be productive as well as to respect proper limits.

The fourth stage is industry versus inferiority. This is Freud's latency period, not a period ushered in by new drives. Rather, it is the time the child begins a long period of apprenticeship or education, when it takes up the task of learning and mastering the technology of the society. As Erikson writes:

> It makes sense, then, that a period of psychosexual latency should permit the human to develop the tool possibilities of body, mind, and thing-world and to postpone further progress along sexual and sensual lines until they become part of a larger area of social responsibility. (1964, 123)

The successful outcome blends learning with creativity and self-initiative with working with others, achieving the hopeful result Erikson terms "competence." The unsuccessful outcome implies that the self cannot master a space, and that the individual's sense of worth cannot be confirmed in the world of others.

Erikson is certainly best known for his discussion of the fifth stage, which he designates identity versus role confusion. At this stage, which is the period of adolescence, the social world of the individual expands again. Identity is a bridging of past and future, of self and other. It seeks to combine the lessons of childhood with the future promise of the adult: the individual's developing sense of who she or he is, with the possibilities for work and life that the society offers. There is a clear ideological component, for the individual is "seeking after an inner coherence and a durable set of values" (1964, 125). This is a time to try to find one's sexual identity as well as a career. The positive meeting of the dual axes of inner and outer, self and other, is a sense of identity to be carried on, while the failure in this stage means that the person is not sure of who she or he is or where their proper place in the world might be. Finally, Erikson sees fidelity: "the ability to sustain loyalties freely pledged in spite of the inevitable contradictions of value systems" as the virtue of this period (1964, 125).

The sixth stage, intimacy versus isolation, once again builds upon the past experiences and resolutions. Intimacy for Erikson is "the capacity to commit himself to concrete affiliations and partnerships and to develop the ethical strength to abide by such commitments, even though they may call for significant sacrifices and compromises" (1963, 263). As this stage follows upon the engagement with the issues of identity, it means that Erikson posits that a finding of oneself, built out of trust, autonomy, initiative, and industry is the prerequisite for authentic intimacy with others. Only now is the individual able to give himself or herself without a fear of losing everything. Love, the virtue of the "mutuality of mates and partners in a shared identity" (1964, 128), thus refers to others whether they are erotic partners or close friends.

The seventh stage is generativity versus stagnation. At one level it pertains to the individual becoming a parent, nurturing a child. However, the scope is broader than that, as Erikson sees it, for generativity "is primarily the concern in establishing and guiding the next generation" (1963, 267). It is about the virtue "care," passing on something valuable that comes from the self to those who will follow, and about having capacities for "productivity and creativity."

The final stage is perhaps the richest for Erikson, ego integrity versus despair. It, of course, builds upon the working through of all earlier stages. As Erikson writes:

> Only in him who in some way has taken care of things and people and has adapted himself to the triumphs and disappointments adherent to being, the originator of others or the generator of products and ideas—only in him may gradually ripen the fruit of these seven stages. (1963, 268)

The catalyst for this stage is the individual's facing the inevitability, the inescapability, of her or his death. The question is whether life can be affirmed despite death, or whether death erodes all meaning. Wisdom is the corresponding virtue of this test, which Erikson defines as "detached concern with life itself, in the face of death itself" (1964, 133). Erikson sees many social dimensions within this encounter. One comes to appreciate the quality and necessary limits of life, an appreciation that results from examining one's own life as well as individual lives in the past. While the person in the midst of this stage affirms the meaning of what he or she has done, there is also a recognition that the lives of others, both of one's time and earlier ages, also have value. Finally, Erikson believes that if one is able to authentically face death, later generations can learn to have trust in life. Despair haunts the other side of this crisis, the sense that one's life has no meaning and that it is too late to do anything about it.

An assessment of Erikson's psychoanalytic narrative of development might isolate a few issues. His understanding of the nature of the self is certainly less complicated than one finds in some of the other post-Freudians or, clearly, in Freud himself. The interest in the relation between the two poles of the psychological and the social, as in psychosocial stages, often leads to an understanding of the self, or at least the ideal self, as a unity or a whole. For example, the critic Anthony Elliott faults the lack of complexity in this presentation of the self. He holds that Erikson "brackets" the view of the subject as "internally divided—repressing painful feelings, denying parts of the self through projection and splitting, investing distorting self-images through unconscious fantasy" (1994, 67). However, I find that a more complex and textured understanding of the self is portrayed in his reflections on therapy, which we will examine later, and in the large work *Gandhi's Truth.*

Additionally, there has been much controversy surrounding Erikson's depiction of women in terms of "inner space." This treatment of women may appear stereotypical, playing on metaphors taken from biology and cultural arenas. He associates women with the closeness and nourishment of the maternal matrix from the first stage of life, and also with an acknowledgment of human embeddedness in nature and the environment. Still, it departs radically from Freud's view that women are intrinsically deficient. Erikson writes, for example:

> Religious presence, however . . . has an affinity to the experience of women, who in their hereness and practical religiosity weave together in the chores of daily life what really "maintains the world," and who—while heroes court death—can experience death as an intrinsic part of a boundless and boundlessly recreative life. (1969, 401)

One of the problems here is precisely its idealization, Erikson's hope that women can revivify a world that men's aggression, illusions, and self-aggrandizement have brought to the edge of extinction.

This concludes the presentation of Erikson's very detailed narrative of development. In the context of this book, part of its contribution lies with the wider personal and social context that it demands for understanding the development of the subject. As part of this, the place of the mutuality of interaction in the form of recognition between infant and mother, and even self and society, is extremely suggestive. For example, Erikson has written in *Toys and Reasons*: "The human being which at the beginning wants to be gazed upon and to respond to the gaze, to look up to the parental countenance and to be responded to, continues to look up, and to look for somebody to glance, lift him up" (cited in Capps 1997, 183). Finally, Erikson has shown a deep appreciation for religion, and indicates a way that the languages of the two areas, psychoanalysis and religion, can be examined together in discussing such enduring human features as trust, hope, identity, integrity, and death. Some of the specific treatments of psychoanalysis and religion in later chapters will build upon these last insights.

Melanie Klein

Melanie Klein marks one of the most crucial developments in or departures from the Freudian narrative. After the first group of those who disagreed with Freud, including Adler and Jung, Klein represents a later critical stage. She was trained by some of the first generation of psychoanalysts. These were Sandor Ferenczi in Budapest, and, later in Berlin, Karl Abraham,[8] who was writing papers with Freud at this time. Her most important work was done in London, where, in the late 1920s, she became the pivotal figure of the emerging object relations theorists. As with other developments in psychoanalysis, she opened up a new path by giving a different emphasis to features in the Freudian corpus. Among the most outstanding discontinuities within continuities, she kept Freud's focus on instincts as driving psychic life, but, in tension with this,[9] she understood them in terms of passions and believed that their objects were absolutely crucial. The narrative of mental life is presented almost as a play of such objects/persons. As one critic described this, Klein portrayed "the id as a person or collection of persons in passionate relationships to other persons or parts of persons" (Mitchell 1993, 104).[10] She also rearranged Freud's dual instinct theory, giving prominence to the death drive over the erotic or libidinal. This meant that not frustrated desire but overwhelming violence against life itself lies at the genesis, and remains the ongoing basis, of the mind.

Melanie Klein's special expertise was in child development, which brought her to detail the earliest months of life. Her observations and theories were based upon watching infants and very young children playing with toys. She spoke of introjected objects, as if the child also plays with inner figures at the deepest levels of the mind. Her insights came to be seen as plotting the landscape of the pre-Oedipal and, correspondingly, looking at the first level of psychic illnesses, the psychotic rather than the neurotic. Psychotic disturbances point back to problems not of sexuality, but of the stability and integrity of the ego itself.

Klein's ideas, as powerful and unique as they were, still need to be seen in the context of developments in psychoanalysis contemporary with her work. As recounted earlier, the psychoanalytic movement had recognized fairly early that the Freudian account of infancy and childhood required real empirical work, since Freud had gleaned his material about these stages by inquiring of adults. Anna Freud and Klein were two of the leaders in this direction, although they passionately clashed with each other. In addition, the horrendous carnage of World War I had brought Freud himself to speculate about the death drive and reformulate his work in terms of the dual instinct theory of eros and thanatos.

The Kleinian Narrative

Klein's account of psychic development foregrounds two stages, her famous paranoid-schizoid and depressive positions. However, before launching into the narrative it is important to offer a few explanatory remarks and definitions and to speak about what initiates as well as peoples her stories. Her stages are called positions. A position is a specific constellation or pattern of anxieties, defenses against anxiety, and phantasies.[11] The two positions, the paranoid-schizoid and the depressive, chart entire ways of organizing or better experiencing the self and the world. They occur during the very first months of life, and their importance for Klein reinforces her view that the infant remains at the core of the adult. In her words: "Experience has taught me that the complexity of the fully grown personality can only be understood if we gain insight into the mind of the baby and follow up its developments into later life" (1997, 178).

Although the infant has innate instincts of life or love and death or hate, it is the latter which is the main early catalyst for psychic activity, according to Klein. The infant's raging hate, destructiveness, and envy are expressions of this death drive. Both drives are experienced by the infant in conjunction with phantasies about the inner and outer world. In relation to the drive of destructiveness, Klein observes: "I hold that anxiety arises from the operation of the death instinct within the organism, is felt as fear of annihilation (death) and takes the form of fear of persecution" (cited in Phillips and Stonebridge, eds., 1988, 167). For Klein, instincts and feelings are not free-floating. They are always tied to objects and parts of objects. In the first months of life the mother is the central object, and thus, the instincts of love and hate are experienced in relation to her. Klein has written: "The struggle between life and death instincts and the ensuing threat of annihilation of the self and of the object by destructive impulses are fundamental factors in the infant's initial relation to his mother" (1997, 179–80).

Klein is especially well known for the elaborate phantasies that she believes punctuate the life of the infant. For her, phantasy is an inborn, fundamental process in humans: the basic manner of expressing or portraying the two instincts. In phantasy object images are created and manipulated. Corresponding to the two instincts of death and love, the infant at first relates to the mother in terms of images of a good and bad breast. The good breast is seen as loving and caring, while the bad breast is threatening and persecutory. Ultimately for Klein, all experience, whether from within or of the outside, is elaborated through or mediated by way of phantasy.

The paranoid-schizoid position governs the first months of the infant's life and corresponds to Freud's oral and anal phases. It is a shifting constellation of aggression, sadism, fear of persecution, terror, of splitting and idealization that is built into the subject. It is a period of timeless phantasies, when events and experiences are not organized sequentially. The stage is named for the splitting (schizoid) and terrifying fear (paranoid) of being attacked that the infant undergoes. The death drive, that is, the innate destructive impulse that the infant experiences directed against itself, terrorizes and overwhelms. In the face of the powerful feelings of destructiveness and anxiety, the fragile ego attempts some defenses. The mother becomes a major target of the hostile feelings, with the infant experiencing urges to cut up, scoop out, and destroy her. The infant splits the destructive impulses from itself, trying to guard at least a portion of the ego and to maintain some stability. The infant then projects, which Klein describes as projective identification, this splitting and its substances, piercing and wounding the mother. The mother is now seen as having a good side and a bad side, which are identified with the mother's two breasts. The two breasts are then taken back into the infant, or incorporated, so that they become both inner and outer objects. Although the expressions of the instincts, splitting, and projective identification are inevitable processes in the infant, the actual interactions with the mother have some impact, reinforcing them. Times of satisfactory feeding at the breast build up the image and strength of the good breast, while frustration and difficulties in feeding reinforce the strength of the bad breast.

The infant's violent and destructive impulses which were at first directed upon itself have now become identified with the bad breast. The bad breast, seen as sadistic and persecutory, threatens to fragment and annihilate the ego. However, the good breast, which is experienced as the source of love, provides a positive foundation for the strengthening of the ego. The long quotation that follows provides a summary of Klein's understanding of the passions and processes of the paranoid-schizoid position, and also conveys the flavor of her work. She writes:

> In the very first months of the baby's existence it has sadistic impulses directed, not only against the mother's breast, but also against the inside of her body: scooping it out, devouring the contents, destroying it by every means which sadism can suggest. . . . But it is because the baby projects its own aggression on to these objects that it feels them to be "bad" and not only in that they frustrate its desires: the child conceives of them as actually dangerous—persecutors who it fears will devour it, scoop out the inside of its body, cut it to pieces, poison it—in short, compassing its destruction by all the means which sadism can devise. These imagos, which are a phantastically distorted picture of the real objects upon which they are based, are installed by it not only in the outside world but, by the process of incorporation, also within the ego. (1986, 40)

In Klein's later work, and especially in her important essay of 1957 "Envy and Gratitude," she focused on the emotion of envy to portray a number of the features of the paranoid-schizoid position. Envy is directed at the good breast as an outside and as an inner object. It seeks to deny and to spoil the positive forces of the good breast. If envy is not checked or mitigated, it will undermine the ego's contact with the innate and the external sources of goodness. In Klein's words: "It is, however, only more recently that I have laid particular emphasis on the spoiling and destructive quality of envy in so far as it interferes with the building up of a secure relation to the good external and internal object" (1997, 230).

The depressive position follows upon the paranoid-schizoid foundation, and embodies the possibility of partially overcoming its powers of destructiveness. The depressive position represents the effort to reclaim something good, and comes from the infant's remorseful realization of the damage wreaked upon the mother, or at least upon her imago. The characteristic emotions are those of guilt, loss, and reparation. This stage is designated as depressive, because the infant is at times deeply haunted by doubt and depression following all the destruction that the mother has endured. The infant fears that the injuries to her are permanent, and wonders whether the mother can be made whole. Thus, in Klein's view, as early as the second quarter of the first year, out of a concern for the mother, the infant begins to repair its relation to her. It gains a clearer sense of reality, recognizing that many of the passions that it had experienced as coming from the mother and from the mother's bad breast within actually originated in itself. The infant also comes to see that what it had earlier experienced as two dichotomous pieces, within and without, are actually good and bad dimensions of the mother and of the self. In all, the consolidation of the mother, treating her as a whole object, and the integration of the self are the key processes of the depressive stage. Klein writes:

> When the infant reaches the depressive position, and becomes more able to face his psychic reality, he also feels that the object's badness is largely due to his own aggressiveness and the ensuing projection. This insight . . . gives rise to great mental pain and guilt when the depressive position is at its height. But it also brings about feelings of relief and hope, which in turn make it less difficult to reunite the two aspects of the object and of the self and to work through the depressive position. . . . Through mitigation of hatred by love the object improves in the infant's mind. (1997, 196)

Toward the end of the initial emergence of the depressive position, still within the first year, other objects, such as "the father, siblings, etc." enter more deeply into experience. There are negative and positive aspects of this development, which Klein identifies with Freud's Oedipal crisis. Other objects bring out rivalry and jealousy in the infant, but they also expand the infant's possibilities for love and her or his experiences of being loved.

For Klein, the two positions do not lie fallow in the past. They are always there, as the basis for the way that one experiences the inner and outer worlds. The positions are thus not stages overcome, but recurring resources as well as screens through which reality is continuously experienced. In this vein, the good breast, the "primal object" in her terminology, is connected to basic trust, hope, and the belief in goodness. It is a source for patience, generosity, as well as creativeness in the child, adult and even senior (1997, 180). Connection to the good breast is the foundation for a person's "devotion to people, values, and causes" (1997, 187). On the other hand, a sense of loss of contact with the good breast and identification with the bad breast is tied to feelings of persecution, guilt, grievance, envy, the devaluation of the self, and the loss of inner security (1997, 230–31).

The Significance of the Kleinian "Theater"

The topic of reading Klein, by which is meant distilling her significant insights from phantastic/fantastic narratives about sadistic, devouring, cannibalistic infants, is omnipresent in current psychoanalytic literature.[12] On the one hand, Klein has been found to be one of the most fertile post-Freudians in terms of a host of issues including the death drive, violence, object relations, gender, self and other, and phantasy. On the other hand, theorists read and use her by departing from her. As Phillips and Stonebridge wrote: "the best 'readers' of Klein are those extraordinary thinkers who read—really read—and then transformed or departed from her work: Wilfred Bion, Donald Winnicott and W. R. D. Fairbairn" (1998, 2). The circus of objects and parts of objects—what Stonebridge denotes as "the great theoretical edifice of the Kleinian theater of object relations" (Phillips and Stonebridge, eds., 1988, 198)—and the expanding number of mechanisms that are held to go on in the infant psyche, erect a barrier that does not allow the wholesale acceptance of Kleinian theory by most critics. Many thinkers find it difficult to conceive of the infant in the first few months as experiencing such complex emotions as sadism, jealousy, guilt, and remorse. Klein also has the full complement of Freud's structures of id, ego, and super-ego, the stages from oral to Oedipal, as well as such mechanisms as splitting, projection, and introjection all during this same extremely early period. Questions have been raised whether Klein provides any theory at all, or whether she presents an unmediated phenomenology of phantasy. Judith Butler has succinctly formulated one way of putting this issue of the possibility of mining elements from the Kleinian structure without taking up the whole corpus. She wrote: "Indeed, it is unclear to me that one needs to accept the topographical schemes that Klein offers in order to affirm the specific dynamic of sadism, moralization, and self-doubt that she sketches with such skill" (1998, 185).

Although Klein has spoken of love and gratitude as well as the force of the death drive, the great originality of her work is usually tied to her discussion of the latter. This is perhaps the core of the Kleinian "scandal" (Phillips and Stonebridge, eds., 1988, 195), and without doubt the original psychic force in her narrative. The death drive invades, overwhelms, causes anxiety, which in turn initiates the contact with objects and the beginnings of the other basic infantile mental processes. Consequently, it is not much of a conjecture to suggest that for Klein the death drive constructs the self. The narrative of the self begins with the threat to annihilate oneself and that which is most deeply tied to the self, the mother.

The pervasive power of violence is another way of reading the basic Kleinian theme. The death drive is a violence pitted against life. The reaction to it is through still other violence, aggression, seeking to destroy, first directed outward and then taken back within. The super-ego, which for Freud only emerged in the fourth year or so in conjunction with the Oedipal conflict, is for Klein the infant's action against its violence, a power of reaction that through splitting uses the first violence against itself. Since the infantile is the inescapable basis for all that follows, even the most mature processes and actions remain open to passionate eruptions of destructiveness.

Another contribution of Klein, and the reason that she is often portrayed as the founder of the object relations school, is her view that these psychic forces and processes cannot be abstracted from objects. Objects and pieces of objects dominate the Kleinian narrative. Through interaction with the mother, incorporating pieces of her, the self comes to be. Whether through attack and fear of persecution in the paranoid-schizoid position or in guilt and attempted reparation within the depressive position, the object is central. One consequence of this understanding of the inseparability of drive and object, of self and other, is well expressed by the critic Thomas Ogden. Reflecting on Klein's concept of projective identification, and its elaboration by other theorists, he writes: "the subject is conceived of as arising in a dialectic (a dialogue) of self and Other. Paradoxically, the subjectivity of the individual presupposes the existence of two subjects who together create an intersubjectivity through which the infant is created as an individual subject" (1994, 47). The self comes to be, is built up, through the interlinking chain of processes of inclusion and exclusion of the other.

The radical role that objects take up in Klein's narrative has also influenced later discussions of sexuality and gender. Klein narrates gender identity in terms of identification with the mother and, later, other persons. In addition, she added to the Freudian repertoire of (primarily) male/male interactions by exploring the dynamics of specific relations between mother and daughter as well as between sister and sister.[13] These developments have offered a positive legacy for feminist theorists, although the prominence of violence in all of Klein's stories about relationships is a lesson not always remembered.[14]

There is much discussion in the secondary literature surrounding Klein about whether the experience of objects has very much to do with concrete, actual interactions with other persons. Does the particular mother or father have influence on the infant? What role do experiences with the mother and father have on the infant's primary processes and phantasies? While Klein insists that satisfactory experiences reinforce the life-affirming drive, and frustrating experiences the negative drive (1997, 229), the answer to this important question is not clear. Mitchell and Black summarize Klein's ambiguity as "her tendency to derive all important psychological processes from constitutional factors" (1995, 100).

Klein's narrative exposes the psychological instability of the dichotomy of inner and outer. Such processes as projection and projective identification demonstrate the insubstantiality of this dichotomy to master or order psychic life. The self is both itself and pieces of another and the experience of the other always contains pieces of the self. The idea of the autonomous self is acutely shattered by Klein. Similarly gone or failed is the haughty Cartesian intellectualism or rationalism of the "*cogito ergo sum*." It is replaced, obviously, by phantasy. Originating phantasy/fantasy arises prior to the integration of the self, and to all contact with the outside, including the influence of language/culture. In terms of the latter, since the drives of death/hate and life/love and the phantasies they give birth to are innate, the impact of language and culture cannot have the definitive role that it does for many post-moderns and other post-Freudians, including those who follow Lacan. Again, destructiveness, jealousy, and rage, as well as love and gratitude, emerge independent of culture. The splitting, fragmentation, that is, alienation, of the self is similarly prior to any outside influence.

Klein's depressive position appears to promise a stage of reality testing, where the infant no longer sees the mother in terms of the good and bad breasts, but as a single, mixed attractive and dangerous object. Phantasy thus seems to be mediated, but it is never replaced. The question of the extent to which one can gain an approximate sense of reality remains murky. What would constitute objectivity, when the infant/adult reads everything through images and attachments? Even the concern for truth is expressed as or through an attachment, deriving from the relation to the good breast.

Klein's narrative is enticing and stimulating as well as deeply disruptive. The play of drives through fascinating objects reverberates with great suggestiveness. This powerful and unsettling legacy will be taken up again soon.

W. R. D. Fairbairn

Fairbairn was one of the early contributors to the British object relations school. He was trained in England in the 1930s, which already was under the impact of Klein's powerful critique of Freudian theory. While many of Klein's views influenced Fairbairn, he challenged both her and Freud. He is one of the first to completely discard drive or instinct theory and replace it with an object relations foundation. As we saw, while Klein spoke of the centrality of objects rather than of libido, her focus was primarily on internal objects that dominated the psyche, perhaps even independently of relationships to external objects or persons. For Fairbairn, motivation, development, psychopathology, and analysis can fully be explained in terms of the success and frustrations of relationships to other persons. The thoroughness and consistency of this philosophy or vision of object relations adds a crucial perspective to this survey. However, since Fairbairn never consolidated his many years of research into a single presentation, some areas within his narrative are rather sketchy.

Unlike Klein and Winnicott, Fairbairn was not hesitant to proclaim that his work constituted a fundamental departure from Freud. A familiar refrain in a number of his pivotal essays is echoed in "A Revised Psychopathology of the Psychoses and Psychoneuroses" of 1941, where he wrote: "it would appear as if the point had now been reached at which, in the interests of progress, the classic libido [drive] theory would have to be transformed into a theory of development based essentially upon object-relationships" (1986a, 74).[15] Fairbairn insisted that the central motivation for humans was to relate to other persons, or in his parlance: "The real libidinal aim is the establishment of satisfactory relationships with objects; and it is, accordingly, the object that constitutes the true libidinal goal" (1994, 138). He claimed that to fixate upon libido was to falsely look at the psychic energy that the ego used, rather than to understand the goal and dynamics of mental life. Similarly, to designate developmental stages in terms of erotogenic zones erroneously overemphasizes the particular means that were used to express the relationships, rather than the nature of the relationships themselves. This Fairbairn stated as: "Erotogenic zones are not themselves primary determinants of libidinal aims, but channels mediating the primary object-seeking aims of the ego" (1994, 162).

Fairbairn is well known for his substitution of a three-stage developmental narrative for the Freudian libidinal model of oral, anal, phallic, and genital. Fairbairn's stages are not only characterized, but labeled, in terms of the types of relationship that dominate: infantile dependence, transitional (quasi-independence), and mature dependence.[16] Further, it is noteworthy that Fairbairn's narrative of development goes all the way back to intra-uterine life. During this (pre)stage of development the fetus is obviously completely dependent on the mother. Since Fairbairn equates dependence with identification, it can also be said that during this period the fetus exists in the most extreme form of identification (and merger) with the mother. There is no differentiation between self and m/other: the other is "not only his world, but also himself" (1986a, 90). The developmental stages follow upon or extend this type of relationship. In Fairbairn's words: "Identification [and dependence] may thus be regarded as representing the persistence into extra-uterine life of a relationship existing before birth" (1986a, 90).

In the stage of infantile dependence, which Fairbairn generally equates with Freud's oral stage, the infant's extreme dependence on the mother is both physical and psychological. In terms of the latter, it identifies with her ("primary identification") and relates to her as a part-object, the breast. For Fairbairn, the infant relates orally not because the object/breast brings nourishment and security, but because the infant's access or channel to the world/mother is through the mouth at this point. Put in another way, the relationship to the mother through sucking is understood not in terms of sexual gratification, but as the first "social relationship" (1994, 24–25). The basic features of infantile dependence are "an attitude of primary emotional identification," and "a one-sided attitude of incorporation" (1994, 145). There are two phases within the stage of infantile dependence, early and late oral. In the first phase, the mode of relating is exclusively taking or sucking, and it is through sucking that the mother is incorporated within. In the late oral phase, an aggressive element is included in the relationship, which is expressed in biting. This activity also represents the infant's first steps at disengaging from the mother.

In Fairbairn's narrative, the basic elements of the psyche, what he describes as the "endopsychic structure," develop during the period of infantile dependence. Freud's three-piece structure of id, ego, and super-ego is replaced with five elements.[17] For Fairbairn the ego does not emerge from a dominant id, but appears very early in infancy, at least in the capacity of the infant to relate to the mother. Unsatisfactory relations to the mother splits the ego in three, each part identifying with a feature of the mother that has been incorporated into the infant's psyche. Thus, inner objects are inescapable for Fairbairn, not because they spontaneously emanate in the earliest stages—as with Klein—but because experiences of early relations are always to some extent frustrating. The endopsychic system includes three ego elements and two inner objects. There is the libidinal ego, which is bound to and identified with the exciting object (aspect of the mother) and perpetually seeks for the enticing promise of relatedness. The anti-libidinal ego is attached to the rejecting object, which emerges from the infant's experiences of rejection. This anti-libidinal ego, which Fairbairn often calls "the internal saboteur," is hostile toward any possible contact or gratification. A central ego remains after the two other ego pieces have been split off. This third part of the ego is still available for relations with persons in the external world. The ego-parts (central ego, libidinal ego, internal saboteur) and objects (exciting object, rejecting object) are repositories of dependence, hostility, destructiveness, and false hope. Inner life is filled with attacks and illusions because of them. These features and their attachments persist throughout life and are obstacles to fulfilling relationships in the world. The more one is tied to inner dependencies, scenes, battles, and compensations, the less one is available to have fulfilling relationships with real persons. Fairbairn believes that dreams and waking fantasies directly reflect, or are dramatizations of, this overall structure and the ways that the different elements and objects interact (1994, 170).

Between infantile dependence and mature dependence lies a transition, a period of "quasi-independence," which corresponds to Freud's anal and phallic stages. It appears that during this period the infant relates to the mother as a whole object and not just to her breast, but the inner attachments, or incorporations of the mother, are still very strong. Thus, ambivalence and vacillations plague this period. In harmony with Freud's and Abraham's characterization of the anal stage, this is a phase of excretory processes. The infant attempts to get rid of the internalized objects without, however, totally losing contact with its important early objects (1994, 146).[18]

At the stage of mature dependence, which begins at the time of Freud's genital period, the emerging adolescent has more successfully overcome the initial merger with the mother. She or he engages with the mother and other persons as objects outside of the self. There is thus the possibility of cooperation, with the individual being able to both give and receive. Fairbairn defines mature dependence as "a relationship involving evenly matched giving and taking between two differentiated individuals who are mutually dependent, and between whom there is no disparity of dependence" (1994, 145). However, the simplicity of the narrative (infantile dependence, quasi-independence, mature dependence) is deceptive in a number of ways. For example, the early stages are never fully left behind. Fairbairn has written: "no one ever becomes completely emancipated from the state of infantile dependence . . . or who has completely escaped the necessity of incorporating his early objects" (1986a, 99). Further, the ideal of mature dependence is never fully actualized in reality.

The movement through the stages is influenced to a tremendous extent by the quality of parental care. The infant has a natural inclination toward a deeper and mature relationship, just as he or she does toward relationships overall. Through satisfactory "mothering" the parents foster this inclination. Put in another way, Fairbairn holds that there are two fundamental psychological requirements that the parents provide. As he relates it:

> the greatest need of a child is to obtain conclusive assurance (a) that he is genuinely loved by his parents, and (b) that his parents genuinely accept his love. It is only in so far as such evidence is forthcoming in a form sufficiently convincing to enable him to depend safely upon his real objects that he is able gradually to renounce infantile dependence without misgiving. (1986a, 82)

What mitigates the inclination toward maturity is a failure of parental satisfaction, which Fairbairn believes is at least to some extent inevitable. Frustration in the earliest relationship to the mother brings the infant to create, turn to, and depend upon inner objects instead of the outer one(s).

Thus, Fairbairn is saying that the infant/child seeks and is deeply formed by the relationship to the parents. The negative as well as positive dimensions of the experiences of these relationships are internalized. The infant bonds to whatever patterns of relationship the parents provide and is trained, as it were, to seek or repeat these in the future. In this way, the isolating, negating, obstructing, punishing, or threatening elements in the earliest relationship experiences are kept alive within and color both the internal life and future relationships.

Reflections on Fairbairn

In naming the developmental stages in terms of the style of relatedness, Fairbairn creates a full-blown object relations narrative. Since the movement is from infantile dependence to mature dependence, maturity is not for the sake of autonomy and self-sufficiency, but for deeper and richer relationships. It is also diagnostic that Fairbairn labels the last stage "mature dependence," indicating that he does not believe that independence or a total escape from dependence is possible in relationships.

The foundation for Fairbairn's vision is already given in the view of intrauterine life. While Freud had the fetus turned in upon itself, Fairbairn has it merged with, which is the same for him as total identification with and dependence upon, the mother. Thus, for Fairbairn, the period before birth and extending into the first weeks of infancy is characterized by a relationship that is so intense that there are not even two distinct partners. This is a far cry from Freud's narrative about the primary narcissism of the libido. Paradoxically, it appears that the label of narcissism is used by Fairbairn for this period because the infant identifies with the mother, and it loves its self, as it were, only because the mother and the self are one (1994, 48).

While Fairbairn keeps the notion of libido, its description is no longer in terms of pleasure or the release of tension. Connection is fundamental to the libido. Fairbairn continues in his departure from Freud in terms of the sequence of the pleasure and reality principles. Freud's narrative featured the movement from pleasure principle to reality principle, but Fairbairn's infant begins by seeking relationships with the outside (reality), and only turns within for satisfaction (pleasure) when the outward quest is not adequately fulfilled.

Finally, it is important to note that the role of aggression in the infantile makeup, an expression of Freud's death drive, is somewhat ambiguous in Fairbairn's narrative. It is not present in the earliest oral stage, but appears to arise only as a result of the infant's frustration at the later oral stage. This represents, thus, not only a departure from Freud, but from Klein also. Similarly, he sees neither inner objects nor fantasy as innate. They are inevitable, again because of frustration, but arise as a result of unsatisfactory experiences. This raises a question about whether Fairbairn has overdrawn the importance of parental care and underestimated the possible constitutional factors of aggression, inner objects, and fantasy. Since Fairbairn represents the fullest or purest relational narrative of the important figures of post-Freudian psychoanalysis, one is left pondering whether the possible lacunae in his account are symptomatic of his work or the overall relational position when narrated in its full consistency.

D. W. Winnicott

D. W. Winnicott is one of the best-known psychoanalysts of what has come to be known as the British object relations school. Like others, including Klein,

Winnicott's interest in and experience with the earliest period of the mother-infant relation reoriented Freudian psychoanalysis in dynamic ways. Winnicott was a pediatrician even before being trained as an analyst and he continued in this field. This background is highlighted in what is probably his most cited statement: "There is no such thing as an infant," by which he meant that "without maternal care there would be no infant" (1986, 235). He has expressed this insight in an equally emphatic, if not as well known, way: "It is not possible to state what takes place [in terms of development] by reference to the infant alone" (1965a, 145). While Winnicott's focus on the dynamics of the mother-infant experience profoundly affected his views of the earliest stages of infant development, the etiology of psychopathology, and the nature of analysis, he did not formulate a whole narrative in the fashion of Klein, for example. Thus, there is no full developmental narrative with Winnicott, but the pieces are extremely evocative and have had a great influence on later psychoanalytic theorists.[19]

In Winnicott's writings the environment or external object relations almost dissipate both Freud's focus on drive/instinct and Klein's on inner objects. From this perspective it is interesting that he introduces early in one of his most important articles, "The Theory of the Parent-Infant Relationship" of 1969, a quotation from Freud. Freud was discussing the power of the pleasure principle on the infant, as against the "reality of the external world," when he added that even though one is treating the infant as a closed system, this is a "fiction" unless one "includes with it the care it receives from the mother" (cited in Winnicott 1986, 235). What for Freud is a footnote, for Winnicott is a programmatic declaration.

In terms of Klein, Winnicott broke from her use of inner objects as the fundamental explanatory mechanism. The actual mother and her specific care decide the psychological health of the infant and later person. He spoke of the parameters of maternal care in terms of "good enough" and "not good enough." He thus correlated the dynamics of maternal care with the infant's coming to be as a person, that is, its psychological centeredness, stability, quality of relationship to the outside, and even creativity.

While the role of the "environment," that is, maternal care, is deepened to the highest degree in Winnicott's formulations, the other side of this is his interest in the inner or "central self." The tie between the two is seen in the following:

> The central self could be said to be the inherited potential which is experiencing a continuity of being, and acquiring in its own way and at its own speed a personal psychic reality and a personal body scheme. . . . Any threat to this isolation of the true self constitutes a major anxiety . . . [and] defenses of early infancy appear in relation to failures on the part of the mother (or in maternal care) to ward off impingements which might disturb this isolation. (1986, 242–43)

He believed that the psychological health of a person was dependent on a sense of integrity, the meaningfulness of one's life, and a confidence in the ability to be creative. When one possesses a true self, one is able to live with others without the feeling of being taken over or lost in the outside. Without a sense of one's integrity, a "false self" dominates, and the individual accommodates to the outside without a centered inner core. At the end of this treatment, the tension between Winnicott's relational model of development and his focus on the separateness and integrity of an inner self will be explored.

Before looking at the details of the stages within the first months of the infant's psychological development, two dramatic features of Winnicott's overall relational orientation should be highlighted. The first is that while the mother's care has always been recognized by psychologists as crucial to the physical survival of the infant—this is certainly what Freud had in mind in the quote above—the importance of this physical side pales in comparison with the emotional component of the relationship for Winnicott. The baby's physical need and instinctual gratification are not the essence of maternal care. The mother's emotional nurture of the infant is what Winnicott sees as crucial and what he believes is often ignored. It is this emotional dimension that he had in mind in writing: "If maternal care is not good enough then the infant does not really come into existence, since there is no continuity of being" (1986, 251). Or more explicitly he wrote:

> It would be wrong to put the instinctual gratification (feeding etc.) or object relationships (relation to the breast) before the matter of ego organization (i.e. infant ego reinforced by maternal ego). The basis for instinctual satisfaction and for object relationships is the handling and the general management and the care of the infant, which is only too easily taken for granted when all goes well. (1986, 246)

Second, Winnicott's recognition of the particular psychological ways that the mother or "mother-substitute" is linked with the infant is without parallel. At times he refers to the mother-infant dyad as the "original two-body relationship" (1965a, 29). The details of this relation will be examined below, but the general import needs to be underlined. At first the mother identifies with the infant to such a great extent that the infant's needs do not even have to be communicated to her; they are intuited as immediately as her own. Further, the mother gives form to both the infant itself and to its experience of the world. The mother patterns, as it were, the infant by supporting its engagement with its inner drives and providing a sense of its integrity through mirroring. The baby's sense of self develops, it knows itself, through seeing itself reflected in its mother's face (1971, 112–13). The mother also brings the world to the baby. Winnicott writes that at the earliest stage "a human being [the mother] has to be taking the trouble all the time to bring the world to the baby in understandable form" (cited in Greenberg and Mitchell 1983, 192). The intriguing link between maternal care and individual development is paradoxically framed by Winnicott as: "It is only when alone (that is to say, in the presence of someone) that the infant can discover his own personal life" (cited in Greenberg and Mitchell 1983, 193).

Narrating the Earliest Stages

Winnicott depicts early development in terms of two broad stages; one is the dependence of the infant and another is the developing independence of the child. He sometimes breaks this up somewhat differently as absolute dependence, relative dependence, and toward independence (1965a, 84; 1986, 242).[20] More specifically, during infancy there are two types of experience and in early childhood there is a period that Winnicott describes in terms of the transitional object and transitional experience. He also insists, as we find in most psychoanalytic narratives of development, that the first stages do not abruptly end, to be relegated to "history," but have an enduring impact upon mature life and experience.

At the beginning of the stage of absolute dependence the infant lives in a kind of free-floatingness of undifferentiated sensations, with no distinction between inside and outside. The infant experiences the mother as at one with the self or as part of the self. What exists is the mother-infant dyad. The mother through her interactions slowly brings a patterning to the infant's life that allows the inner urges to be recognized and organized. Winnicott speaks of the infant's illusion of omnipotence as the prevailing condition of this stage. The infant is born with an orientation to the breast. Out of her or his need, the infant hallucinates the appearance of the breast, and the mother, in intuitive response, brings the breast forward in harmony with the infant's illusion. The infant regards this circumstance as if it created—the illusion of omnipotence—the breast out of its desire. Winnicott describes this as:

> The mother, at the beginning, by almost 100 percent adaptation affords the infant the opportunity for the *illusion* that her breast is part of the infant. It is, as it were, under magical control. . . . In another language, the breast is created by the infant over and over again out of the infant's capacity to love or (one can say) out of need. (1986a, 266)

Three basic processes occur within the infant during the period of absolute dependence. The ego begins to be integrated, the tie of body and person is developed ("personalization"), and relationships to objects begin. The mother facilitates and supports each of these through her holding, handling, and object-presenting to the child (1965a, 60). In a wider sense, Winnicott speaks of the mother providing a "holding environment." She must protect the infant from two types of impingements, from the outside and from the inside. The mother ensures that the outside world, including herself, does not make excessive demands on the infant, so that its slowly developing ego can coalesce. In addition, she gives stability and security to the infant in his contact and struggles with his raging inner drives.

The infant begins to move from the stage of absolute dependence to relative dependence as the harmony of infant and mother begins to wear thin, even in the first weeks. The mother's almost obsession with the infant cannot last, as she begins to experience her own needs. From the infant's side, the seamless fit between need/expectations and reception is opened, and the first frustrations are felt. These teach the infant that the mother and the self are not indeed one, that there is an external reality beyond illusion. From six months to two years, the child is aware of maternal provision and his or her dependence upon the mother.

In his later writings, Winnicott took up more of Klein's work in describing the infant's attitudes toward the mother, particularly in the movement from the illusion of omnipotence to the recognition of the mother as separate (Greenberg and Mitchell 1983, 204–5). At first, with "object-relating," the infant's projections upon the mother do not allow her breast or herself to be seen as separate. As the immediacy of the mother's relationship dissipates, the infant reacts to the challenge to its sense of omnipotence with hatred toward the mother, but this is soon somewhat sidetracked (1986a, 90). Along with this comes the recognition of the reality of the breast. However, the powerful erotic and aggressive drives in infancy lead to the "ruthless usage of objects" and, subsequently, to guilt. Through the mother's providing "the opportunity for giving and for making reparation" the infant slowly comes to terms with his drives, overcomes guilt, and develops a sense of concern (1965a, 77). Winnicott's narrative shows important differences from that of Klein in this context. In his narrative the aggression is not pervaded with hatred, and the attitudes toward the mother are not instinctual drives but pieces of a relation to the particular mother (Greenberg and Mitchell 1983, 204–5).

There are a variety of processes that characterize the movement toward independence in Winnicott's somewhat fragmented narrative of development. The child cultivates the ability to be alone by internalizing important objects, especially the mother. A sense of self, including contact with one's impulses, allows the widening ability to identify with other adults and social groups. More generally, Winnicott speaks of such "tendencies that gradually reveal themselves in health, such as . . . the capacity for a sense of concern and guilt;

the capacity to love and to like the same persons; and the capacity for happiness at appropriate times" (1965a, 68–69). He summarizes the movement from dependence to independence in the following:

> One half of the theory of the parent-infant relationship concerns the infant, and is the theory of the infant's journey from absolute dependence, through relative dependence, to independence, and in parallel, the infant's journey from the pleasure principle to the reality principle, and from autoerotism to object relationships. (1986, 238)

Winnicott is saying that with absolute dependence, the infant is motivated by pleasure and turned in upon herself or himself. Independence is defined in terms of the reality principle, that is, being able to deal with outside objects without illusion. Actually, the treatment of independence is less prominent in Winnicott's work than his explorations of dependence or the transition to independence.

One other important feature of the early mother-infant relationship should be introduced, although the period of its occurrence is not clear. Winnicott includes an important scene of the mother giving shape to the baby's sense of self through her being a mirror (1971, 111–18). The baby looks into the face of the mother and sees itself, because the mother's face was affected by what she saw in the baby. The integrity of what the baby sees adds to the crucial process of integration. This occurrence is summarized in one treatment of Winnicott's thought in the following way: "As Winnicott describes it in his later writing, the mother functions as a mirror, providing the infant with a precise reflection of his own experience and gestures, despite their fragmented and formless qualities. 'When I look I am seen, so I exist'" (Greenberg and Mitchell 1983, 192). Even though Winnicott has acknowledged his indebtedness to Jacques Lacan's work on the mother as mirror (1971, 111), Winnicott's sense of the positive coming to be of the baby through the mother is in deep contrast to Lacan's treatment. For Lacan, the mirror stage provides a false sense of the unity of the baby. The mirror represents the beginning of the alienation of the infant/child from itself, an alienation that is never overcome.[21]

Transitional Phenomena and the Mother's Side

The interval or transition between inner illusion and conscious interaction with the outside world is very significant for Winnicott. The child's relation to the transitional object, which often is a blanket, is a new type of relation, neither of illusion nor of negotiation with the outside world as a person with others. The object is still tied to the wellsprings of the child's fantasy, but it can to some extent also be recognized as separate and as something belonging to the outside. It is intermediate and retains its power as long as there is no need, from the child or from the outside, to clearly determine its status. Thus, as one might suppose, the transitional object is a bridge, but one that once crossed can be crossed again. In his classic paper of 1953, "Transitional Objects and Transitional Phenomena: A Study of the First Not-Me Possession," Winnicott wrote:

> I have introduced the terms "transitional object" and "transitional phenomena" for designation of the intermediate area of experience, between the thumb and the teddy bear, between the oral eroticism and true object-relationship, between primary creative activity and projection of what has already been introjected, between primary unawareness of indebtedness and the acknowledgment of indebtedness. (1986a, 255)

In the period of transition the mother and other parental caretakers must again facilitate certain ego tasks. Winnicott speaks of the collusion of the caretakers with the child's use of the transitional object. The caretakers allow the in-between status of the object to be unquestioned or undetermined. Thus, the transition period is crucial in the development of the ego in terms of what Winnicott sees as the perennial task of every person in relating inner and outer reality. In summary, Winnicott writes: "the task of reality acceptance is never completed, that no human being is free from the strain of relating inner and outer reality, and that from this strain is provided an intermediate area of experience which is not challenged (arts, religion, etc.)" (1986a, 269).

The relation to the transitional object develops into the child's play. With play, it appears, illusion and fantasy remain, but the objects are no longer part of the self. However, more important than the distinction between transitional experience and play is that the one is the introduction and basis for the other. As such, transitional experience is a perennial part of human life. It is the first gleanings of the creative use of fantasy that may be translated into reality. It, thus, bears the seeds of humans' use of fantasies, ideas, words, and symbols to make original, transformative contributions to the world. As we saw, Winnicott ties transitional experience to religion and to culture overall. In his words: "I am therefore studying the substance of *illusion*, that which is allowed to the infant, and which in adult life is inherent in art and religion" (1953, 256).

Examining the earliest periods of infancy from the perspective of the infant is only half of the story. Outside of some feminist psychoanalysts, Winnicott has given more attention to the mother's experience than any other prominent psychoanalytic theorist. While there has been much criticism of Winnicott's notion of "good enough" and "not good enough" mothering, the controversy itself points to the supreme importance of the mother in the developmental narrative.[22] Winnicott notes that the changes that the mother undergoes in terms of the infant begin, of course, before the birth itself. The mother is prepared for the baby through physiological and psychological changes that occur while she is carrying him or her. Psychologically, she becomes more attuned to the fetus' movements and her own changes. She identifies with the fetus, as Winnicott stresses: "mothers do in one way or another identify themselves with the baby that is growing within them, and in this way they achieve a very powerful sense of what the baby needs" (1986, 250). This intensifies right after birth into a state that Winnicott describes as "primary maternal preoccupation." At this point, the mother identifies so closely with the baby that she "knows what the infant feels like" and is able to intuit its needs (1986, 251). In suspending her own autonomy and subjectivity, in experiencing the infant and herself as one, the mother is no longer in her right mind. One commentator alludes to Winnicott seeing this as a type of "madness" (Mitchell and Black 1995, 126), and Winnicott does speak of the psychopathology of the mother's orientation (1969, 250).

The mother's inevitable and necessary "failure" to continue in this state occurs as she feels her own concerns arise. Interestingly, Winnicott sees the change in terms of the movement from the mother's empathetic intuition of the infant's needs to her reading of the infant's signs of these needs. The mother interprets the infant's actions, expressions, and cries, and then responds. This indicates a separation from the prior immediacy of mother and infant, but it also allows the baby to develop, to learn about its dependency, and not omnipotence, and to communicate.

In conclusion, Winnicott offers some very important insights, models, and metaphors for an understanding of the interhuman, even though it is not all systematically completed and the narrative exhibits tensions. First, he powerfully brings forward a narrative of the way that persons are formed by other persons. The infant is wired, as it weie, for interaction. The essential narrative of infancy is about developing the inner or central self and not about meeting drives. It is only through the mother's self—body and psyche—that the foundation of another person comes to be. She even teaches the infant to know about its own needs and feelings. In all, Winnicott speaks of the intricacies of the maternal tie in very deep ways and these have a direct and profound effect upon the person's ability to live with others, to participate in cultural life, and to find meaning.

However, it is also striking that while Winnicott's narrative is so relational, his view of the "true self" is in some ways so substantial, non-relational, and "modern." The fact that the central self, this solid hidden entity—as it were, is so important to Winnicott does mitigate to some extent the full relational understanding of who persons are. As much as we are formed by another, Winnicott still wants to isolate a hidden inner self. In a listing of features that characterize "personality growth," he writes: "The development of a capacity to make relationships with objects in spite of the fact that in one sense, and an important sense, the individual is an isolated phenomenon that defends this isolation at all costs" (1965, 68). The "isolation" of the person may also be in the background for his depiction of adult love. Winnicott sees love in terms of the abilities of two partners to allow one another to get in touch with their own deepest emotions and illusions, even though this is a type of use of the other. One treatment of Winnicott summarized his view of love: "Adult love . . . entails periodic mutual object usage, in which each partner can surrender to the rhythms and intensity of his or her own desire without having to worry about the survivability of the other" (Mitchell and Black 1995, 129). Certainly love is this, but are its relational components adequately covered by the terminology of usage?[23]

While Winnicott has been faulted in terms of the demands put upon the mother through the notion of a good enough mothering, at least this earliest relationship is not left in darkness. Feminist critics recognize the importance of the experience of this dyad that is finally brought out in Winnicott and other object relations theorists. In addition, Winnicott gives voice to the "other side," the side of the mother in the infant-mother unit. His close examination of the changes within the mother, from the beginning of gestation, is important. However, once again, the description of this feature is not left unproblematic. Is it helpful to see the mother's deep identification with the infant as a pathological state? It is only unhealthy if one equates health with the fundamental self-concern of the person. Further, should we not try to understand what the processes undergone by the mother mean to her (psychologically and in other ways) even after the infant grows to be a baby and then a child? Perhaps the experience of this relationship means that she will never come back fully to "her senses" (or self-concern). Since having children is a rather common event in human life, to understand the meaning of this experience might entail that none of us recover our old "senses."[24]

Conclusion: A Vast Panorama

The psychoanalytic narratives of development that we have surveyed portray a wealth of positions concerning the place of others in the early and later life of each person. This section will provide an overview of this panorama focusing, of course, on object relations. After a summary or schematic of the positions, some of the symptomatic scenes of interaction will be explored. The chapter will end with a brief reflection on the contributions of each narrative to a psychoanalytic understanding of the interhuman.

While Freud's work accounts for development primarily in terms of instincts or drives, his discourse provided a vocabulary for later psychoanalysts to increasingly emphasize the role of objects, both inner—images and fantasies—and outer—tangible persons. Freud actually began with an account of pathology or neurotic activity in which the actions of others had tremendous impact (Greenberg and Mitchell 1983, 25). This was his theory of infantile seduction, that is, that at the heart of neuroses lay a traumatic sexual encounter that occurred in childhood. However, Freud came to believe that such accounts were not reliable, and he eventually constructed a system whereby both health and illness could be understood in terms of the two drives and the defenses built against their unacceptable desires. In the end, he provided an incomparably rich but essentially closed system in terms of drives—libido and death; structures—id, ego, super-ego; and stages defined in terms of erotogenic zones.

Erikson appears to widen the scope of Freud's narrative by emphasizing the specific familial and cultural context. The substitution of psychosocial for psychosexual stages does not constitute the significant break with psychoanalysis' founder that later theorists forged. He does not change the role or meaning of the basic instincts, but reconfigures the developmental narrative so that it pivots around the fit between individual and society/culture. The ego's stability, identity, fruitfulness, and integrity are the foci for the challenges or "crises" commencing with the basic requirement of trust and concluding with the ultimate threat of despair.

Klein represents a more thorough transformation of the Freudian narrative. Her telling retains the term "instincts" but the referents are almost unrecognizable in relation to the original. There are still two drives—eros and thanatos—but these cannot possibly be seen as amounts of energy: they are transformed into phantasies that overwhelm. The tale in infancy of raw destructiveness, hate, envy, sadism, and, concurrently, persecution is welded to the bad breast/mother, and of guilt, reparation, and gratitude to the good breast/mother. The inner life of phantasy of the paranoid-schizoid and depressive positions dominate all relations that follow. Yet, despite the prominence, the almost omnipresence of objects, all of this is a constitutionally, that is to say, innately, choreographed theater. The question of whether actual persons have roles is left unresolved. The message that the interplay of inner objects/images pattern the first relations and those that follow is disquieting.

With Fairbairn the narrative of object relations takes full flight from Freud. Critics acknowledge that he represents the most consistent exploration of the possibilities of narrating development in terms of "outer" objects, of actual persons. The infant is, first and foremost, object-seeking. Fairbairn constructs an all-encompassing chronicle of contact, security, and assurance. In the uterus the nature of the relation is one of total dependence, but even in maturity it is still mutual dependence. Departing also from Klein, inner objects are not innate, but only appear as residues of unsatisfactorily met relational needs.

Winnicott again sees the intra-uterine, the inseparable unit of mother-fetus, as the precursor for the centrality of relationships in every life. The psychological need for other persons is also primary in his account. The mother's indispensable support for the infant's developing ego is powerfully described in terms of the infant's illusion of omnipotence. The realm of fantasy is portrayed in terms of object relations and usage, and later through transitional experience. A counterbalance to the impact of the maternal environment on the infant/child in Winnicott's narrative comes through by way of his interest in the true self. Early relationships allow this self to coalesce, with the subsequent integrity and continuity of inner experience. Winnicott's narrative adds an important position in the points along the line of possible ways of narrating object relations.

A more revealing way of presenting the meanings of the above narratives might be to explore details of the relation of self and other in a representative series of "intriguing scenes." For Freud what might be the most symptomatic is the characterization of the Oedipal crisis. Certainly the dynamics of this period are significant, since, as noted a number of times, as important as the earlier stages are, they are still depicted as pre-Oedipal. This account begins with the libidinal instinct being expressed as the desire for the mother. It continues with the son's anxiety about the threat of castration coming from his rival, the father. The son relinquishes his pursuit of the mother, acknowledging the overwhelming power of the father. The father's influence or stricture upon desire continues through the formation of the super-ego, which Freud ties to the death/aggressive drive and often portrays as excessive and vindictive. Finally, Freud sees the taboo against incest as the foundation for all society.

The Oedipal crisis witnesses to fundamental perspectives within Freud's psychosexual narrative. The original driving force, the desire for the mother, touches upon both libidinal instinct, that is, biology, and also the importance of the mother as an object, hence, the psychological. Desire is portrayed as naturally disruptive, inevitably coming into conflict with father and culture. This conflict between (libidinal) desire and reality (culture) is made perennial by being structured into the psyche as the conflict between id and super-ego. Thus, Freud is portraying the seminal event of individual and society in terms of a number of conflicts. These are innate conflicts between love and hate/aggression: between pleasure and reality. Further, the narrative emphasizes the realm of the innate, including inner objects. Overall, despite the significant place of the individual's personal history in the process of analysis, the narrative does not allow much space for the specific experiences of a concrete child, mother, father, or society.

With Erikson it would be appropriate to look again at the crisis of identity for which he is renowned. Identity is the fifth psychosocial stage, which builds upon preceding physiological and psychological developments, as well as the acquisition of skills and experiences. It is midway between childhood and adulthood. The adolescent must now begin to establish who she is, by bridging past and future, inner and outer. Objects figure here in terms of prior exchanges with the family and negotiations with those in the wider world of school, work, play, and love. The central task of this period is to balance old identifications and identities with new ones. For the adolescent, at least in the West, the peer group, its styles and judgments, are tremendously salient. Identity is about fidelity, but also about love. Here is the way that Erikson describes this: "To a considerable extent adolescent love is an attempt to arrive at a definition of one's identity by projecting one's diffused ego image on another and by seeing it thus reflected and gradually clarified" (1963, 262).

In this sketch of identity, Erikson reveals the foci and parameters of his developmental narrative. It is first of all about fit. On the one hand, there are the inner physiological and sexual dimensions, and on the other hand, the social. Adolescence is defined by physical powers, sexual interests, and the allure of the wider world. Erikson maintains his interest in the correspondence between how the self sees itself and how the world assesses the person. A person cannot forget either side, and the intricacy of the tie is exquisitely expressed in the above quote, where the way one sees/finds oneself is "reflected" and "clarified" by the other. Erikson's expansion of Freud's narrative is clear.

The major difficulty in selecting one scene of object relations in terms of Klein is because of the overabundance of possibilities. Since the earlier presentation in this chapter focused on the paranoid-schizoid position, it might be good to now look at the depressive position. In the second quarter of the first year, many changes occur in the life and experience of the infant. The range and types of relations to the outside expand. There is a strengthening and integration of the ego, as well as a more realistic integration of the good and bad sides of both internal and external objects. Most importantly, the infant acquires more power over the aggressive, persecutory and early defensive phantasies in which he or she was first engulfed. All of this comes to the fore in the changing quality of the relationship to the primary object. Drawing upon the loving and life-affirming drive, the infant feels guilty about its violent and sadistic impulses that were earlier directed toward the mother. In Klein's words: "When the infant feels that his destructive impulses and phantasies are directed against the complete person of his loved object, guilt arises in full strength and, together with it, the over-riding urge to repair, preserve or revive the loved injured object" (1997, 74). There is thus a concern with the mother's condition, and reparative efforts are made. The infant shows care and tries to revive the injured mother. There is also an inner fight with depressive anxieties about the mother's ability to survive the earlier onslaught directed at her. If all of these positive developments can be nourished, then a constructive foundation for all future relations has been poured.

Upon reflection, there are a number of remarkable features of this Kleinian phantasy. The narrative is still about eros and thanatos, but these are translated into pictures or inner objects. The life-affirming and loving features of the inner life follow upon the life-denying ones of the first quarter. For Klein, although desire always is tied to an object, as we have seen repeatedly, these are internal objects and the play of forces is innate. Finally, it is precisely the explosive quality and intricacy of Klein's descriptions—the infant life of desire, aggression, sadism, love, reparation; objects and part-objects; ego splitting and integration; the super-ego—that perhaps undermines their full plausibility.

The relationship of inner and outer objects in the transition stage between infantile dependence and mature dependence might well be seen as the diagnostic scene for Fairbairn. At first the infant, who is inherently directed to seek the mother, completely identifies and merges with her. Maturity describes a situation where there is both some separation and the ability to give to and take from one's other. In the period of transition what allows the child to move from one stage to the next is the parent's double assurance of being loved and of having its love accepted. Where this is lacking, and it can never be fully forthcoming, infantile dependence expresses itself in attachment to inner objects. In such a case, both the ego and the other are fragmented in various forms of alienating ties. Fairbairn secures this dynamic to a complete scheme of psychopathology in writing: "It is this trauma [frustrated desire for connection] which creates fixations in the various forms of infantile sexuality to which a child is driven to resort in an attempt to compensate by substitutive satisfactions for the failure of his emotional relationships with his outer objects" (1986a, 83).

Analysis of Fairbairn's above scheme is straightforward. The dominating characteristic of infants, and persons, is the need for relationships. The stages are characterized by the quality of the relationships, and illness by the creation of their substitutes. A mature person is one who can relate to actual others in a give and take. However, because of inadequacies of the past, people are always stuck in patterns of withholding or withdrawing. Thus, for Fairbairn, fantasy is always, and only, a symptom of, a poor substitute for, outer connection. In comparison with either Klein or Winnicott—or Freud—this view of fantasy rings somewhat hollow.

The portrait of the mother's role in the mother-infant dyad during the first months is a fascinating element in Winnicott's narrative. The mother prepares/is prepared for this as she carries the fetus. Her attention focuses on what is happening within her and lags in terms of her own concerns with the outside world. Thus, at birth she is powerfully attuned to the infant's inner developments and needs. Her contribution to the infant is two-fold. She helps the infant organize and identify the mass of inner events and also conveys or communicates the outer world in a way that can be accepted. These tasks define her holding of the infant. From the infant's side, the match of anticipation, expectation, and what is forthcoming is experienced as an omnipotent power over the world, the "illusion of omnipotence."

Winnicott has here provided a most powerful psychological view of how persons are formed by others. This is really far from Freud's isolated infant, caught in narcissism. Winnicott is saying that the other puts together one's entire world, inner and outer. There is no sense of oneself, nor a connection to the outside, unless both are given. Without this, the inside is amorphous chaos, and the outside threatens with an overwhelming cacophony of demands. Stepping outside of this scene a little, one wonders whether the narrative requires a "true self" to balance all that the mother/other at first means.

What have these narratives contributed to an understanding of the nature of the human? Jane Flax, in a statement quoted at the beginning of the chapter, provided an overview of what one can expect from these "philosophical" contributions/reminders. It is completely appropriate that her point of departure is Freud. In comparing Freud's narrative to typical philosophical portrayals, she underlined the former's view of mind as "fully embodied, inherently conflictual, dynamic, nonunitary, and constituted in and through processes that are intrinsically different and cannot be synthesized or organized into a permanent, hierarchical organization of functions or control" (1990, 60).

The unforgettable in the Freudian narrative, his first lesson, is about the unconscious. Humans are not aware, usually do not have access to, the forces that drive them and permeate their experiences. Consciousness and self-consciousness are thus less reliable guides to who we are than are dreams, slips, errors, and neurotic symptoms. Freud also reminds us that persons do not stand as whole beings in the world. Conflict is innate. To be a person is to be torn, to be in-between desires, and also to find an inherent tension between inner and outer. Further, as Klein takes up, one of the determining drives appears to be for the self to unmake, to destroy itself and the wider world. Klein deeply informs us about phantasy. Relationships, and even thought, are grounded, or alternatively, mediated through innate phantasies of love and hate, of aggression and reparation. In addition, Klein demonstrates the ways that fantastic pieces of others haunt and enrich the self. Coming to be and relating is also identifying with and introjecting the other. For Erikson the exchange between self and other whether in childhood or in later society appears as his most important message. Throughout life, there are basic crises that the developing person faces by negotiating innate drives with what is provided and possible from the outside. Fairbairn demonstrates all the powers and limits of a narrative where connection to others is almost the single theme. The characterization of connection in terms of infantile through mature dependence underscores the significance of this way of conceptualizing relationships in all psychoanalytic narratives. Finally, Winnicott informs about the necessity and creativity of the in-between. Fantasy and later reflection emerge from a dimension of living where no solid boundaries between inner and outer, self and other, are to be found. Winnicott reminds us that only if the other properly prepares us can we find this situation tolerable, can we creatively mine the riches of ambiguity.

Together these narratives highlight many complex and intriguing psychoanalytic processes in overlapping stories of the personal and the interpersonal, such as fantasy, dependence, projection, identification, and mirroring. In the next chapter we will begin to compare these ways of narrating relationships with the insights generated through the Jewish philosophical narratives of the life with others.

Notes

1. Freud wrote: "I can say that in the course of my work I have modified my views on important points, changed them or replaced them by others, and have of course in each case published the fact" (1969, 219). There are many accounts of Freud's changes. See, for example, Greenberg and Mitchell's account of the changes relating to Freud's "drive/structure model" (1983, 24–25).

2. Loewald has written: "Freud, like any man who does not sacrifice the complexity of life to the deceptive simplicity of rigid concepts, has said a good many contradictory things" (2000, 255).

3. Paul Ricoeur's classic work on Freud as well as the more recent book by DiCenso indicate some of the resources that Freud's writings provide for contemporary explorations in philosophy, religion, and culture.

4. It is interesting in this regard that Fairbairn sought to justify his argument that libido could not be treated as a type of energy independent of structure and object by referring to changes since Freud's time in the scientific understanding of energy (1994, 176–77). Fairbairn's remark shows a recognition of the influence of outside narratives or models on psychoanalysis.

5. Freud also distinguished between positive and negative Oedipal crises for each gender. See Hughes (1989, 50–54).

6. This last statement is an example of Freud's dramatic use of words and overall narrative mastery. No wonder that he saw a knowledge of literature and religion as part of the background required to be a psychoanalyst. Freud discusses this background in his *The Question of Lay Analysis* of 1926.

7. Irigaray's discussion of these points is the core of the first part of *Speculum*, "The Blind Spot of an Old Dream of Symmetry" (1985, 13–129). Essays by Jessica Benjamin, Nancy Chodorow, and Adrienne Harris in *Relational Psychoanalysis* (Mitchell and Aron, eds.), indicate some of the critiques that other feminist psychoanalysts have offered. Harris also discusses Freud's contributions to the psychological study of women and gender.

8. Klein saw her work as extending Abraham's and also possibly leading to a greater appreciation of its significance. See *Envy and Gratitude* (1997, 176–77).

9. Klein stands as a transitional figure between the drive/structure model and the relational/structure model for Greenberg and Mitchell (1983, 136).

10. Mitchell saw this description as accurate for Fairbairn and some other psychoanalysts not treated here, but I think that it is most appropriate in terms of Klein.

11. As Ogden indicates, Klein and other English psychoanalysts regularly use this spelling (phantasy), especially to distinguish the unconscious side of fantasy (1997, 10). I will utilize the term only in conjunction with Klein, who used it consistently.

12. The introduction to *Reading Melanie Klein* (Phillips and Stonebridge, eds., 1998) and the chapters that follow strongly make this point.

13. See Eli Zaretsky's article in Phillips and Stonebridge, eds. (41).

14. See Flax's reflections on the problem of "sanitized" versions of female relations (1993, 65–66).

15. Fairbairn's break with Freud's libidinal theory is again announced in an important later essay (1986, 102–3, 115).

16. There are some minor differences in terminology and characterization in Fairbairn's treatment of the stages over the years. One overall treatment is summarized in an article of 1941 (1986a, 81–84).

17. Fairbairn's cast of ego structures and objects is not fully consistent throughout his writings. At times it appears there are six structures, with the sixth being an (ideal) inner object somewhat corresponding to Freud's super-ego. See Fairbairn's essays "Object-Relationships and Dynamic Structure" of 1946 and "A Synopsis of the Development of the Author's Views Regarding the Structure of the Personality" of 1951, both in *Psychoanalytic Studies of the Personality*. There is a helpful treatment of Fairbairn's "Psychic Structuralization" in Greenberg and Mitchell's book (1983, 163–69).

18. Fairbairn's description of the subject trying to get rid of the internalized objects without losing contact with them is ambiguous in the original (1994, 146).

19. The many important references to Winnicott in the essays included in *Relational Psychoanalysis* (Mitchell and Aaron, eds.) witness this influence.

20. In order to provide a sense of the continuity and elasticity of the stages, Winnicott has depicted them in the "series": extreme dependence, dependence,

dependence-independence mixtures, independence-dependence, independence, social sense (1965a, 66).

21. A number of interpreters of Lacan note the alienation in his portrayal of the mirror stage. See, for example, Jane Gallop's treatment (1985, 59–60).

22. Jane Flax has an extensive discussion of Winnicott in her *Thinking Fragments* (107–32).

23. Emmanuel Ghent also sees the language of usage as not being particularly "felicitous" (Mitchell and Aron, eds., 228).

24. In a number of writings, Jessica Benjamin has focused on the mother's side of the mother-infant relationship, rejecting what she has termed the "infantocentric viewpoint" (1998, 32).

3

Of Gifts

The PHENOMENON OF GIFT-GIVING has intrigued anthropologists, sociologists, political scientists, philosophers, and psychologists. It has been explored in terms of the ways that gift-giving engenders social relationships of reciprocity and obligation; symbolically articulates identity, love, and power; and discloses self-interest or altruism. Factors such as class and ethnicity, familial relations, the public/private dichotomy, and gender roles are salient. Gift-giving can thus be seen as a fertile paradigm for the multi-faceted dynamics that underlie the interhuman. The gift is the leitmotiv for this chapter. Gifts make us and change us. We develop through, are nourished by, a web of gifts, as receivers and as givers. Without this web of others, there is no person; or, once again, as Buber put it: "There is no I as such . . ."

The term "gift," even if not directly spoken, evocatively reverberates through the foundational scenes of interaction—the mother's giving birth and caring for the infant, and the love relation between God and the soul—in the discourses of post-Freudian psychoanalysis and of modern Jewish philosophy. It is the gift "of life" that is alternatively attributed to the mother and/or to God. A constitutive gift, the ultimate gift, from one whom through it becomes the highest symbol of altruistic action, the ultimate giver. As the plot of this chapter unwinds, we will see in what ways the metaphor of the gift illuminates features in both discourses.

A number of similarities have probably been noted in traversing the first two chapters, the narratives of the interhuman of Rosenzweig, Buber, and Levinas and the narratives of development of Erikson, Klein, Winnicott, and Fairbairn. This chapter endeavors to make the case that the obvious is not superficial, that the similarities between these narratives of modern Jewish philosophy and post-Freudian psychoanalysis are indeed profound. When put into dialogue with one another, in this chapter, the one encouraging the other, the two groups of thinkers sketch a portrait of the interhuman of invaluable richness. The chapter will begin with an overview, reexamining the prominence of the interhuman in each of the thinkers' narratives. It will then turn to the issue of what allows persons to interact with others, that is, how openness to the other is understood. The main body of the chapter will explore the particular gifts from others that constitute a person. Identity and meaning are especially celebrated in this regard, but among the host of other gifts/constituents are trust, language, love, self-consciousness, and even reason. The chapter that follows this dialogue about the common or the shared will focus on the differences between the two sets of narratives. These differences converge around the processes, rather than the gifts, of relationship, and are symbolically expressed in the tension between "transference and transcendence."

Significance of Relations

As mentioned earlier, the autonomous individual is often the unchallenged point of departure in the modern West for thinking about the nature of the human. This dominant portrait is contested by the thinkers in the two intellectual streams that we have examined: modern Jewish philosophers and post-Freudian psychoanalysts. They provide a distinct account of the human that is built upon the gifts of the interhuman. For them, the interhuman is at the heart of the genesis of the human. Genesis may have two meanings, the birth or very beginning and also the foundation for the most essential attributes of a person.

Martin Buber finds that the interhuman pervades almost every feature of the human. He conceives of the ability to address and respond to others as innate, in terms of an "innate Thou" in every person. For him, the infant first lives in the context of a rudimentary "I-Thou" world with the mother, and only later does he or she see the two participants as separate. In this sense, even identity and self-consciousness emerge only after the awareness of being with another. The centrality of relationships in the genesis of each person is repeated by Buber through such statements as "Man becomes an I through a Thou" (1970, 80), and "Persons appear by entering into relation to other persons" (1970, 112). It is only in relation that a person gains freedom, lives in the present, learns of her or his task, and finds meaning in life.

With Franz Rosenzweig, at least in *The Star*, the prominence of the interhuman appears as a later development than it does for Buber. Rosenzweig does not lay a foundation for the importance of relationships by looking to birth and the first few months or years of the child's life. His description of the first years of life up through, perhaps, early adulthood seems to be in terms of the individual's isolation and alienation from others. This is a basic condition for him. Thus, the interhuman is that later dimension that both overcomes alienation and breaks the individual out of death-like limitations. Still, in his words: "Only in the discovery of a Thou is it possible to hear [as well as to be] an actual I" (1972, 175). While character and personality develop outside of relationship, for Rosenzweig, receiving a name, pursuing truth, fulfilling one's task, facing death and finding meaning result from being called by and responsible for others.

For Emmanuel Levinas, the other impinges upon the self from the very beginning, though this cannot be synchronized with time, such as the event of birth. The ethical obligation, that breaking into the self by the other is, in Levinas' words, rather: "an anachronous birth, prior to its own present, a non-beginning, an anarchy" (1981, 139). However, the importance of this ethical birth cannot be underestimated. One's uniqueness as a person is constituted by the singular conjuncture of one's responsibilities. Many of the most important human attributes such as language, self-consciousness, reason, justice, objectivity, and even one's sense of time arise out of consciousness of responsibility. More generally, Levinas has written: "And the proximity of the neighbor in its trauma does not only strike up against me, but exalts and elevates me, and, in the literal sense of the term, inspires me. Inspiration, heteronomy, is the very pneuma of the psyche" (1981, 124). Responsibility is thus the very essence of being a person.

The increasing significance given to relationships in psychoanalytic theory has been seen by many critics as the outstanding development since Sigmund Freud. For both Freud's topographical (unconscious, preconscious, conscious) and his structural models (id, ego, super-ego) the individual was portrayed as basically a closed system, in which the unconscious drives, and their repression, sublimation, and engagement with the ego's defenses, accounted for human motivation, psychological development, and character. Reality, especially the limitations of the social world, did affect drive expression, but it is only in terms of the super-ego that others impacted the structure of the psyche itself. Here the image of the parents was incorporated into psychic structure, which is the source, among other things, of conscience.

Erik Erikson's narrative of development, the eight psychosocial stages, reveals the beginning, at least in terms of the theorists we are examining, of a Freudian revision in terms of the self and others. Each stage outlines a crisis and (ideal) resolution in terms of a symmetry between the poles of Freud's psychosexual scheme and the social arena. In clear and concrete ways, psychological health requires that an expanding circle of others nourish, encourage, reflect back, support, share, and receive the needs and efforts of the individual. Erikson recognizes that not just receiving from but giving to others is required for a person to achieve fullness. In commenting about this dynamic in the crisis of generativity he writes: "Mature man needs to be needed" (1963, 266–67). While motivation is not ostensibly relational in Erikson's narrative, since health is, so must be health's opposite, pathology. The infant's basic trust is undermined without the mother's consistent and dependable, that is, trustworthy, responses; and in the years that follow, inadequate responses by others threaten shame, guilt, inferiority, confusion, isolation, stagnation, and despair.

Melanie Klein's work, even during her lifetime, was recognized as a substantial break with Freud, but it is still ambiguous in terms of the significance of other persons. The autonomous force of the drives in Freud, which remains at least a pole in Erikson, is now itself a relational phenomenon for Klein. Eros and thanatos are no longer the abstract drives of attraction and disintegration, but are necessarily coupled to specific others in love and hate, or alternatively, envy and gratitude. In her words: "The object-world of the child in the first two or three months of its life could be described as consisting of hostile and persecuting, or else of gratifying parts and portions of the real world" (1986, 65–66). Drives are transitive verbs. However, the phantasmagoric spectacle of love and hate, envy and gratitude, takes place within the psyche with inner objects and pieces of objects (the good and the bad breasts) as the protagonists. Still, motivation, health, and illness are relational in the two definitive paranoid-schizoid and depressive positions, and other persons, as inner objects, have a much greater role within the psyche than they did with Freud.

With W. R. D. Fairbairn all of the parameters of psychoanalytic discourse take up a relational coloring. Fairbairn's clarion call concerns the issue of motivation: "Libido is essentially object-seeking" (1994, 162), or more expansively: "The real libidinal aim is the establishment of satisfactory relationships with objects; and it is, accordingly, the object that constitutes the true libidinal goal" (1994, 138). His naming libido as object-seeking is probably a misnomer, for there is no place for anonymous energies in his psychoanalytic narrative.[1] What "drives" the infant, child, and adult is the quest for deeper and more mature relations, culminating in the full give and take of the adult. His narrative is holistic, personal, and relational, as is articulated in the stages: infantile dependence, quasi-independence, and mature dependence. The ambivalences or tensions within relationships to concrete others constitute the fundamental explanatory mechanism. Even "inner objects" are seen as an epiphenomenon. In harmony with this picture, psychopathology ultimately concerns a failure in the quality of parental care.

Winnicott's presentation continues to affirm the overwhelming significance of others, even if his concern with an inner self decenters Fairbairn's more consistent relational symmetry. The stages of dependence, transition, and independence show his difference with Fairbairn, but the tremendous prominence of the mother-infant dyad, and the preceding focus on the intra-uterine in both, are better guides to their fundamental similarities. Winnicott's relational foundation comes through clearly in his famous declaration "There is no such thing as an infant" (1986, 235). Health is defined in terms of the mother providing the "holding environment" for the inner self to crystallize. More profoundly, the mother is the vehicle through which the world is seen and the infant comes to know even of itself.

Overall, what can one conclude about the significance of the interhuman in these two discourses? Paraphrasing both Buber and Winnicott one can say that there is no self, there is no such thing as a self, without the other. Another way of saying this is that they find that the unit of study, for understanding the human, is always plural. The psychoanalysts concentrate on the pivotal early periods in the life cycle, especially the first months and years of life. The Jewish philosophers focus more consistently on the middle and later stages and how integrity and authenticity, which Erikson calls virtues, are gifts from the other. The clearest overlap brings together Buber with Fairbairn and Winnicott in terms of the mother's formative place in the development of the infant. Buber's description of the infant, who has a "longing for relation" (1970, 77) and "a drive to turn everything into a Thou" (1970, 78), seems to translate directly Fairbairn's and Winnicott's language of the infant being "object-seeking." Yet, from a variety of angles, the correspondences are still more extensive. Erikson explicitly describes the role of others in bestowing the later gifts that are the major topic of the Jewish philosophical narratives. In addition, since the infant's early stages are never left behind, but color all succeeding actions and relationships for the psychoanalysts, the significance of the interhuman in the maturing person's life is clearly evoked in both sets of narratives.

Openness to Others

There are a variety of ways that the philosophers and psychoanalysts justify the profound significance that they attribute to the interhuman. Their narratives include detailed accounts of the nature of human openness, that is, the origins and motivations for human attachments. The three Jewish philosophers express the factors behind human openness in distinctive ways. There are two angles in Buber's work that are relevant to this issue. First, Buber believes that human life is always relational. The first line of *I and Thou* states: "The world is twofold for man in accordance with his twofold attitude" (1970, 53). There are two "basic words," that is, two attitudes or orientations that characterize every human experience, activity, and reflection upon the world. One form of this is dominated by use and objectification—I and It, the other by mutuality and reciprocity—I and Thou. While this second form of interaction is often ignored and made difficult in the modern world, it is still one of humans' basic features. No matter how much it is abandoned, it is always a possibility and persons seem to know its creative and liberating power even in the jaws of the most nightmarish despair or "waking dream" (1972, 120). Second, Buber speaks of there also being an innate craving for intimate or meaningful relations. He writes: "In the beginning is the relation—as a category of being, as readiness, as a form that reaches out to be filled, as a model of the soul; the *a priori* of relation; *the innate Thou*" (1972, 78). As we saw, in the earliest stages of life the infant is driven by a "longing for relation." In a possible response to Freud, Buber utilizes the term drive, as in the infant's "drive to turn everything into a Thou" (1972, 78) or its "drive for contact" (1972, 79), and holds that this drive is independent of other drives and requirements, such as that of nourishment (1972, 77).

With Levinas, both egoism and relation appear to be innate. He recognizes that enjoyment and pleasure are powerful features of all aspects of living, such as eating, working, feeling comfortable in a place of one's own, and in these circumstances the "other" is only a means. However, there is also a "metaphysical desire" for the other, for relation with other persons, which is not based upon the egoism of enjoyment. This is a desire "without satisfaction" and "for the absolutely other" (1981, 34). Individuals are open to what is beyond, what cannot be understood or described in terms of, their needs and requirements. This is a direction that is ethical in-itself, that is, it places the needs of the other before the interests of the self. Levinas writes: "Subjectivity . . . obligated with regard to the neighbor, is the breaking point where essence is exceeded by the infinite" (1981, 12). Thus, the ethical concern surpasses or rises above usual ways that persons describe or calculate their nature ("essence") and interests. From perhaps another direction, Levinas phenomenologically describes human openness by referring to the way that the skin of the body is passive and vulnerable to the outside. One's being-for-another is even uncovered in the passivity of fatigue and aging (1981, 55). Thus, for Levinas, openness to the other is both an expression of the ethical dimension of human existence and seems to be inherent in or structured through human corporeality itself.

For Rosenzweig openness toward other persons is neither inherent as a basic possibility of address nor immanent because humans are also ethical creatures. At the beginning of his narrative in *The Star* about the genesis of the human he finds that even as a created form, a creature, to be human is to be cut off from others. This viewpoint is not merely stylistic, an outgrowth of the creation-revelation-redemption plot of *The Star*. Turning toward others in the fullness of speech and love is for him a human transcendence or a transcending of the human, not totally explained in terms of the ordinary powers of persons. It results from the love of God, either directly, or through another's love. Openness is a gift from the outside, rupturing the fearful enclosure of death. It results from a call, a "Where art Thou?," and in answering the individual is opened, "unlocked," becoming a soul (1970, 176). Rosenzweig might be saying, then, that one is surprised that humans can deeply connect, and that this can only be understood as something both extraordinary and given. However, once the human has been opened up, the life of relation, the tremendous possibilities of the "dual," can never be forgotten. A fascinating account of openness! Distinctive, even if Levinas also features some of Rosenzweig's insights here.

Many psychoanalysts following Freud viewed the infant as inherently turned toward others or adapted to interaction. This development is well expressed in the critical statement "All the important contemporary psychoanalytic schools view the human infant as less alien, more suited and adapted to the world into which he or she is born, than Freud did" (Mitchell and Black 1995, 113). Freud's basic account of psychic development and functioning focused on a system dominated by instincts. The outside world clashed with instinctual gratification, just as the father did with the son's Oedipal desires. Further, in the concept of primary narcissism, Freud rendered the infant as first seeking and finding release or gratification through itself. Actually Freud distinguished between autoeroticism and primary narcissism. Autoeroticism characterizes the very first months of life, when the infant finds pleasure in its own body alone. Following this, the energy of libido is invested in the ego. This is Freud's description of primary narcissism: "an original libidinal cathexis of the ego, from which some is later given off to objects, *but which fundamentally persists*" (my emphasis, cited in Greenberg and Mitchell 1983, 58). Even loving others is self-referential. One chooses (loves) another because she or he is similar to oneself, to what one ideally is, or to someone who was part of oneself—all three are "narcissistic object choice"—or because one is loved by the other—anaclitic choice (Freud 1986, 33). In all, Freud's understanding of primary narcissism forcefully embodies his global understanding of the human as turned upon itself and closed to direct and deeper connections with others. As one critical assessment concluded: "Freud's concept of primary narcissism is a stumbling block for any relational/structure model, since it explicitly presupposes that the infant is at first *not* oriented toward others, thereby making object relations secondary and derivative phenomena" (Greenberg and Mitchell 1983, 205). Those psychoanalytic theorists who describe the infant's primary openness to others were thus forced to minimize or outright reject Freud's account of narcissism.

The critic Stephen Mitchell has argued that post-Freudians, and especially object relations psychoanalysts, pursue one of three options in characterizing the infant's, and later person's, fundamental orientation toward connection (1988, 20–35). Humans are viewed as relational by either design, intent, or implication. *Design* refers to the biological and psychological composition of the infant. Here data from psychological studies of infants is used to argue that there is a basic biological need for the other, and that this drives the infant's interactions of sucking, smiling, clinging, crying, and following. This position also draws upon conclusions about the ways the infant's perceptual organs are structured to recognize human faces and voices. Those theorists who speak of *intent* hold that there is an autonomous motivational drive or craving for relatedness. From this perspective, persons are understood to "seek and maintain relatedness at any price" (Mitchell 1988, 26). Pursuing relationships is not an activity deriving from the need for nourishment or sexual release. Finally, some theorists insist that relationships to others play a crucial role in such larger projects as the development of the ego/self or the establishment of identity. They suggest that others are indispensable by *implication*.

This present study does not afford good examples of psychoanalysts who have concluded that humans were relational by design, their work deeply influenced by biological and perceptual studies. John Bowlby's investigations of response patterns and the perceptual capacities and preferences of newborns brought him to take up the "design" option in his formation of "attachment theory." The early interpersonal psychoanalyst Harry Stack Sullivan also belongs to this category (Mitchell 1988, 21–25).[2]

The implication model fits well with Erik Erikson, whose writings on identity are renowned and who is often categorized as a "self psychologist." For Erikson, other persons are necessarily implicated in the narrative of the eight psychosocial stages. Such building blocks for the self's development and health as its sense of its own goodness, self-esteem, initiative, creativity, identity, responsibility, productivity, and integrity all require support, encouragement, reciprocity, and intimacy with other persons. In this scheme, a person is a working connection between inner and outer, self and other. The lack of other persons supplementing and mirroring the inner is tied to a loss of faith in oneself: shame and doubt, guilt, inferiority, confusion, isolation, stagnation, and ultimately, despair. Still, Erikson's portrayal of the infant searching for the gaze of the mother—looking for a glance that will lift it up—seems to evoke Bowlby's findings concerning the human as structured for relationship.

The other psychoanalytic discussions that we have recounted belong to the intent stream. With Klein this comment refers to something somewhat subtle, but still significant. The language of anxieties, of inner objects and pieces of objects, does not seem to resonate well with the notion of motive or intention. Actually, however, inner objects and outer objects, and the processes that link them, such as introjection and projective identification, are ways of describing intense attachment to real and/or fantasized other persons. Every feeling and action is motivated by relation to the other. Others are so important that they must be taken into the psyche, becoming part of the constellation of forces that govern feelings and behavior. Further, changing unhealthy behavior requires abandoning old identification and shifting the constellations of objects and part objects. The intensity of the need for the other, the others having become part of the self itself, is attested by the way patients in analysis stubbornly fight against moving out of even extremely painful patterns.

In addition, it is possible to suggest within Kleinian theory that both the death and life instincts reveal a type of intent turned toward others. Clearly, at least, these drives are always tied to such "objects," since this link constituted Klein's primary departure from Freud. For example, the catalyst for the movement from the paranoid-schizoid to the depressive position is a change in the infant's attitude toward the mother. Klein is saying that by the second quarter of infancy, pieces of the ego and of various objects have been integrated enough so that one can speak of the infant's change in attitude. The infant demonstrates a (natural) attempt to rectify, redeem, and repair the earlier relationships poisoned by hate, envy, and paranoia. She describes this shift as: "the tendency to make reparation [which] ultimately derives from the life instinct" (1997, 74). Of course, the question of whether Klein's "theater" is composed of fantasized or real persons clouds the impact of her intuitions about the motivation of connectedness.

In Fairbairn's work, the feature of desiring relations, that is, intent, is preeminent, as is demonstrated in his affirmation that libido is object seeking and not pleasure seeking. Fairbairn makes contact with others the single motivation for behavior, and other explanations such as libidinal and destructive instincts, or the quest for the self's integrity, are rejected. Even Freud's narrative of psychosexual stages becomes transformed into a chronology of paths or vehicles for attachment. Satisfactory experiences with the parents allow the infant to embark on the progression from infantile dependence to mature dependence. Even painful and destructive interactions are internalized and treasured. Despite the pain and distortions that the latter signify, moving beyond destructive early interactions is felt by the patient to require abandoning the parents, an almost impossible task. Finally, with the motivation for attachment as the singular explanatory mechanism, behavior, health and pathology are accounted for totally in terms of the conflicts and vicissitudes in relations.

Winnicott's narrative appears to include descriptions of relatedness to others in terms of all three orientations: design, intent, and implication. First, he holds that the infant is born, designed, with an orientation to the breast. Second, the drive or craving to be related to others is clearly seen in Winnicott's progression in the status of the mother from inner object to outer object. Intent is also featured in Winnicott's discussion of the transitional object, for he is saying that the need to be attached to others is so dominant that the infant depends upon an object—a personalized or anthropomorphic object, a blanket, for example—to move toward the outside world. Third, Winnicott's discussions of the mother providing a holding environment for the infant show the strong tendency to make relationship (the holding environment) a means for the higher end, which is the development of the central self. "Good enough" mothering is in this case a necessary condition for the emergence of an authentic self.

Winnicott's statement that there is "no such thing as a baby" needs to be examined in its own right. For him, as well as for Fairbairn, both in the uterus and during the first days of life, the fetus/infant is totally merged with the mother. The infant and mother are one unit, infant-mother. He is saying that in these periods, the psychic boundary between the two is not clear. The infant is thus structured or designed, in the most impressive way, for relatedness. Intriguingly, the mother is also structured/designed for this psychological relatedness, which is termed "primary maternal identification." Thus, this type of relationship is not "just" infantile for a great number of female persons.

Despite some differences in discourse and vocabulary, the three Jewish philosophers and the four psychoanalysts affirm that being human is synonymous with being open to the other. One way of bringing together the different languages is to re-introduce the concepts of design, intent, and implication to explore both sets of thinkers. In this wider context, the most helpful of the three categories is intent, which had earlier brought together Klein, Fairbairn, and Winnicott. Along with the object relations thinkers, Buber and Levinas have characterized persons as those, who at the most fundamental level, desire the other. There is an array of articulations in Buber's writings that satisfy the notion of humans being fundamentally motivated to seek others. The I-Thou orientation of humans as well as the notion of the "innate Thou" as a "readiness" (1970, 78) expresses this. Even more impressive are his statements about the infant, who has a "drive to turn everything into a Thou," or a "drive for contact" (1970, 79), and for whom the "craving" and "longing for relation is primary" (1970, 78, 79). Levinas explores this motivation to be related to the other through the distinctive terminology of "metaphysical desire." This is an insatiable desire for the other that celebrates the other's distance and separateness (1969, 34).

When the claim is made that humans are oriented toward the other by intent, or motivated by relatedness for its own sake, then other motivations are often explicitly rejected. For example, Buber writes that the infant glances and reaches toward the other "at times when there is obviously no desire for nourishment" (1970, 77). In this way Buber differentiates the craving for the other from hunger. Fairbairn argues somewhat similarly that it is the intense quest for the object, rather than other motivations, that explains the infant's basic behavior. Neither the goals of pleasure nor need define this quest, in Fairbairn's view (Mitchell 1988, 27). Taking up what would seem to be a difficult case, Fairbairn does not regard thumb sucking as motivated by pleasure, but by the need to find an alternative to the unavailable breast (1986a, 76–77). For him, autoeroticism results from the failure to find a satisfactory relation with another—the complete reversal of Freud. Finally, the force of Levinas' use of the phrase "metaphysical desire" is its differentiation from "need." The search for the other is "metaphysical," that is, outside of the explanatory categories of pleasure, nourishment, or security. For Levinas, "metaphysical desire" is independent from the basic human needs, and, unlike every other desire, it does not have its own satisfaction as the goal (1969, 33–34).

The idea that humans are physiologically and psychologically structured to seek the other, so that the infant is designed or attuned to human faces and voices, does have some echo in both discourses. Buber's discussions of the "innate Thou," appears as a psychological expression of the notion of relatedness by design. Levinas' phenomenological account of the skin as showing a vulnerability to the outside, as well as his overall treatment of human "sensibility," may be his way of describing an almost physiological openness to the other (1981, 51–56). As mentioned before, Erikson's description of the infant looking for a glance from the mother does have a resemblance to the findings about the infant's perceptions being attuned to the human face. He interprets this "physiognomic detail" as a "search for experience and assurance" (1964, 116). Finally, Winnicott's characterization of the infant as being oriented toward the breast, with the concurrent spontaneous process of the infant believing that it had actually created it (1986a, 266), is also a relevant example of the human as structured for relation.

Among the post-Freudian psychoanalysts, the idea that the centrality of relation is best understood in the context of important developmental tasks, that is, by implication, is most clearly exemplified in the works of Erikson and Winnicott. For Erikson, the other is needed throughout all of the psychosocial stages, for the sake of the identity and integrity of the person. Broadly speaking, one might suggest that whenever a developmental narrative gives prominence to the other throughout the stages, as also found in Winnicott and Fairbairn, then the notion of implication is active. Winnicott's concern with the true self, and his depiction of the mother providing a holding environment for the emergence of this, demonstrates that he is very clearly saying that relations are especially significant in the wider context of the self's development.

The Jewish philosophers have a special stance toward the language of relation by implication. All three of them describe the ways that fundamental features of the human, especially those that coalesce around integrity, require the other. More generally, the idea that the self requires the other for the sake of integrity bridges the philosophical and psychoanalytic presentations. However, the narratives of the Jewish philosophers do not affirm that relations with others are a means to bring about the authenticity of the self. For them, relations are narrated solely as ends in themselves, a position that is not as clear at least in the narratives of Erikson and Winnicott.

Finally, one way to accentuate the openness of persons to each other is to give the intra-uterine and the mother-infant dyad a forceful role in one's narrative. As we have seen, this is the case in the presentations of Buber, Erikson, and the two object relations theorists, Fairbairn and Winnicott. Buber turns his attention to the mother-infant dyad as a way of demonstrating the priority or "natural association" of one to another, as the embryonic foundation for the I-Thou attitude. He writes: "The prenatal life of the child is a pure natural association, a flowing toward each other, a bodily reciprocity; and the life horizon of the developing being appears uniquely inscribed, and yet also not inscribed, in that of the being that carries it" (1970, 76). There are remarkable passages where Buber is both poetic and very concrete in his description of the infant reaching out and looking for the other, grasping, trying to converse with inanimate objects, in all, turning everything into a Thou (1970, 77). He adds that the image of the intra-uterine remains with us in later life, but not as a longing to return (a reference to Freud?), but as a reminder of the experience of association (1970, 76–77). The exchange of glances between infant and caretaker, inspiring an exchange of hope, is a comparable illustration of the "experience of mutuality" within Erikson's first psychosocial stage (1964, 116). Fairbairn's first stage of infantile dependence is described in terms of total identification, of merger and almost symbiosis. As we saw, this initial period within the first stage is dominated by orality. Yet, Fairbairn does not use the term orality to refer back to a bodily or erotogenic zone, but to observe that the earliest relation/identification with the mother is achieved by taking her in orally. For Fairbairn, the openness of the human toward others is noted by claiming that the infant starts not isolated, but merged, and that infantile dependence lays the foundation for mature dependence/relations (1986a, 78). Winnicott provides an extensive treatment of the earliest months of the infant-mother's life, beginning with the intra-uterine. His particular interest is the holding environment that the mother provides to allow the integration of the infant's ego. Holding means being the vehicle through which the infant experiences the inside and outside. Only with satisfactory care by the mother, sensing the infant's psychological and physical needs as her own, does the infant slowly develop as something distinct. Although relationships have a supporting role in his narrative, relational by implication, the closeness and dramatic character of the merger/interaction between mother and infant adds material to the overall portrait of humans' basic openness to the other. In the context of these four presentations, it is perhaps a misnomer to speak of the intra-uterine; the prefix should almost be some form of "inter-."[3]

What are the consequences when the intra-uterine and the mother-infant dyad are not given a place in one's narrative of the human? Freud's omission is fully consistent with his view of the asocial character of the human. From a different perspective, it is not surprising that Levinas does not feature this relation in his narrative,[4] for he argues that the ethical relation is a break with being/nature. For Rosenzweig, full relations are, once again, a break or a rupture with the original isolation of the individual. While he uses the mother-infant image to allude to the relation of soul and God, the progression of his narrative would be obscured if the mother-infant dyad had a pronounced place. Luce Irigaray's charge that philosophy has its *own* very good reasons for ignoring this period of life will be seriously taken up later.

Gifts: Identity and Integrity

This section inaugurates an extensive examination of features of the self that originate in or are nourished by the interhuman. The first property or achievement is certainly one of the central dimensions of being a person, combining aspects of what has often been explored in terms of such concepts as identity and integrity. In this context, integrity alludes to someone being whole, coherent, or integrated. Although post-modern theorists have encouraged notions of the self as fractured and maintaining multiple identities, it is hoped that they are not challenging the idea that when persons have no coherence or stability, as in the borderline personality disorder of schizophrenia, they are in a serious and dangerous situation.[5] Jane Flax provides a general description of the borderline: "Lacking an ability to sustain coherence, one slides into the endless terror, emptiness, desolate loneliness, and fear of annihilation that pervade borderline subjectivity" (1993, 102–3). As opposed to this, to possess identity/integrity means that one sustains an overall sense of distinctiveness, wholeness, and integration. The narratives of the modern Jewish philosophers and post-Freudian psychoanalysts ground this essential feature of identity/integrity in the interhuman. Put another way, what many might regard as the most individual, personal, and even autonomous dimension of being a person these theorists claim is one of the greatest gifts that can be received from the other.

How does Rosenzweig speak of identity and integrity? With Rosenzweig it may be said that these are the products of two processes, one inherently part of the self and the other requiring the other. Personality and character form in isolation. Personality is Rosenzweig's way of saying that a person is part of a species, the human species, but also a specific expression of the species. Character is a non-comparable characteristic. It is not an attribute but an overpowering pattern of being: a one-sided, self-regarding acting and relating. Rosenzweig gives us a sense of its power and direction by linking character with defiance, and of its depth by suggesting it coalesces with the confrontation with one's own death. These are the rudiments of both identity and integrity, but neither in their fullness. However, his understanding of a whole individual, a person, is tied to the language of the soul as in: "It is only . . . in the love of God that the flower of the soul begins to grow out of the rock of the self" (1972, 169). A person becomes a soul when she or he is called by another. The other calls one out, opens one up. The call that opens is personal, between persons, in the second person verb form, by a thou. This insight is reinforced by Rosenzweig's tying the call to the activity of love. In his words: "Previously man had been a senseless and speechless introvert; only now is he—beloved soul" (1972, 169). However, since Rosenzweig sees love and speech as almost synonymous, the call of the thou is not necessarily synonymous with romantic love, but represents some type of deep concern. The calling to another, the attitude of addressing and deeply caring for another individual, transforms the other's self into a soul, the other's being an individual into being a person. Beyond the features of personality and character, there is now identity and integrity. This process is completed with the newly developed person turning in address to her or his neighbor. A full person is both beloved and lover, addressed by a thou and addressing another thou. The two-fold process of love or speech is represented by Rosenzweig in God's dual commandments to love God and to love the neighbor. Here we see not only how being a full self is a gift, but also the way that Rosenzweig understands identity and integrity. These not only arise out of relation but are definable totally in terms of someone being able to relate. What specifically distinguishes being a self from being a soul, or what relational attributes the person acquires from the thou, will be explained below.

Identity and integrity are also products of relation for Buber, or better put, the I crystallizes through relations to a thou. Buber's basic proposition remains: "Man becomes an I through a Thou" (1970, 80). In *I and Thou* there are two processes that combine to constitute personal integration, both of which are surrounded by periods of relation. The sense of a distinct self is not there from the beginning. Put in another way, Buber is quite clear that deeper relations with others are not possible from the position of embeddedness that first appears between the infant and mother. Self-consciousness, "I-consciousness," slowly emerges out of the infant's "natural association" with the mother and with everything that is touched. Through nascent I-Thou relations the self begins to dawn, and this development allows for the detachment necessary for the first I-It relations as well as for more developed I-Thou relations (1970, 80–81). The second process, which may correspond to adolescence, is a repetition of the earlier occurrence, another dawning of I-consciousness from out of prior relations. Buber writes of this as an event where "the soul may become one" (1970, 134). In "this decisive moment" the person "stands alone in itself," "concentrated into a unity" (1970, 134). This second process of concentration seems to complete the integration or identity of the person. However, it also has a wider context, for the concentrated I must now turn to others in a way: "wholly successful only now—with mystery and perfection" (1970, 134). In all, Buber presents an insightful view of a two-staged systole and diastole of the I and others, offering an impressive variation on the theme of the I as a gift.

For Levinas, to be means to be for others. He has many ways of putting this. Being a person, an "I," requires a process or attitude of answering, of standing with a "here I am . . . for everything and for everyone" (1981, 114). This is detailed further in his dramatic sentence "The subjectivity of the subject is persecution and martyrdom" (1981, 146). To be a person requires an accountability for the other which reaches all the way to being hostage to the neighbor. Thus, basic integrity for Levinas is not the natural outcome of just existing, of merely having a center or being an ego. It is more than living under the rubrics of satisfaction and enjoyment. Rather, to be a person arises out of the recognition and acceptance that the human has, is meant to be, and lives in, a transcendent-ethical dimension, beyond the natural and animal. With such recognition and acceptance one becomes a soul. Underlining the view that this is not self-engendered, Levinas writes that the "soul is the other in me" (1981, 191).

Audaciously, to the last, Levinas has another way of asserting that the I proceeds from relation. Here he argues through the language of uniqueness. For him, the specification of being a distinct person, this one person, is not a natural attribute. It is linked to the other through a transitive verb: to be this particular person is to be chosen. In his words: "exposedness is the one-in-responsibility, and thus the one in its uniqueness," or: "uniqueness means the impossibility of slipping away and being replaced" (1981, 56). Responsibility calls one out: it establishes, through demand, oneself as just this person and no other. Additionally, perhaps, just as the points around the circumference of a circle specify one and only one mid-point, the array of responsibilities designate the distinct one that a person is.

If being a person is being just this one in a state of persecution, obsessed by responsibility, then it is not mistaken to see identity and integrity as gifts from the other, gifts through "election." The idea here is that these features obviously cannot be achieved by oneself, they require others. Then, these are gifts, but, as is sometimes the case in such matters, not wholly welcomed initially. On the other hand, as with gifts generally, the reception of identity and integrity entail obligations or demands; the greatest gifts, the highest demands.

The narratives of the post-Freudian psychoanalysts explicitly detail the ways that identity/integrity requires the other. For Erikson, the crisis of identity constitutes the fifth psychosocial state, and it emerges around the period of adolescence. In all of his writings, he emphasizes the relational aspect of this ego strength or "virtue." Identity requires the confirmation of one's inner sense of who one is by the world. As Erikson explains: "The sense of ego identity, then, is the accrued confidence that the inner sameness and continuity prepared in the past are matched by the sameness and continuity of one's meaning for others, as evidenced in the tangible promise of a 'career'" (1963, 261–62). From the adolescent's point of view, he or she is "primarily concerned with what they appear to be in the eyes of others as compared with what they feel they are" (1963, 261). In addition to the peer group who must confirm the self's definition of itself, Erikson discusses the role of the intimate other, who becomes salient with the onset of puberty. He writes: "adolescent love is an attempt to arrive at a definition of one's identity by projecting one's diffused ego image on another and by seeing it thus reflected and gradually clarified" (1963, 262). Thus, Erikson suggests that different types of others have a central role, through the processes of mirroring and confirmation, in achieving the all-important virtue of identity.

Klein, Fairbairn, and Winnicott explore some features of identity/integrity by turning to earlier times and by introducing such concepts as identification and integration. They all see the foundations for identity, which includes the integration or consolidation of the ego, in the emergence of the second stage of the infant's development. Although the issue of actual "others" is always ambiguous for Klein, it is perhaps in her narration of the transition between the two "positions" that we come upon the notion of identity. In this period the mother is addressed because the infant is driven by the "urge to repair, preserve or revive the loved injured object" (1997, 74). She is no longer seen as threatening and persecuting, but as the injured victim of one's own attacks. In terms of the issue of identity, it is important to note that the process of projective identification dominated the earlier paranoid-schizoid position or attitude toward the mother. This process is characterized by splitting of the infant's ego, projecting bad parts upon the mother, and then taking these back into the psyche. At that time the mother was also treated as a part-object and not as a whole. With the dawn of the depressive position the integration of both infant and mother begins. In a crucial statement Klein writes: "the child comes to know the mother as a whole person and becomes identified with her as a whole, real and loved person" (1986, 66). The process of becoming a whole, of uniting split-off good and bad pieces of the ego, occurs as the infant turns toward, and identifies with, her. The mother is seen as a single person, rather than as good and bad breasts. In addition, for this process to succeed, for the infant's doubts about the possibility of reparation to be overcome, he must have a sense that his efforts have been accepted. This occurs as the infant, in Klein's words: "obtains reassurance over and over again in the love of the mother" (1986, 67). Thus, the role of the m/other is paramount in Klein's narrative about identity. Integration of the ego commences with the infant treating the mother herself as a whole. In this sense, integrity follows from the recognition of, and identification with, the integrity of the other. Further, the infant's efforts, and the resulting ego consolidation, can only succeed with the gift of the mother's reassuring love.

For Fairbairn the issue of identity revolves around the movement or transition from the earliest stage of infantile dependence to the later period of mature dependence. The first stage is a continuation of the type of deep dependence—Fairbairn calls it "absolute dependence"—of the intra-uterine state. During the first weeks of life the identification with the mother is so intense that the infant has no separate identity. In Fairbairn's words: "In so far as identification persists after birth, the individual's object [the mother] constitutes not only his world, but also himself" (1986a, 90). What later allows the infant to become whole, seeing itself, as well as relating to the mother and others, as independent? This is the essential assurance, which Fairbairn has described as: "that he is genuinely loved by his parents, and . . . that his parents genuinely accept his love" (1986a, 82). Through the double gift of assurance a separated identity appears. A new, mature type of relationship with others now also becomes possible. This new possibility is described by Fairbairn as: "mature dependence involves a relationship between two independent individuals, who [ideally] are completely differentiated from one another as mutual objects" (1986a, 84). Mature dependence also indicates that the split-off pieces of the ego are somewhat reintegrated and do not have the dominant position that they earlier held in the psyche. Finally, Fairbairn saw the origin of the most serious mental illnesses as arising out of the trauma that resulted from the lack of this double assurance. The consequences of the failure to assure were so serious that Fairbairn could state: "Frustration of his desire to be loved and to have his love accepted is the greatest trauma that a child can experience; and indeed this is the only trauma that really matters from a developmental standpoint" (1986a, 83). Thus, for Fairbairn, identity is so tied to the other that it is proper to suggest that to feel loved and to be accepted as loving determines whether there is a self at all.

Winnicott's notion of the mother's provision of a "holding environment" for the infant is the main feature through which the other's role in one's identity and integrity are portrayed. The nomenclature of "holding" is both helpful and somewhat misleading in its passive connotations. The mother not only introduces the infant to the world but also introduces it to itself, by reflecting, ordering, and identifying its inner experiences and movements, even helping in the discrimination between inner and outer. By supporting the infant's ego through her ego, "ego-relatedness," the infant is able to master his inner (id) drives as well as the requirements that are external. Overall, reliable maternal care is the sine qua non for the infant attaining integrity or "unit status," that is, becoming a "person, and individual in his own right" (1986, 241). The language of the "true self" provides another perspective on the importance of the holding environment. Winnicott believes that this inner self is the embryonic foundation for personal existence. With satisfactory care her natural development proceeds, while if it is not guarded and supported a "false self" surfaces instead. The gifts of identity and integrity by the mother are vividly summarized by Winnicott in the following:

> With the care that it receives from its mother each infant is able to have a personal existence, and so begins to build up what might be called *a continuity of being*. On the basis of this continuity of being the inherited potential gradually develops into an individual infant. If maternal care is not good enough then the infant does not really come into existence. (1986, 251)

The philosophical and psychoanalytic accounts above, arranged around the topic of identity/integrity, are in harmony in voicing the need for the other in the becoming of the self. In all of the cases, distinctiveness, wholeness, and integration, the very integrity of the self, are understood to be gifts from the other. The various chronologies suggest both similarities and differences. There are striking similarities in the narratives of Buber, Fairbairn, and Winnicott about the emergence of the infant from out of the earliest merger with the mother. In these cases, relation to the mother precedes the birth of the I, and early relations continue some of the basic features of the intra-uterine. In the narratives of Fairbairn and Winnicott, the other then supports the dawning self by providing the assurance of love given and accepted, or by protecting and guiding the innate movement toward personal existence.

With Rosenzweig, Buber, Levinas, and Erikson the chronology is not as clear. Rosenzweig and Erikson have these central processes of identity/integrity occurring later in life. Buber features an earlier and later stage, while Levinas refuses a set chronology at all. Together, these thinkers present narratives about the mature self or identity in its strongest sense. Rosenzweig and Buber frame this in terms of the dialogical self, Levinas portrays it as the ethical self, and Erikson treats identity at the stage of adolescence. For these thinkers, the development of the self is linked with mature intimacy with another. Rosenzweig discusses this through the exchange of love and speech, Buber through the dialogue of "I and Thou," for Levinas it is the intimate tie of responsibility, and for Erikson it is the intimacy of love and a mate. Further, Rosenzweig and Levinas find that the mature self develops only when called. Rosenzweig has the call embedded in love, in the call to love the other, whether God or the neighbor. For Levinas it is the call of the widow, orphan, poor, and stranger: that is, the ethical call of the neighbor.

Among other important insights about identity and the other in the accounts of the psychoanalysts, the role of identification and mirroring are especially prominent. Erikson's examination of identity speaks of the role of mirroring in adolescent love as important in the coming to be of the individual. For Klein, Winnicott, and Fairbairn one becomes whole through identifying with the intimate other as well as seeing one's future wholeness reflected in her face.

Despite significant differences in the chronologies, processes, and even the types of identity that are being described, there is a pervasive sense that identity is linked with deep concern. This may be the concern by the other or concern for the other. For Rosenzweig the love/concern of the other is required to open the self. Buber's self is innately open to the other, but requires many I-Thou relationships, and their manifestations of exclusive concern, to become an I in the fullest sense. Levinas features (obsessional) concern for the other in one's responding to his or her face. With Klein the self begins to be integrated as it attempts reparation for its fantastic injuries to the other. Fairbairn insists on the double assurance of loving and being loved in order for the self to coalesce. Finally, for Winnicott, in narrating the first stages of the development of the ego, he portrays the mother's concern for the infant as so deep that it is almost pathological!

Meaning

The next quality or "virtue" that the narratives of the Jewish philosophers and the psychoanalysts attribute as a gift from the other is meaning. Together, identity/integrity and meaning are probably the two most important features of human life. If the first quality touches upon the senses of distinctiveness, wholeness, and integration, the second alludes to the feelings of trust, confidence, purpose, and direction. Through looking at these two sets of narratives insight is gained not only into the ways that the self is given a trust in itself, a trust in others, and a direction in the world, but also into the nature of the quality of meaning itself. As was the case with the issue of identity, a difference in chronology between the treatments is quickly apparent. The Jewish philosophers explore the basic sense of the meaningfulness of one's life and of life overall in terms of the mature individual, while the psychoanalysts investigate the foundations or rudiments of meaning in the first months and years of life. What constitutes meaning and how is it given by the other?

The nature of that sense of life's meaningfulness, its basic constituents, and the dynamics of its being given by the other are prominent in the narratives of the Jewish philosophers. Buber directly addresses the issue of meaning in *I and Thou*, in the key section on revelation to which we have often turned. He writes:

> nor does association [with the divine Thou] make life any easier for us—it makes life heavier but heavy with meaning . . . the inexpressible confirmation of meaning. It is guaranteed. Nothing, nothing can henceforth be meaningless. . . . What could it intend with us, what does it desire from us, being revealed and surreptitious? . . . it wants to be demonstrated by us in this life and this world. . . . The meaning we receive can be put to the proof in action only by each person in the uniqueness of his being and in the uniqueness of his life. (1970, 158–59)

There are a number of constituent elements in Buber's portrayal of meaning. He suggests here that meaning is inseparable from the sense of purpose, direction, and the recognition that one is assigned things that must be done. Meaning is about one's life and life overall. One has a unique task in the wider arena of life. Further, throughout Buber's description of what a person receives from the encounter with the divine, he insists that no "content," "formula," "image," "prescription," or specific ethical teaching is involved. Meaning is not tied to a static object or announcement, but a direction about which one has only a sense. One receives only by appropriating, that is to say, by answering and acting.

For Buber meaning is not self-engendered or part of one's natural development. It is not included in some developmental cycle, as if it were to inevitably just spring forth one day. In narrating meaning as a divine gift, he is maintaining that it transcends what is inherent to the self as well as what is natural and everyday. Further, meaning is an orienting gift that makes demands upon the receiver. Unlike some gifts that ease or simplify life, this gift makes life heavier.[6] The highest gift, the one that gives meaning to the self, world, everything, entails a life filled with obligations.

Rosenzweig is particularly helpful in understanding some of the constituents of meaning. His discussion of this most important virtue is also in the context of revelation. In the section that is "the heart" of *The Star of Redemption*,[7] he writes about the way that the beloved soul is transformed by the divine lover, or alternatively, of what the soul receives from this lover. As we saw, prior to this, the individual is an isolated, alienated self. While having a personality and unique character, its fearful obsession with death imprisons it in an angry defiance. This is a good description of the effects of meaninglessness. Defiance is the appropriate (Kleinian) position, when one is dominated by, when all that one has to look forward to is, death. The movement out of this situation comes with the divine call to love (God). God's commandment to love elicits, in turn, the love of the beloved.

Rosenzweig offers a number of elements that ensue from God's love. There is the awakened love of the beloved, which he characterizes as: "An awe compounded of humility and pride, together with a feeling of dependence and of being securely sheltered, of taking refuge in the arms of eternity" (1972, 168).[8] An additional result of the divine love is opened through Rosenzweig's analysis of humility. Of this Rosenzweig says: "humility which is conscious of being what it is by grace of a Superior . . . rests secure in the feeling of being sheltered. It knows that nothing can befall it. And it knows that no power can rob it of this consciousness which carries it wherever it may go" (1972, 168). Other gifts received are featured in Rosenzweig's concluding epigram about revelation: "Revelation teaches us to trust in the Creator, to wait hopefully for the Redeemer" (1972, 382).

Is this description of the effects of God's love in revelation pertinent to the issue of meaning? Rosenzweig is speaking about something one is given by the other. Although a gift, it is about new qualities of the self, not something external. As something given, one is dependent on "grace," on the transcendent giver. Thus, the quality Rosenzweig is describing is certainly not something one could make, find, do, or give oneself. What one receives is a complex gift of humility and trust. Humility is a transformation out of the defiant obsession with death. It is the sense of being secure. Humility comes from a trust: a trust in oneself, because of the other's trust. Further, this trust extends to life, in life/the world itself, for the phrase "nothing can befall it," encompasses all of life. The trust is even beyond life, because it includes the hope—a kind of far-reaching, future trust—in the Redeemer. So Rosenzweig's portrayal of the love of the beloved is about meaning: the meaning of one's life and life itself.

For Levinas, the ethical relationship to the other, which is symbolized in the biblical injunction to care for the widow, orphan, poor, and stranger, grounds meaning. It, uniquely, grounds meaning. There is the life of being or ontology, of pleasure and satisfaction, but this is deadening, ennui, and not renewing and purposeful. All that is meaningful and new issues from the appearance of the other. This proximity brings into question pleasure and satisfaction—my whole existence, and through the infinite tasks, responsibility allows meaning to break out. Stated in another way, the other breaks down the door of the ego with her or his irreplaceable gift. Levinas' statements about the ethical "approach" to the other demonstrate that this meaning is comparable to what has just been seen in Rosenzweig and Buber. He writes:

> The self inasmuch as, in an approach, it abrogates the egoism of perseverance in being, which is the imperialism of the ego, introduces meaning into being. . . . The approach, inasmuch as it is a sacrifice, confers a sense on death. . . . In it life is no longer measured by being, and death can no longer introduce the absurd into it . . . we can have responsibilities and attachments through which death takes on a meaning. That is because, from the start, the other affects us despite ourselves. (1981, 128–29)

Thus, according to Levinas, the meaningfulness of life issues from that lifelong attitude, approach, or position of being for the other.

It is inescapable that for Levinas the other who introduces meaning is the neighbor. There may be various traces of the divine in her ethical height, but it is clear that it is not a direct relation with the divine that bestows meaning, purpose, orientation. Levinas' attribution of the gift of meaning to the ethical encounter with the neighbor may reinforce some less explicit features in the two other Jewish philosophers. Meaning also revolves around the neighbor in the narratives of Rosenzweig and Buber. For Rosenzweig, the love between God and the soul is both simile and more than simile of the love between persons. Additionally, God commands that the soul's love of the divine be supplemented by the love of the neighbor. Finally, it can be argued that the neighbor experiences this love by the other as God's love. Buber enhances this last statement, in that the encounter with God is both preceded and followed by turning to others as thou. Further, Buber's statement "Extended, the lines of relationships intersect in the eternal Thou" (1970, 123) reinforces the inseparable connections between meetings with humans and meetings with the divine.

There are many psychosocial stages in Erikson's narrative that are relevant to the issue of meaning, but there is no one single stage that he labels in terms of the crisis, or identifies explicitly with the virtue, of meaning. Taking the lead from the discussions of the Jewish philosophers, it may be helpful to look in Erikson's work for equivalents to such features as that double trust in oneself and the world, as well as a sense of purpose and mission. Erikson places the issue or crisis of trust at the beginning of the life cycle, and reiterates that this crisis, as every other one, continues to arise in later periods. He also notes that what is described by him in terms of trust, others may wish to label as confidence (1963, 247–48). The goal or achievement for this first stage Erikson sees as "an essential trustfulness of others as well as a fundamental sense of one's own trustworthiness" (1968, 96). The two-fold referents of trust appear again in the quasi-religious language of "faith in the goodness of one's strivings and in the kindness of the powers of the universe" (1963, 251). The eighth stage of the life cycle, which Erikson presents in terms of the tension between ego-integrity and despair, is also relevant to his understanding of meaning. It is occasioned by the confrontation with death, and he defines integrity as "the ego's accrued assurance of its proclivity for order and meaning" (1963, 268). The achievement of integrity is also described in terms of a sense of the "meaning" of one's strivings and of the "dignity" of one's life as a whole (1963, 268). Since both the first and last stages of life are directly implicated in the issue of meaning, Erikson seems to suggest that life cannot begin without an elementary sense of this, but that the issue of meaning ultimately touches upon the whole life.

There are a number of ways that Erikson indicates that meaning requires the other. In a general statement about the first stage he writes: "Mothers create a sense of trust in their children" (1968, 103). Trust also precipitates through the interchange with, the giving to and receiving from, the other. Erikson writes that the baby learns to receive by being given, and, more intriguing, that it also learns to be a "giver" through identifying with the mother and eventually becoming "a giving person" (1968, 99). Finally, that aspect of meaning tied to the last stage involves others in significant ways. Here the reference to others is expressed in the widest possible sense as well as one more narrow and immediate: "comradeship with the ordering ways of distant times and different pursuits" (1963, 268), and: "participation by followership as well as acceptance of the responsibility of leadership" (1963, 269).

Those qualities that seem to correspond to meaning in the narratives of Klein, Fairbairn, and Winnicott are attributed to the second phase of the infant's development. With Klein meaning becomes possible with the onset of the depressive position. Prior to this, the infant's experience was dominated by the anxieties, defenses, and phantasies engendered by the death drive. That drive with its overriding envy endeavors to spoil whatever good the infant might experience, and is ultimately an envy about the other's life, or life itself, according to Klein (1997, 189). Gratitude, envy's opposite, is the major emotion of the depressive position. It is, ultimately, a thankfulness for the goodness or meaningfulness of life. Some of Klein's characterizations of the depressive position, with this primary virtue of gratitude, echo ideas that we have just seen in the preceding discussions of meaning. She writes of trust, security, and confidence in the following comments concerning gratitude and the depressive position: "Gratitude is closely linked with the trust in good figures" (1997, 188); there is "a greater trust in one's capacity to love and a lessening of the paranoid anxiety of the bad objects" (1986, 69); "a feeling of greater security ensues" (1997, 75); and "the infant gradually gains a greater confidence in his objects and in his reparative powers" (1997, 75). In summary, the depressive position is the early basis for that feeling of having a "share in the experiences and pleasures of life . . . much more able to believe in the continuity of life" (1997, 203). Here then is that trust or confidence in other "objects" and in oneself that combines into the overall sense of the meaningfulness of life.

Of course, what is distinctive of Klein's presentation is that both positions are narrated in terms of complicated drives/instincts and objects. Satisfactory experiences with the mother reinforce (1986, 66), but still come across as secondary to, the natural developmental expression of the drives. In her words: "Since the tendency to make reparation ultimately derives from the life instinct, it draws on libidinal phantasies and desires" (1997, 74). Thus, the use of the metaphor of gift to describe this fundamental developmental achievement is somewhat ambiguous, because the place of the mother's actual care or response is problematic.

There does not seem to be a direct discussion of the quality of meaning in Fairbairn's narrative. Still, meaningfulness might be related to the transition toward and inception of mature dependence. One of the possible pathologies, the schizoid state, within the stage of infantile dependence reveals what is at stake in the movement toward mature dependence. Fairbairn found that schizoid individuals do not have faith in their power to love and respond to this by turning within. The isolation and withdrawal, in Fairbairn's words: "may even go so far that all libidinal links with outer reality are surrendered, all interest in the world fades and everything becomes meaningless" (1986a, 93). However, if the child's experiences of being loved by the parents are sufficient, then the sense of meaninglessness is held off. Another hint concerning the link between meaning and mature dependence may be found in Fairbairn's understanding of the mutuality that characterizes this later stage. One loves, trusts, depends on the other, and allows the other to love, trust, and depend on oneself (1994, 145).

The question of meaning is a paramount concern for Winnicott. The entree to the issue is his concept of the "central or true self" (1965a, 140–52). The central self refers to the inner potential of the infant to experience and live reality in his or her "own way" (1986, 242): it is the foundation for having a personal life at all. In Winnicott's words: "Only the True Self can be creative and only the True Self can feel real" (1965a, 148). The opposite to this is a "false self," a self of facade and compliance that is lost in the world. The false self sees only the futility of existence, and feels that "life is not worth living" (1971, 65). The singular place of the "true self" in Winnicott's work is confirmed by the critical literature on this important psychoanalyst. One finds, for example: "Winnicott was concerned with the quality of subjective experience: the sense of inner reality, the infusion of life with a feeling of personal meaning, the image of oneself as a distinct and creative center of one's own experience" (Mitchell and Black 1995, 124).

What is the role of the other in the development of an individual's sense of her or his personal meaning? Winnicott answers this in terms of two different stages. During the period of absolute dependence the mother is crucial. She provides the holding environment, protecting the infant from impingements from the outside that would overwhelm and fracture the inner self.

Winnicott directly connects the holding environment with a person's meaning. He writes:

> individuals live creatively and feel that life is worth living or else . . . they cannot live creatively and are doubtful about the value of living. This variable in human beings is directly related to the quality and quantity of environmental [maternal] provision at the beginning or in the early phases of each baby's living experience. (cited in Greenberg and Mitchell 1983, 196)

The term "holding," which for him is "a form of loving" (1986, 245), once again hides the active and positive nature of maternal care. This care includes the exquisite sensitivity to every feature of the infant's developing physical and psychological being, the twenty-four hour holding, handling, and object presenting tailored to the specific infant.

Winnicott's narration of the transitional stage provides another opportunity to uncover the role of others in the emergence of personal existence and meaning. At this time, the infant is turning its attention from the inner world to the outer world. "Subjective omnipotence," that is, the infant's sense that the world magically appears at its behest, must slowly give way to the child's more realistic, objective stance toward the outside. However, it is possible for the demands of the outside to crush the infant's burgeoning psyche. The task of protecting the infant widens beyond the mother during the transitional stage, although the importance of the "others" is no less decisive. They must collude with the infant's half fantasy/half realistic use of objects. They protect the child's play from questions about reality. How important is this parental role? The arts, religion, and creative work originate in and are extensions of the child's earlier play-world. Winnicott sees illusion and fantasy as the basis for one's sense of purpose and meaning. In all, for Winnicott, while meaning is not given by others, it never crystallizes unless nurtured by them.

The narratives of the Jewish philosophers and the psychoanalysts portray the constituents, "origins," and scope of that sense of the meaningfulness of one's life. While meaning can be described in terms of confidence and security, confidence in the self and security in facing the world, it is more closely allied to trust. The trust in oneself concerns one's capacity to love and to care (be responsible) for others. Without this trust, life is meaningless. However, despite the significance of trust, it is not within the individual's own control. It is given by the other. Through the other's love/trust in oneself, and the other's acceptance of one's love—again trusting oneself—meaning is generated. For some theorists meaning appears as a gift totally at the initiative of the other—Rosenzweig, Levinas; for some it is rather more like an exchange between partners—Buber, Erikson, Fairbairn; and for Winnicott, meaning lies as a seedling within the self and the gift from the other is one of nurture.

There is also a difference in the presentations in terms of the scope of meaning. For the Jewish thinkers, individual meaning is coterminous with the meaning of all of life. In this case, a transcendent reference or origin seems to be required. Erikson explicitly ties meaning to an identification with whole generations of persons, while the other psychoanalysts do not seem to require such a wide base. For them, meaning is engendered by mother, parents, and the wider social world and there is no need to widen the base for individual meaning beyond these social circles.

Other Gifts

One of the benefits of juxtaposing the Jewish philosophical and the psychoanalytic narratives is to gain a fresh, relational perspective on many of the most important features of human existence. In these narratives, there is a plenitude of gifts, beyond identity and meaning, that are attributed to the interhuman realm, that is, to what the self receives from the other. Among other qualities, there are references to language, love, and hope, as well as surprising allusions to self-consciousness and reason. To see these latter attributes, which are at the very core of the ubiquitous Cartesian notion of the self, as gifts from the other, reinforces what is at stake in these relational narratives. In presenting convincing narratives of the interhuman origin of even self-consciousness and reason, these philosophical and psychoanalytic theorists challenge, at the most fundamental level, alternative views of the self as autonomous and self-engendered.

For Buber, the growth of the infant occurs in the context of the deep relations with the mother, both in the womb and during the first months of life.

This brings him to regard all of the major attributes of the individual as having a basis in and naturally emerging out of relation. In Buber's language, the I-Thou relationship, at least in its nascent form, precedes the realm of the I-It and all the human attributes and skills that define the latter. These would include, for example, self-consciousness. Of self-consciousness, Buber writes: "Man becomes an I through a Thou. What confronts us comes and vanishes, relational events take shape and scatter, and through these changes crystalizes, more and more each time, the consciousness of the constant partner, the I-consciousness" (1970, 80). Buber is saying that the I begins as embedded within a relation to the other and it slowly becomes conscious of itself only in the wake of many events of encounter.

Other aspects of the I-It realm that unfold through these early relations include the sense of objects as distinct from the self, and also such attributes as reason. In terms of the former, Buber states: "But the genesis of the thing is a late product that develops out of the split of the primal encounters, out of the separation of the associated partners—as does the genesis of the I" (1970, 78). A reference to productive skills, reason, and analytical skills is seen in his statement that the "inventive drive," to "produce things synthetically or . . . analytically," "emerges later" than and is determined by the drive for relation (1970, 79). All of the rational skills—to compare, analyze, synthesize, and make judgments—thus follow, in Buber's eyes, from the "natural association" to the mother and other things.

In light of the chronological priority of the relational drive to the inventive drive, is it proper to speak of self-consciousness, reason, and other features as gifts from others or of the interhuman? The answer is ambiguous. We can conclude, at least, that for Buber one does not give oneself, as it were, either self-consciousness or reason. Further, these attributes do not ground or determine relationships with others. Buber's treatment of language is telling. Language appears to be a natural feature of the I-Thou world (1970, 56–57). It does not emerge from reason, from some kind of desire to communicate ideas or messages. As we will see, Rosenzweig and Levinas offer a much more explicit understanding of language as gift.

Love and speech or language are the major features of the human that Rosenzweig attributes to the appearance of the other.[9] Love is the capacity to move beyond obsession with the self and its fated death, which was Rosenzweig's understanding of the "natural state" of human existence. It is seen as transformative. In being loved by the other, the self emerges in its fullest sense. Rosenzweig refers to these two aspects of love in his statement "love is man's momentary self-transformation, his self-denial" (1972, 163). Actually, love is doubly transformative: in loving the other, both the other and the self change. The exchange of the lover and the beloved thus makes each fully real for the first time. In *The Star*, Rosenzweig formulates this insight as: "In this belief of the beloved in the lover, the lover first really becomes a human being. True, the soul awakes and begins to speak when it loves, but it attains being, a being visible to itself, only when it is loved" (1972, 182). In addition to becoming real, Rosenzweig believes that only through love does the self live in the present. Without the experience and effects of love, persons are doomed to live a life defined by a closed past and a menacing future.

Since becoming a full person is not something an individual can do on her or his own according to Rosenzweig, love, that catalyst, is a gift. The self becomes what it could not be through its own initiative, a lover, and the other becomes what it could not be on its own, a beloved. For Rosenzweig, the exchange of love, as well as the acceptance of love, between lover and beloved, is thus the story of gift and return-gift. In his words: "Only the love of a [initiating] lover is such a continually renewed self-sacrifice; it is only he who gives himself away in love. The beloved accepts the gift. That she accepts it is the return gift" (1972, 162).

Rosenzweig's reference above to the soul's speech as a response to its being loved exemplifies the way that he has the subject of speech or language naturally arising amidst the discussion of love. Love and language become synonymous for Rosenzweig. Both are divine gifts, expressions of God's turning to each human in revelation. *The Star*, whose "center-piece" is "the wholly real employment of language" (1972, 174), testifies to the divine aspect of both love and language:

> Love simply cannot be "purely human." It must speak, for there is simply no self-expression other than the speech of life. And by speaking, love already becomes superhuman, for the sensuality of the word is brimful with its divine supersense. Like speech itself, love is sensual—supersensual. (1972, 201)

All of the social interactions between humans are seen by Rosenzweig within the purview of language. Its grammar—of persons (I, Thou, he, she, we, they); tenses (past, present, and future); and moods (declarative, interrogative, imperative, and subjunctive)—plot out all the ways that humans bring forth, guide, and care for each other. Language is the medium of social contact: its capacities delimit the parameters of human life. However, if language is a divine gift, among other things, human life that lives off language reveals itself as incalculable and inexhaustible.

All the features of human life in their fullness are consequences of the transformative gifts of love and language. For example, Rosenzweig holds that the authentic use of reason as well as the pursuit of truth have their source in language/speech. Reason is not to be understood as the individual's soliloquy, but as "speech-thinking," that is, as a way of thinking with and for the other (1999, 86–87). It is in conversation that the new appears, and even when the other is silent she or he draws one out, has a unique influence on the speaker that cannot be calculated beforehand. For Rosenzweig the pursuit of the highest truths is ultimately "messianic," for it requires the fervent commitment of persons, of groups, of communities over years, decades, and millennia. Rosenzweig's "messianic theory of knowledge" provides an astonishingly relational criterion of truth, for it "evaluates truths according to the price [in 'sacrifice' and 'commitment'] for its verification and to the bond that they establish among human beings" (1999, 99).

The list of the gifts from the other is as far-reaching in Levinas as in Rosenzweig, since both of them believe that all the features of an authentic life ultimately derive from the other. Levinas narrates the transcendent meeting with the other not, in the first instance, in terms of divine love, but as the shattering burden of responsibility that the neighbor thrusts upon the self. Responsibility for the other, which is the very opposite of the natural state of egoism, arises when the other orders through his or her face. Most importantly, when a person responds to the face with a "*here I am* . . . for everything and for everyone" (1981, 114), not only is one made responsible, but one is *granted* the powers to fulfill that life of responsibility.

What are these powers bestowed by the other? The first is language. In fact, Levinas finds that the encounter with the other is the very meaning of language. He writes: "Meaning is the face of the Other, and all recourse to words takes place already within the primordial face-to-face of language" (1969, 206). Language and the face are synonymous for Levinas. Thus, it is equally correct to say that either—or both together—the face and language ground those attributes that issue out of the social realm. The link between language and love is also tightly woven in Levinas' accounts. Of this gift, that is, love, from the other he writes: "The metaphysical event of transcendence—the welcome of the Other, hospitality—Desire and Language—is not accomplished as love. But the transcendence of discourse is bound to love" (1969, 254). In *Totality and Infinity*, the welcoming of the other stands as the foundation for a long list of attributes, including rationality, freedom, intelligibility, signification, universality, justice, objectivity, fraternity, and the consciousness of time (1969, 204–24). For example, more directly than Rosenzweig, Levinas sees reason as a gift from the other. Reason arises out of and is nourished by language. In his words: "reason lives in language . . . the first rationality gleams forth in the opposition of the face to face" (1969, 208). He even includes self-consciousness as following other-consciousness. In this regard Levinas writes: "Conscience and [metaphysical] desire are not modalities of consciousness among others, but its condition" (1969, 101).

The narrative of the origin of many of our most essential human attributes is somewhat different in Levinas' second text, *Otherwise Than Being*. He holds that these qualities follow from the recognition of the "third person" and justice. Levinas' argument is that while responsibility to the neighbor is infinite, since one lives with more than a single other, there are third parties to which one is also responsible. The relationships to these parties, and their relationships to still others, must certainly affect what can concretely be done for the immediate other. The issue of third parties and of the wide circle of others is treated under the label of justice in Levinas. Levinas holds that reason, calculation, and even some dimensions of self-concern originate in the need to determine what is owed to, or what constitutes justice for, the more distant others. He writes, for example: "The fact that the other, my neighbor, is also a third party with respect to another, who is also a neighbor, is the birth of thought, consciousness, justice and philosophy" (1981, 128).

How does self-consciousness arise from the meeting with the other? There may be two answers to this in *Otherwise Than Being*. Subjectivity, being a subject and being aware of oneself as a subject, comes from the call of the other. Subjectivity is understood as a being-chosen, elected, or designated. One discovers oneself by being assigned responsibility for the other (1981, 112). As Levinas states it: "This book has exposed the signification of subjectivity in the extraordinary everydayness of my responsibility for other men" (1981, 141). In a second way, self-consciousness, in the senses of knowing the self, thinking of the self, or taking the self into consideration, arises out of the context of the third party and justice. One takes oneself into consideration when one calculates what must (justly) be given to the proximate other, what must be given to third parties, and, finally, what must be given to oneself as the others' other. In Levinas' words: "The act of consciousness is motivated by the presence of a third party alongside of the neighbor approached" (1981, 16); "Consciousness is born as the presence of a third party" (1981, 160); and finally, "The foundation of consciousness is justice" (1981, 160).[10]

For Levinas, every response, every assessment and judgment, follows under the theme of responsibility. Overall, since the relation of the face-to-face with the neighbor precedes all relations, including the self's relation to itself as well as to the more distant others, the list of gifts that is received or derived from the relationship to the other appears almost limitless. The following statement from *Totality and Infinity* might summarize this all-important point: "The establishing of this primacy of the ethical, that is, of the relationship of man to man—signification, teaching, and justice—*a primacy of an irreducible structure upon which all the other structures rest* . . . is one of the objectives of the present work" (my emphasis; 1969, 79).

There is still one other important feature of human existence that Buber, Rosenzweig, and Levinas see as a product of the interhuman, which is life within community.[11] For each of them, authentic communal life is not just the project of a person or a group, it must be nourished by genuine relationships. Buber states this as:

> True community does not come into being because people have feelings for each other (though that is required, too), but rather on two accounts: all of them have to stand in a living, reciprocal relationship to a single living center, and they have to stand in a living reciprocal relationship to one another. The second event has its source in the first but is not immediately given with it. (1970, 94)

Buber is saying that a relationship to the divine, that "single living center" of a group, is needed in order to provide a foundation for communal life. In addition, community requires reciprocal relationships between its members. The first relation implies, perhaps, that a group needs to have a concern for more than itself and its members for it to become a true community. The second relation implies that in addition to a shared meaning, there must be authentic relationships among the human participants.

For Rosenzweig, authentic communal life is only possible when members have a relation to the divine. There is an openness to others and a trust in life within religious communities that is not found in natural forms of community such as political states. The latter are characterized by fear of the other and doubt about the future. This doubt and fear are translated into the many forms of state violence that seem so often to be inevitable. However, true (religious) community—"the realm of brotherliness, the bond of supernatural community" (1972, 204)—is directed by that transcendent divine love of neighbor that works toward and anticipates an all-inclusive kingdom (1972, 205–53).

Justice is the platform for community in Levinas' account. Living in a large group or community requires that persons think about justice and thus put limits on the infinite responsibilities that originate in the more direct face-to-face relation. However, there is a danger that the calculations concerning justice necessitated by communal life may completely overshadow or overwhelm the individual's awareness of the infinite demands of the neighbor. This danger appears to result in Levinas' skepticism about the possibility of establishing authentic, responsible communities. To the extent that responsible communities are possible, the concern for the poor, the stranger, the widow, and orphan would be prominent. Said in another way, responsibility for the other is the only possible foundation for authentic communal life.

The post-Freudian psychoanalysts also find that, in addition to the attributes of identity and meaning, many of the most essential qualities of personal life are given or nourished by the other. The scope of the psychosocial narrative of Erikson touches upon a litany of features: trust, autonomy, initiative, industry, identity, intimacy, generativity, and integrity. The individual acquires some sense of these as she or he interacts within expanding social circles. One of the last of the psychosocial crises, which revolves around the issue of generativity, provides an impressive example of the relational challenges to and requirements for personal development. It also reveals a relational dynamic that is different from the usual ones featured in object relations accounts. This stage often commences with the raising of children. Erikson writes:

> The fashionable insistence on dramatizing the dependence of children on adults often blinds us to the dependence of the older generation on the younger one. Mature man needs to be needed, and maturity needs guidance as well as encouragement from what has been produced and must be taken care of. (1963, 266–67)

Erikson is focusing on a very important feature of the interhuman. The sense that one has been and can continue to be productive and creative very much comes from others. In the specific terms of a mother and father, it is obvious that a child can give one a sense of being productive. For any mature person, the others could be members of the younger generation or a variety of persons in need. Erikson regards stagnation as the negative counterpoint to generativity. The self requires others to accept and appreciate its contributions, or else a feeling of stagnation ensues. It is important to note that this description of the relationship between older and younger generations in terms of "dependence" is fully representative of the ways that psychoanalysts characterize human relations and interactions overall.

All three of the object relations theorists see the subject emerge within the dialectic of infant and mother. Thomas Ogden's statement about the Kleinian infant is fully appropriate to the other two psychoanalysts: "The infant as subject is present from the beginning, although that subjectivity exists largely within the context of the psychological-interpersonal (containing/contained) dimension of the relationship of infant and mother" (1994, 48). Both identity and self-consciousness would thus evolve from this matrix. For Klein, the psychological processes of identification with the mother and the good breast bring to the fore many qualities in the infant. The relation to the mother is the source/resource for love, "hope, trust, and belief in goodness" (1997, 180,), and for "the devotion to people, values, and causes" (1997, 187).

Even reason is included in the personal attributes that originate in this early relational dynamic, according to Klein. In her scheme, since the two positions—paranoid-schizoid and depressive—and their accompanying objects and passions mediate all interactions with the outside world, the use of reason is not regarded as independent of relationships. One critic has tied instrumental reason, concerned with guarding the self and the self's interests against all threats, to the first position. In this case, the other is seen in paranoid fashion and reason is utilized in the service of "prediction, manipulation, and control" (Alford 1989, 152). "Reparative reason," which is based upon a concern with the other for its own sake, is a product of the second position. It is "sensitive to the complexities and nuances of objects" (Alford 1989, 138), which it experiences "as they are mediated by a richer, more creative set of phantasies" (152). Klein's provocative notion of the passionate and relational basis for rationality is summarized by the critic Donald Meltzer, who writes: "love for truth becomes very strongly allied to the capacities to appreciate the beauty and goodness of objects" (cited in Phillips and Stonebridge, eds., 1988, 39).

Fairbairn powerfully demonstrates that the movement beyond infantile types of relations outstrips the innate powers of the self. Paradoxically, it is only through the aid of another, that is, by depending upon another, that one can overcome debilitating and limiting types of dependence. It is particularly in terms of the stage of mature dependence that Fairbairn indicates the results of satisfactory maternal and familial care. Thus, the capacities for seeing others as having inherent value, and for relating to other persons as entities in their own right, ultimately derive from the infant's support by the mother. The ability to act co-operatively with others, another characteristic of mature dependence, also develops out of this earlier positive basis. Finally, Fairbairn emphasizes the importance of the earliest interactions with the mother in the development of the ability to love and to maintain complex social relations. He writes:

> The child's oral relationship with his mother in the situation of sucking represents his first experience of a love relationship, and is, therefore, the foundation upon which all his future relationships with love objects are based. It also represents his first experience of a social relationship; and it therefore forms the basis of his subsequent attitude to society. (1994, 25–26)

As we have seen, Winnicott's narrative of the developments made possible by the mother as a holding environment and the parents in the transitional stage touch upon an extensive array of powers. Along with features already examined, Winnicott has written about "the capacity for concern" (1965a, 73–86) and "the capacity to be alone" (1965a, 29–36). With the former he has looked into the sense of responsibility, and in terms of the latter he has written about the virtue of trust. More expansively, Winnicott has suggested: "Maturity and the capacity to be alone implies that the individual has had the chance through good-enough mothering to build up a belief in a benign environment" (1965a, 32).[12] However, it is perhaps out of the dynamics of the transitional stage and transitional phenomena that some of the most important personal qualities are developed. In these cases, the parents must collude with the child's refusal to be strictly aligned with reality. The inner and outer world are brought together, but this is through the liberating activities of fantasy, imagination, and play. Thus, without the support of others, the creative life and the deeper possibilities of existence are forfeited. Winnicott acutely appreciated the importance of play, which is seen in his statements "There is a direct development from transitional phenomena to playing, and from playing to shared playing, and from this to cultural experiences" (1971, 51); and "It is in playing and only in playing that the individual child or adult is able to be creative and to use the whole personality, and it is only in being creative that the individual discovers the self" (1971, 54).

Conclusion: Evaluating a Metaphor

A final assessment of the two discourses will take up once again the nomenclature of gifts. How helpful is the metaphor of the gift in understanding the narratives about the interhuman offered by modern Jewish philosophers and post-Freudian psychoanalysts? One instance of the term "gift" has been noted, in Rosenzweig's poetic description of the love exchange between God and the soul: "Only the love of a [initiating] lover is such a continually renewed self-sacrifice; it is only he who gives himself away in love. The beloved accepts the gift. That she accepts it is the return gift" (1972, 162). Rosenzweig's statement alludes to a number of issues that have been explored by philosophers, psychologists, sociologists, and anthropologists in the literature concerning "the gift." In that literature, issues about reciprocity, of the relation between gift and return gift, and the way that a web of relationships is established by giving and receiving are most prominent. Also important is the question whether a gift is a true self-sacrifice, that is, a matter of altruism, or an expression of self-interest.

There are many insights about gift-giving that are in harmony with or substantiated by the narratives that we have examined.[13] Marcel Mauss argued in his famous essay "The Gift" that gift exchange was the very basis for society. Claude Levi-Strauss also saw the origin of society in the ties created through gift giving, although he, as well as Freud, believed that women were the objects exchanged.[14] While this wider social vision is not primary in the philosophical and psychoanalytic narratives, within their own contexts they agree that gifts stand at the basis for the development of a person. Further, it is interesting to note that Georg Simmel identified gratitude as an important residue of gift-giving. He believed that this feeling, along with faithfulness, was one of the foundations of the social order, and that it had a central role in initiating and preserving social relationships. Simmel's ideas about society are closely paralleled by Klein's views about the importance of gratitude in the infant's development. For Klein, the emergence of gratitude for the gifts that the infant has received from the mother is the basis for all future positive relationships. Without this appreciation and gratitude, the infant is cut off from others, lost in its paranoia and its rage.

Bronislaw Malinowski's insight that the closer the human relationship, the less reciprocity is expected, certainly is relevant to the psychoanalytic narratives that feature the mother and infant. Equally applicable to the psychoanalytic presentations are other conclusions in the critical literature about gifts that have come out of the examination of gender roles. It has been noted that gift-giving is an important activity between intimates that usually takes place in the private sphere. In these cases, women are clearly the principal participants.

The question of whether gifts reveal self-interest or altruism has a long history. There is an ancient Roman saying "*do ut des*," that "I give in order that you will give in return" (cited in Komter 1996, 3). Neither the philosophical nor the psychoanalytic accounts explain human relationships through this direct reciprocity or calculation of giving and receiving. One critic's discussion of three types of altruism may be helpful in understanding why these accounts eschew the motive of self-interest. Christopher Jenks has argued that altruism can be classified in terms of "empathy (unselfishness derived from identification with concrete others), . . . community (springing from identification with a collectivity . . .), and . . . morality (internalized moral ideals)" (Komter 1996, 8). The mother's total dedication to the infant, that maternal preoccupation which is the milieu out of which she provides for the infant, seems to correspond to the first variety of altruism. In this case, the mother's providing for the infant is deeply tied to her identification with it. The second type of altruism is relevant to the philosophers. Their focus on what must be given to the neighbor is at least partially based upon the understanding that all humans are linked together as a family. Finally, the third variety of altruism is especially appropriate to Levinas, where the vision of what is owed to the other originates in the optics of ethics.

What is distinctive to the narratives of the Jewish philosophers and the post-Freudian psychoanalysts is that the self itself is portrayed as a gift. This insight is a progression beyond the statements "There is no I as such" (Buber 1970, 54) and "There is no such thing as an infant" (Winnicott 1986, 235), for it alludes to more than humans' social dimension. If the self is a gift, then without gift-giving there is no I or infant at all. For both sets of theorists identity and meaning are the fruits of relationships. In their works what one receives escalates to include love, trust, direction, language, reason, and creativity. This array of gifts that the self requires and receives confirms Rosenzweig's conclusion that we are "dependent on the other for what is ours" (1999, 87). As noted previously, this portrait of the relational self that depends upon the other for self-consciousness, reason, and orientation forcefully challenges the hegemony of the Cartesian self with its autonomy built upon self-engendered consciousness, reason, and direction.

Still, there are important differences between the two sets of narratives, in terms of the nature of the gifts, the period of offering, the participants involved, and the types of relationships that the gifts establish. On the whole, the modern Jewish philosophers explore gifts that fulfill a life, and the post-Freudian psychoanalysts focus on gifts that provide an initial foundation for a life. The philosophers look at meaning, orientation, purpose, and mission, while the key terms that the psychoanalysts examine include identity and integration. The philosophers see the gift as occurring, or at least being fully recognized, after adolescence. The gift, of meaning, comes unexpected upon a life already begun. It is a radical surprise, a shattering occurrence. The giving points to the transcendent, that is, directly or indirectly to the divine. For the psychoanalysts, especially the object relations theorists, the gift is primarily about the support that enables the infant/person to go on. Their emphasis is on the first weeks and months of mother-infant unit, with its antecedents in the intra-uterine and its consequences for the future.

In the discourses of Buber, Rosenzweig, and Levinas, the gift is often depicted as rising out of and/or creating responsibility. Whether it is the love of neighbor, the requirement to turn to others in the address of I and Thou, or in the face-to-face relation, the gifts involve responsibility. Responsibility ties one to the other, but, especially in Levinas, it is the individual's responsibility for the other, rather than the two-sidedness of responsibilities that is primary. The three thinkers also explore the gift in terms of both love and language. Why love? Love in its freedom, spontaneity, power, intensity, and association with responsibility describes the essential dimensions of the relationships that are created. Language is a synonym for love, because it mirrors and facilitates the variety of relationships that a full life requires.

In the psychoanalytic discourse, within the framework of the various developmental narratives, the category of dependence is often salient. The gifts that the mother/caretakers give and the infant/child receives occur within the context of partners who are not equal in power or experience. The relation of dependence does not mitigate the gift. Further, it also alludes to the fact that nothing is expected in return. In all of the cases, the psychoanalysts see a mutual dependence, the ability to give and receive, as both a gift from the other and the highest statement of maturity.

The psychoanalysts provide one very important reminder in understanding the ways that relationships constitute the self. Just as some gifts are ambiguous or even harmful to the recipient, relationships to others are not always positive in the formation of an individual. The deleterious effects of some early relationships are well emphasized by Winnicott's exploration of "not good enough" maternal care, and Fairbairn's tracing all psychopathology to failure in parental satisfaction. Especially for these psychoanalysts, it is in analysis that the effects of these early mis-relationships, and others, are faced and, hopefully, partially redressed.[15]

Finally, in at least one significant way, the metaphor of gift is inadequate to describe the dynamics of the interhuman.[16] The particular dimensions of relationships that are obscured by the metaphor are advanced through the philosopher's language of "soul" and "spirit," and the psychoanalyst's discussion of "inner objects." Levinas poignantly has said: "The soul is the other in me" (1981, 191). For him, the responsibility or obligation to the other is so intense and persistent that it is nothing less than the presence of the other in the very heart or soul of the self. Although not in as strong a sense as Levinas, Rosenzweig and Buber also argue that the soul is more than a gift or possession from the other. Rosenzweig holds that the self cannot give itself soul. Soul is the transformed self that arises when the other loves. Perhaps this love could be seen as somewhat equivalent to the other in me? Buber's use of the word "spirit" in *I and Thou* is close to the other philosophers' term soul. He writes: "Spirit in its human manifestation is man's response to his Thou," and: "Spirit is not in the I but between I and Thou" (1972, 89). Thus, for Buber, while in a lesser sense one has spirit, in a truer sense one "lives in the spirit," that is, in the flow of the relationships of I and Thou. All three philosophers agree that what stands as the very essence of a person is also that which is a part of, or in relation to, the other.

The psychoanalysts' vocabulary of "inner objects" directly and eloquently expresses the notion that the influence of the other is so pervasive, one's own identification with significant others so long-lasting, that the other lives within the deepest recesses of the self. In this regard, they strongly parallel Levinas' insight. The language of inner objects is found in psychoanalytic literature as early as Freud, in his structure of the "super-ego," but it is especially prominent in the three object relations theorists. For Klein, Fairbairn, and Winnicott, relationships to others constitute as well as haunt the self, that is, others live in the self in both positive and negative ways. For them, inner objects are implicated in both the health and pathology of the person. Through all of these expressions, terms, and notions, the philosophers and psychoanalysts register the insight that the relationship to the other is more than even the matter of the essential gifts that are received from the other. Perhaps the philosophical and psychoanalytic language of "the other in me" can also be extended to the wider literature of "the gift" to describe some aspects of what the gift creates in the receiver?

Notes

1. In *Relationality*, Mitchell assesses Fairbairn's position in terms of that of Freud and of those relational psychoanalysts of the 1990s and later. He sees Fairbairn as "struggling toward a different way of understanding the nature of human beings, as fundamentally social, not as *drawn* into interaction, but as *embedded* in an interactive matrix with others as his or her natural state" (2000, 105).

2. Also see Daniel Stern's treatment of the newborn's patterns of perception and response (38–42).

3. In a fascinating interview between Luce Irigaray and the biologist Helene Rouch, a critique is offered of the intra-uterine phase as presented in psychoanalytic narratives. In Freud, the post-Freudians Fairbairn and Winnicott, as well as many others, the fetus is seen in fusion with the mother before birth. Consequently, birth and later development are equated with moving toward separation and various ranges of dependence/independence. Rouch's study of the fetus and the placenta indicates that the mother recognizes the fetus as other, and thus, their connection is one of relationship and not of fusion. This provides material for a new psychoanalytic narrative of relationship, of self and other, that begins even in the earliest stage (Irigaray 1993, 37–44).

4. In *Otherwise Than Being*, Levinas often offers "maternity" as an example of ethics (1981, 75). The complex issues that surround his use of this term will be examined in chapter five.

5. Jane Flax addresses this issue in *Disputed Subjects* (102–3).

6. Thus, Buber, as well as Rosenzweig and Levinas, contest such treatments of religion as those of Marx and Freud, that see religion as something—a drug or crutch—that makes life easier.

7. Rosenzweig speaks of the treatment of revelation as the heart of his book in "The New Thinking" (1999, 86).

8. This description, first looking at awe, including dependence, is perhaps a reference to and critique of Rudolf Otto's the *Idea of the Holy*.

9. As we have seen, the prototype of the love exchange takes place between God and the soul. The implications for God being the initiatory actor in this event will be explored in the next chapter. There it will be argued that this divine-human love narrative does not lead to a devaluation of the human.

10. Levinas is acutely aware that this priority of ethics over, or as the basis for, knowledge and consciousness constitutes a fundamental revision of philosophy's traditional chronology and predilection. Instead of philosophy defined in terms of knowledge and self-consciousness, Levinas speaks of it as "the wisdom of love [ethics] at the service of love [ethics]" (1981, 162).

11. Their views about community will be briefly presented here, and explored in more depth in the final chapter.

12. In a different sense, Erikson ties the feeling of being alone to an earlier state of being with another: "But aloneness, too, is often dominated by a deep nostalgia for fusing with another, and this in an exclusive and lasting fashion, be that 'Other' mentor or a god, the Universe—or the innermost Self" (1969, 41).

13. There is a group of classic and contemporary essays in *The Gift*, edited by Komter. The introduction is especially helpful and the brief presentation of theories about the gift in the conclusion of this chapter relies on that discussion.

14. Irigaray's use and critique of this insight well be explored in the fifth chapter.

15. Hans Loewald is especially eloquent in writing about the need to confront, accept, and take responsibility for the ways that others may have injured oneself. He writes:

> To begin with we were more or less fortunate victims, and it may be claimed that in some sense this remains true as long as we live, victims of our instincts and those of others, not to mention other forces of nature and social life. . . . Responsibility to oneself . . . involves appropriating or owning up to one's needs and impulses as one's own, impulses and desires we appear to have been born with or that seem to have taken shape in interaction with our parents during infancy. (2000, 392)

16. There is another shared insight of the philosophers and the psychoanalysts that does not easily translate into the language of gifts. Many of them suggest that guilt or shame is an inherent part of the interaction with the m/other. For example, Rosenzweig has the beloved admit its shame at not loving before the divine had turned to him or her (1971, 180); Levinas insists that the individual recognize that she or he is not innocent in the face of the other (1969, 84); Erikson sees some shame as unavoidable in the second stage (1964, 119), as well as in "the inexorable succession of generations (1969, 129); Klein has guilt as part of her second stage (1997, 74), as does Winnicott (1965a, 68–69). Perhaps seeing guilt and shame as inevitable (and not totally negative) outcomes of the life with others also constitutes a critique of—actually, an affront to—the notion of the autonomous self. Many of the discourses that give prominence to this notion of the sovereign and free self contend that the awareness of guilt and shame is foreign to the "natural" life of a person. Guilt and shame are regarded as false teachings of religion or some other outside authority.

4

Transference and Transcendence

THE STRIKING PORTRAIT OF THE interhuman brought together through the narratives of the Jewish philosophers and the post-Freudian psychoanalysts in the previous chapter came at a cost. Many important differences between the two discourses had to be repressed in order to reach that common account. This chapter will constitute a return of the repressed, as it were, by engaging the distinctive and the different. It will begin by exploring the particular ways that each of the two discourses presents the relationships between the self and others. This examination will focus on the specific narrative structures and the basic vocabularies. The next section surveys three themes that each of the discourses treats in characteristic ways: illness/alienation, transformation, and health/fullness. The conclusion of the chapter will assess the accounts of the psychoanalysts and the philosophers in terms of two questions: What features of the lives between persons have been illuminated in particularly insightful ways by the specific discourses? What lacunae haunt each of them?

The earlier chapter used the nomenclature of gifts, that is, the attributes and qualities of personal life that are given by others, to underscore the similarities in the presentations. This treatment will highlight the processes that distinguish the descriptions within the two fields. The chapter also marks a change from the forgoing analyses by reversing the order of approach: first the psychoanalysts and then the philosophers. The reversal is reflected in the title: transference and transcendence. The altered order of treatment follows from the recognition that many of the foci of the chapter are more clearly delineated in the field of psychoanalysis than in the writings of the Jewish philosophers. The genre of the psychoanalytic narrative of development has been a constant staple in the works of psychoanalysts, and is identified and studied throughout the secondary literature. The subjects of psychopathology and analysis are prominent in the presentations of all the major theorists. By beginning with the more defined topics in the psychoanalytic presentations and literature, the corresponding themes will be more easily identified in the work of the Jewish philosophers.

Distinctive Discourses

How are discourses and narratives distinguished in this chapter? A discourse is the total manner and content of a presentation or presentations in a particular field, including the literary genre, metaphors, categories, and topics as well as the ideas, presuppositions, and conclusions. Narratives are the accounts that organize the material that a theorist or group of theorists wishes to present. The first two chapters of this book introduced Jewish narratives of the interhuman and psychoanalytic narratives of development. However, the two are not symmetrical. The genre or conceptional scheme of a narrative of development is an indisputable feature of psychoanalysis since Freud's depiction of the psychosexual stages. However, Rosenzweig, Buber, and Levinas did not themselves utilize the narrative structure studied in the first chapter. It was introduced to present and organize some of their most important views. The three-stage literary structure of alienation, the God-relationship, and the transformed interhuman illuminates the material, and it is an often used formula in religious writings, but it is not overt, that is, intentionally and explicitly utilized, in the writings of these three Jewish philosophers.

While the discourse of psychoanalysis might be regarded as an integral whole, it incorporates terms and models from a large variety of other discourses. Freud's writings reflect his medical training in neurology, an indebtedness to Newton and Darwin, and allusions to philosophy, history, zoology, literature, and religion. All of these dimensions or languages become the heritage of psychoanalysis and affect the understandings of the nature of persons. Persons are seen as embodied organisms, concurrently living in the animal, social, and cultural planes. There are additional empirical fields that have an impact on psychoanalytic theory, including studies in developmental psychology (especially the study of infants in the case of object relations theorists) and the whole phenomenon of analysis or therapy. Of course, the conclusions from these fields are not to be taken as "pure" data, but are themselves dependent on and correlated with selected psychoanalytic theories and models.

The most prominent feature of psychoanalytic discourse that the earlier chapters featured is the developmental narrative. In a statement quoted previously, Jane Flax linked this structure to Freud:

> Psychoanalysts from Freud on have seemed to feel the need to develop teleological narratives of subjectivity. These narratives begin with the premise that there is a unitary substance (or potential) present from the beginning. Given "good enough" environmental conditions, this substance will unfold in definite, innate stages toward its "natural" end or purpose (adult maturity/health). (1993, 99)

Flax's analysis of the developmental narrative is analogous to Susan Kirschner's notion of the "developmental spiral" (1996, 63–94), which she found especially characteristic of the discourses of object relations and self psychoanalysis. Both Flax and Kirschner indicate that a particular narrative framework is used by psychoanalysts in both their theoretical and clinical work. The framework puts material into complex narratives of psychoanalytic development, featuring the unconscious and conscious mind, as well as drives, passions, fantasies, repressions, defenses, and interpersonal experiences. There is a set of stages aligned chronologically and teleologically from a beginning to a conclusion. Each stage is defined in terms of specific challenges or crises. The resolutions in each stage affect how later crises are confronted and settled. Thus, the earlier infantile stages are the foundation for the later mature ones. As Flax noted, the narratives presuppose that persons are naturally driven through the stages toward some goal, whether sexual maturity and the continuation of the species for Freud, ego integrity for Erikson, or mature relationships with others for the object relations theorists. The idea that satisfactory care by the mother provides the requisite conditions or environment that facilitates the natural progression through the cycle of stages is especially central to the object relations theorists, as we have seen.

Stephen Mitchell distinguished two different types of psychoanalytic paradigms: the drive model and the relational model.[1] Mitchell's models typify two types of developmental narratives. In this light, Freud's drive model portrays the human organism as basically autonomous, in the sense that psychological development is accounted for in terms of basic sexual and aggressive drives (libido, death) and their expression or blockage. The individual is an enclosed system. The stages of development are arranged around the changing seats of the individual's drives: oral, anal, phallic, leading through the Oedipal crisis, to the genital, and ending with propagation. Inner conflict is seen as inherent in the organism. Conflict results from the tension between the drives and what is deemed acceptable by the individual and society, or between the different structures (id, ego, super-ego) that refer to the irreconcilable poles of inner satisfaction and outer reality.

The relational model defines the stages in terms of distinctive forms of relatedness. There are Klein's paranoid-schizoid and depressive positions, Fairbairn's stages of infantile dependence, transitional (quasi-independence), and mature dependence, and Winnicott's absolute dependence, relative dependence, and toward independence. Individuals are naturally structured or motivated toward deeper, that is, more holistic and equal, types of relationships. They begin in an intense relationship of dependence and merger, and work toward both separation and interdependence. Conflict is not seen in terms of the battle between satisfying the drives and reality, but as an inevitable feature of all relationships themselves. The individual is continually negotiating the relational polarities of dependence/autonomy and attraction/repulsion. In less abstract language, each person attempts to find that elusive balance between the need to be close to another and the fear of losing one's separateness or integrity. There is an alternating environment, which Erikson depicted as an ever-widening circle of others, from mother, parents, family, school peers, intimate other, through the intergenerational.

An outstanding feature of psychoanalytic discourse is the language of the unconscious. The unconscious is not a place or an organ, but a language to account for the desires, feelings, and memories, of which the individual appears not to be aware, behind behavior. Freud saw the unconscious expressed through normal and everyday occurrences such as dreams and slips of the tongue, as well as pathological behaviors such as "hysteric" and neurotic symptoms. The latter were seen as the return of the repressed, that is, as seemingly alien incursions of the hidden desires and feelings into behavior.

Post-Freudian theorists often utilize the language of fantasy and inner objects in their narratives. Fantasies are objectively false, but psychologically real, vivid, and powerful unconscious scenes. For Klein phantasy and inner objects are the innate expression of drives and the bedrock for all feelings, behavior, and relations. For Fairbairn, at the other end, they are the inevitable residue of unsuccessful early relationships. Some type of language of "the unconscious" seems endemic to psychoanalytic discourse, although there are contemporary critics, such as Stephen Mitchell and Roy Schafer, who are suspicious of the way that this language is sometimes reified, and want to speak of unacknowledged motives and feelings rather than the unconsciously repressed.[2]

Beyond the scope of the developmental narrative, psychoanalytic discourse also features the topics of the genesis and nature of psychological illnesses or psychopathology, and treatment or analysis. Psychoanalytic theorists endeavor to explain the origin, dynamics, and symptoms of illness as well as the treatments that they hope will bring some type of working health. For Freud, analysis was about bringing to light (of consciousness) the depths of (unconscious) conflict between desire and socially acceptable feelings and behavior. He viewed the major activity of analysis as the interpretation of unconscious material for the sake of making this accessible, and somewhat acceptable, to consciousness. For relational theorists, the goal is not to transform material from the unconscious to consciousness, but to repair past relationships in order to allow new, healthy ones to emerge. The topics of psychopathology and analysis will be treated in more detail later in this chapter. Jane Flax's statement that psychoanalytic theory portrays the self as "simultaneously embodied, social, 'fictional,' and real" (1990, 16), is a good concluding statement for this brief exposition into the parameters of psychoanalytic discourse and the particular characteristics of its developmental narrative.

There are vast differences in the major works of the three Jewish philosophers, Rosenzweig's *The Star of Redemption*, Buber's *I and Thou*, and Levinas' *Totality and Infinity* and *Otherwise Than Being or Beyond Essence*. Still each is an experiment with creating a discourse that combines the languages of Judaism, philosophy, and ethics. In none of the books are the three fields brought together in a seamless manner. Rosenzweig's *The Star of Redemption* provides a good introduction to this topic.

Rosenzweig wrote in "The New Thinking," an essay that once stood as the introduction to *The Star*, that the book was not a "Jewish book" (1999, 69). He meant by this that the book might well disappoint those who thought it would treat popular Jewish topics. However, he saw it as a Jewish book in a much deeper sense. It "narrates" a Jewish perspective on the world, the human, and the divine, through the categories of creation, revelation, and redemption. In addition to these categories, it continually utilizes and dialogues with Jewish sources, and alludes to Jewish strands or traditions—such as Kabbalah, that is, Jewish mysticism—in its presentation. *The Star* does not present an ethics in the standard philosophical sense. In fact, Rosenzweig labels one of his treatments "metaethical" (1972, 62–82), by which he means that he will initially look at the nature of the human outside of its definition as subject to ethical law. However, the book addresses ethics in two ways. It regards encounters between persons—including the divine—as the key to understanding the nature of God, humans, and the world, and central to the text is the notion that obligations arise out of these encounters. Rosenzweig considered *The Star* to be a philosophical text, because it places itself in the context of the history of philosophy—from Iona (the Greeks) to Jena (Hegel) and beyond, as well as including such standard philosophical fields as ontology, epistemology, ethics, aesthetics, and religion.

Buber believed that the original portrayal and primary source for his I-Thou philosophy was the Jewish Bible, and that the Jewish mystical movement, Hasidism, was one of its latest communal expressions.[3] It was from these perspectives that Buber saw his book *I and Thou* as an important Jewish text. The claim that *I and Thou* presents an ethical discourse repeats the argument just provided in the case of *The Star*. Buber's text certainly features the importance of the interhuman for understanding what it means to be a person, and it highlights the prominence of responsibility in exploring what human existence encompasses. Finally, it is philosophical, once again, because it confronts the range of philosophical fields, such as ontology, epistemology, ethics, aesthetics, and religion.

Although Levinas sought to distinguish his philosophical writings, such as *Totality and Infinity* and *Otherwise Than Being*, from his Jewish oeuvre, these two texts cannot be so easily separated from his understanding of and commitment to Judaism.[4] For Levinas, the approach of foregrounding the disproportionate responsibility of the self for the other repeats what he saw as the essential message of Judaism. Responsibility for the stranger, orphan, widow, and poor is the fundamental characteristic of Hebraic thinking, according to Levinas, and even in these philosophical books there are brief allusions to Jewish sources. Since Levinas defined the ethical as the realm of the interhuman, it is not hyperbole to suggest that there is not a single line in these books that stands outside of ethics. Finally, Levinas makes the claim that his two main works are philosophical in many ways. He "places" them in one of the streams of modern philosophy, phenomenology, following from Husserl and Heidegger. In addition, the books argue for and demonstrate that a rigorous and challenging philosophy can commence with ethics, which is also the contention of one of his major essays, "Ethics as First Philosophy" (1989, 75–87).

There is a consistency behind the three different Jewish productions, a consistency described here in terms of a Jewish-ethical-philosophical discourse. The writers create a language that emerges from, or is deeply inspired by, Jewish sources. This language empowers an approach or perspective upon the fullest range of philosophical issues that gives prominence to the responsibility that surfaces in the interhuman. Two caveats are required at this point in order to provide some balance. The first is that each of the texts reflect an inner tension that results from the clash of fields that they attempt to weave together. Rosenzweig's text is separated into three "parts" that are not easily united. The first part highlights philosophy, and its featured essences of God, man, and world, but it is only a propaedeutic. It is left behind by the next two parts, which explore the dynamics of the divine-human meeting and the life within the religious communities of Judaism and Christianity. The portrait of the encounter of God and the individual is narrated in a suggestive, poetic style, taking its point of departure from the biblical "Song of Songs." The third section offers a sociological analysis of life within the two religious communities.

Buber's uneasy alliance of philosophy with the other two strands comes through in his unique choice of style. His allusive poetics hides a systematic treatment, but it does not use argumentation or demonstration in any conventional sense. Buber's text presents a great vision spun out. He lightly touches upon philosophical issues and alludes to religious questions. The language often turns poetic or even into a vision or "waking dream."

Levinas frequently discusses the impossibility of using the words—of the logos and philosophy—that are important features of the Greek heritage of the West, to speak the lessons imparted by Hebraic culture. Can infinite responsibility be measured? Can inordinate obligations be systematized? How does one argue for substitution, welcome persecution? In Levinas' texts the tension with philosophy and with reason/the reasonable that underlies Rosenzweig and Buber's works is fully manifest. Together, the thinkers produce a discourse—Jewish, ethical, and philosophical—that is inevitably unstable.

A major element within their discourse is equally responsible for the instability, this element being the divine. The three Jewish philosophers insist that the story of the interhuman—at least the fullness of the interhuman—cannot be told without some reference to the divine. Yet, equally, they acknowledge the difficulties in speaking/writing of this term. With Rosenzweig the language shifts or becomes metaphoric in a special sense. In *The Star* he turns to biblical descriptions of the meetings with the divine. He insists on first-person statements to convey the immediacy of such encounters. For example, encounters with God are narrated in terms of Abraham's answer to God's "Where are thou?," God's command to "Love the Lord with all one's heart . . . !," and the soul's response that "I have sinned." At one of the most crucial junctures in his text, he turns to a line-by-line analysis of the divine-human biblical love poem, the "Song of Songs." Additionally, an essay that extols the unrivaled virtues of biblical anthropomorphisms explains that speaking about God must be done not in the third person, but, as in the Bible, through accounts of how the divine is experienced (1998, 135–45).

Buber's *I and Thou* approaches the issue of speaking of the divine in a different way. He contends that the word "God" has no special importance for him, because there are many names for the transcendent Thou that addresses persons. God is the eternal Thou, that is, the potentially ever-present One, who is encountered as a person. Buber insists that the language of description, of the space and time grids of everyday life, cannot grasp the realm of the I and Thou, which is the only appropriate context for speaking of God. Finally, he acknowledges that even the term "person" when used to speak of God is deeply metaphoric; its meaning only comes through performatively when the source of the voice that directs one's life is experienced as a person (1970, 180–82).

Levinas is even more circumspect about the use of the term "God," as well as insistent that it is appropriate in a philosophical venue.[5] His way of saying this is that God is not encountered, that is, not said, directly. Only persons are met, said, spoken of directly, and the term God is legitimately used only in the context of some special dimensions of those meetings. When a person is speaking about the realm of ethics, of being persecuted by the overwhelming sense of responsibility one has for the other, then the term "God" is appropriate. The more didactic way of saying this is that a trace of God is present in the (ethical) face-to-face relationship. Another way Levinas formulates this is, again, performative: the presence of God is witnessed through the ethical testimony/activity of the self giving itself over to the neighbor. Using the term in other ways is illegitimate, such as in saying that God is with us or even that God exists.

It is important to add that the discourse that Rosenzweig, Buber, and Levinas utilize to portray the divine in relationship to the human is not one that they identify as theological. Each of the philosophers finds that theological discourse—as it is usually understood and practiced—is too literal, systematic, secure, stable and self-contained to convey the transcendent break into the everyday that they regard as so important. Again, their language is metaphoric and performative. It is a language illustrating the ways that the term "God" must be transcribed into the discourse of and about the interhuman.

There are other important characteristics of the Jewish philosophers' language. One of these is the linkage of the terms "person," "soul," and "neighbor." Although English is not the original written language of any of these authors' texts, each of the thinkers does use a term—which is frequently translated as "person," to describe someone who is fully engaged with others. The authors use other terms for individuals, often translated as "self," who are isolated or alienated from others. "Soul" seems to be used in conjunction with the divine, as in the dialogue between the soul and God. The soul, or the human as soul, refers to what has been transformed by God. Rosenzweig, for example, speaks of God awakening the soul. However, the soul is not regarded as a substance, and there is no interest in arguing about its eternity—except that this might designate the person's ability to be in relation to the eternal Thou. "Neighbor" is another crucial term in their discourse. The neighbor is not just another individual. It is someone with whom one is in proximity, and that relationship is defined by obligations. The neighbor is the next one (*der Nebenmensch*) to whom one is responsible. The responsibility is not due to birth, or some obligation by blood, but just to the fact of a human standing nearby. Finally, other features of their unique discourse, including the prominence of notions of obligation and responsibility and the concern with community, have already been described.

In summary, the preceding comparison has highlighted the differences in the literary structures and conceptual parameters of the discourses of the psychoanalysts and the Jewish philosophers. The distinct literary feature of the narrative of development is prominent in psychoanalytic discourse, while the Jewish philosophers endeavored to create a genre combining Judaism, philosophy, and ethics. In turning to the specific topics of alienation, transformation, and fulfillment, the strengths and inevitable fault lines of each discourse will be brought to light.

Alienation

Despite the differences in the discussions of the psychoanalysts and the Jewish philosophers, in both cases the causes as well as the ramifications of an individual's sickness are understood in terms of relations with others. Or put in another way, if there is no self as such—but only the self in relation—then sickness will be relationally expressed both in terms of origin and consequences. Alienation or illness becomes essentially a matter of misrelations. Thus, the differences in vocabulary, perspective, scope, and insight between the two discourses do not subvert the overall similarity of their relational approach. We have, as it were, difference within similarity.

The shift in psychoanalysis from Freud to the post-Freudian stream has dramatically influenced the way that illness or psychopathology is now understood. The critic Anthony Elliott confirms this observation in the following remark:

> In the post-Freudian period, the clinical picture of typical analysands has been, not one of individuals suffering from disturbances in sexual repression and self-control, but rather that of individuals experiencing a deep emotional poverty in relationships with others, coupled with a more general estrangement from the self. (1994, 18–19)

Two types of determinants are prominent in the psychoanalytic accounts of illness, "arrests" in the developmental sequence (Mitchell 1988, 10), and conflicts with or between objects. Just as Freud saw sexual perversion as occurring when the libido was stuck in one of the pre-genital stages of the psychosexual sequence, post-Freudian theorists often refer to arrest within the movement from infantile to mature types of relation. This statement already indicates the second determinant, which constitutes the main departure from Freud. While the notion of the progression of stages is kept, the arena in which both stagnation and progress occur has been transformed. Psychic tension and conflict is no longer detailed in terms of drives, defenses against drives, and conflicts with the outside world. Objects and persons have replaced drives, and conflict is understood within a particular relationship or between relationships. In each relationship there is that tension between dependence and independence, and there are also often conflicts arising out of the attachments to different objects or persons.

For Erikson, who is never included in the object relations school of psychoanalysis, developmental arrest and object conflict do not fully correspond to his understanding of pathology. He seems to present two ways of narrating illness. On the one hand, Erikson remains committed to Freud's libidinal theory and its stages, and addresses neuroses and "other emotional afflictions" in terms of "fixations or repressions to . . . infantile zones and stages" (1963, 61). On the other hand, when illness is discussed in less extreme cases and in the context of the eight psychosocial stages, it is not seen as a matter of arrest or closure of development. Rather, illness is explained as the inadequate negotiation of a particular crisis or the failure to achieve the task of a specific stage, whether that be such a task as trust, autonomy, or initiative. Failure would be seen as the individual tending more toward mistrust, shame, and doubt, or guilt, than toward the positive pole of the crisis. Both success and failure are relative, of course. Still, the negative outcome in the face of a particular crisis, especially the earliest ones, deeply affects all later struggles.

Relations to persons play an important role in the Erikson narrative, which is the reason for his inclusion in this study. However, relationships are not taken as causative factors in the pathology tied to each of the stages, nor are the repercussions of failure necessarily manifested directly in terms of interactions with others. For example, with such stages as initiative versus guilt and industry versus inferiority, others are very important in terms of overall feedback, encouragement, and recognition, but guilt and inferiority refer to how the individual feels about himself or herself and not directly to the nature of a relationship to another.

In addition to the great influence that she had on those who followed, Klein presents an interesting variant in terms of the issue of illness. There are specific pathologies tied to each of her two stages, the paranoid-schizoid and the depressive, and the failure to move from the first to the second also has major pathological implications. Her account is complex, in that it keeps the language of drives—for example, death and life—while securely connecting these to inner objects—the bad and good breasts. Illness results from the inability to rein in the anger, hatred, violence, and feelings of persecution of the first stage, and the guilt of the second. When emotionally laden phantasies become overwhelming, the ego is either not allowed to become whole or is torn apart. While difficulties or the total inability in relating to others may be a symptom or consequence of psychological illness, problems in relating to actual persons are not causative factors. Tension and conflicts of the most horrendous types are innate, the expressions of the death drive and its contest with the instinct for life, and it is these that are causative.

The omnipresence of such phrases as satisfactory mothering and good enough maternal care in the narratives of Fairbairn and Winnicott provide incontrovertible evidence that actual relationships to others have taken over the status of primary causes in terms of both development and pathology. With Fairbairn, unsatisfactory mothering inhibits the movement from infantile to mature types of relation. It splits the ego, brings about immature forms of identification and dependence, and wracks inner life with attacks and illusions. As earlier discussed, unsatisfactory relations to the mother divide the ego into three pieces, at least two of which identify with a feature of the mother that has been incorporated into the infant's psyche.[6] Fairbairn's endopsychic system includes five elements: the libidinal ego, which is bound to and identified with the exciting aspect of the mother; the "internal saboteur," which is attached to the rejecting feature of the mother; and the central ego. The dependency, hostility, destructiveness, and false hopes that accompany the ego's splitting impede successful relations with other persons. Put another way, when the infant/child must look for inner compensations because of the failures of the earliest attachments, then inner dependencies, scenes, and battles between ego parts and objects prevent the ability to turn to others and realistically invest in new relationships.

Since Winnicott puts so much emphasis on the mother's formation of the infant, it is not surprising that he gives a totally interactional account of psychopathology; that is, he traces the psychological illnesses of personality to the mother (the father is always secondary for him) not providing the appropriate care. This can occur in the earliest period in two possible ways. She may fail in the identification with the infant, in which case the infant fails to develop a sense of itself, of the body, and also his or her inner creativity and powers. The mother may also fail to provide satisfactory protection against the outside world—including herself—destructively impinging upon the infant. If this occurs, the infant will be too early directed outside of itself and thus will not find the periods of solitude that are needed to coalesce the slowly developing ego.

Somewhat mitigating the post-Freudian thrust of Winnicott's account is the language of the true self. Still, the "environment," that is, maternal care, is the single causative factor in pathology for Winnicott. Channeling and forming both inner and outer reality, supporting development, and protecting the true self constitute the tasks of the mother during the phase of absolute dependence. Failure impedes development, that is, entails arrest, and in particular it prevents the true or inner self from becoming whole and acquiring its personal psychic reality. Although it does not directly fall under the heading of illness, the impact of others during the transitional period is also vital. By supporting the child's play world of half-reality, half-fantasy, the parents foster the foundation for creativity, in the widest sense, in all of later life. Winnicott's view of the inner self thus adds another element to the impact of others in development and pathology. How are later relations affected by earlier disturbances? The health of the true self parallels the health of later relationships. If a person cannot have basic integrity and a sense of her or his own personal style and meaning, then there can be no mature relationships.

How do the Jewish philosophers understand sickness? While each of the treatments of the three Jewish philosophers is distinctive, they all agree in defining illness or alienation in terms of inadequate relationships. In addition, they share the view that a lack of relation to the divine stands behind sickness, as it were, and that this lack has a powerful impact upon relations with others. Rosenzweig's position is, in some ways, the least complicated. In the natural state, without the love of God and love of neighbor, the self is "solitary" or isolated from others. As life goes on, the individual realizes that death is the only thing that the future holds in store. The individual masks this crushing awareness of the inescapable future with an outward show of pride and defiance. Since death is seen as the defining feature of life, self-regard, that is, fear of one's own death, must overwhelm any concern for the other. Hollowness of relations overall, in speech and love in particular, characterize this solitary life. This is a life suffering from premature dying.

Through Buber's language of the two "basic words" "I-Thou" and "I-It" he immediately shows a different understanding of the natural situation of the human than does Rosenzweig. Humans are always in relation to the world, and he actually considers the I-Thou relationship to be prior to its opposite. Consequently, Buber describes alienation or illness not as a lack of relation, but as an imbalance of one type of relation over another. Illness occurs when the word/world of I and It overwhelms the possibilities for relations of I and Thou. In I-It relations self-concern dominates concern for the other. The other is objectified, an object of one's own design, a pawn in one's plan or scheme. An absence also characterizes I-It relations, the absence of the divine. God can only be approached as a Thou, and all full I-Thou relationships must ultimately refer to this divine other.

It is relevant to this discussion that Buber believes that I-It relations lack wholeness, that in these cases neither the self nor the other are relating in their fullness. The self may see itself in terms of a vocation, an artist, for example, and the other is a mere object of one's interest, with a pretty or interesting face or figure. Thus, only a single or limited amount of dimensions, of both self and other, come into play in the realm of the I and It. As opposed to this, in I-Thou relationships both the self and other are beyond being defined or treated partially. Each faces the other in their fullness and relates with reciprocity and mutuality.

Levinas offers a standpoint concerning illness and relationships that shows some similarities with both philosophic positions, although it is still closer to that of Rosenzweig. Two types of relation are characteristic of human life, but it is a misnomer to say both are natural. Egoism, the pursuit of pleasure and satisfaction, constitutes the path of all life, including the human. Its alternative, the face-to-face relation, is a break with the natural, a metaphysical incursion into the everyday and the ordinary, which, at least indirectly, witnesses a trace of the divine. However, as with Buber, illness or alienation is defined as the preponderance of the relationship of self-regard. In this case, others have the quality of being mere objects, whom I come across in the pursuit of my power and freedom. The other either becomes part of my I—incorporated into my ego, family, or community—or is excluded and persecuted as unalterably alien to me. That which is like me is treasured, and that which is different from me is pursued with violence. Levinas argues that this egoism ultimately translates into a life of ennui, hollowness, and meaninglessness.

What are some of the distinctive features of each of these two discourses about illness? The post-Freudian theorists provide a sophisticated language to describe both the origin and the inevitability, at least some degree, of illness. Within the object relations narrative, humans begin in extremely intense relationships with others. The infant is at first merged with the mother, and soon has pieces of the mother intricately interwoven into its own psyche. Paradoxically for these post-Freudian thinkers, pathology may be said to originate from difficulties in separation. The self is split as it is attached to internal pieces of the other. However, there is an early drive toward maturity that commences in the first months, but this drive requires the support of the mother. If the mother has facilitated the infant's development, the self is made more whole and the other can for the first time be regarded in its integrity. Success in separation is the foundation for fuller, more mutual relations. Thus, the three object relations theorists offer a relational view of the origin and consequences of illness, as well as what constitutes healthy relations.

The Jewish philosophers also describe illness, or really "alienation" in their terminology, in terms of misrelations. When self-concern overwhelms the concern for the other, alienation ensues. Rosenzweig understood the cause of self-concern to be the crushing fear of death, while Buber and Levinas saw it as a result of basic human egoism. Buber and Levinas share a view with the psychoanalysts that illness is synonymous with treating the other as a part-object. For Buber, the other is of interest only in a limited way in the I-It relationship. With Levinas, the I of egoism only finds the other as valuable in the ways that she or he is similar to me. What is distinctive to the narratives of the three philosophers is that they affirm that God is addressed in every full or healthy relationship. Rosenzweig insisted that love and even speech always have a divine referent, while Buber and Levinas hold that true relationships to another must either extend to the divine or in some way witness to the divine.

With Levinas the latter is the case, even if only in acknowledging the ethical prohibition to kill that arises in the face-to-face relation.

Transference and Transcendence

At one point in the narrative for the Jewish holiday of Passover in the *Haggadah*, Rabbi Gamaliel recites the three things that must be said in order to fulfill the mitzvah or obligation of that night: Passover Sacrifice, Matzah (unleavened bread), and Bitter Herbs. In a similar way, from the time of Freud there have been lists of the essential concepts or insights that define psychoanalysis. These often include the unconscious, repression, drives, the centrality of sexuality and discovery of infantile sexuality, the meaningfulness of dreams, the Oedipal complex, and transference. The latter is certainly one of the most powerful resources in the Freudian legacy. As one critic has remarked:

> None of Freud's epochal discoveries . . . has proved to be more heuristically productive or more clinically valuable than his demonstration that humans regularly and inevitably repeat with the analyst and with other important figures in their current lives patterns of relationship, of fantasy, and of conflict with the crucial figures in their childhood—primarily their parents. (Esman, ed., 1990, 1)

Thus, at its basis, transference refers to the ways that humans repeat the patterns of their earliest relationships in their interactions with significant others later in life. In the context of the analytic situation, transference was seen as the primary catalyst for change, and it is in this context that it emerges as so pivotal for our discussion. The question is: How is significant change, that is, transformation, portrayed by the psychoanalysts and the philosophers? If in the first case the focal object is transference, in the latter it is the incursion of transcendence.

As much as with other principal psychoanalytic concepts, the understanding and "treatment" of transference have undergone vast changes since Freud, especially within the more relational streams of psychoanalysis.[7] Among the particular points of contention are those concerning whether transference is a ubiquitous feature of human interactions or an event unique to the analytic setting, whether it is to be understood in terms of the ego and defenses or object relations and infantile fantasy, and whether it should be seen as a corridor to the past or a fundamentally contemporary phenomenon.[8]

Still, the issue of change or transformation is addressed in psychoanalysis in the wider framework of analysis or therapy, and it is starting from that backdrop that the examination of transference will be pursued. For Freud, the goal of therapy was the strengthening of the ego and conscious activity. The analyst uncovers the unconscious desire of the analysand, which has not been allowed to be expressed in anything but distorted form, and makes it conscious. With the break into consciousness, from id to ego, psychic conflict and its accompanying symptoms are overcome. The transformation from unconscious to conscious is thus the fundamental transaction of psychoanalysis. As Freud wrote: "By extending the unconscious into consciousness the repressions are raised, the conditions of symptom-formation are abolished, and the pathogenic conflict exchanged for a normal one" (1969, 377).

However, this change is not easy. It is not enough for the analyst to just tell the patient what is going on within him or her. In this sense, information is not knowledge. The patient resists appropriating the knowledge that will lead to freedom, because of the past and present investment of energy tied to unacceptable desires, their censorship, and their distorted expressions. Only a change of energy will overcome the patient's repression and defenses, allowing the patient to accept or appropriate the needed knowledge (1969, 249). The impetus for change comes from the clinical phenomenon of transference. Freud described transference in this way: "the patient sees in his analyst the return—the reincarnation—of some important figure out of his childhood or past, and consequently transfers on to him feelings and reactions that undoubtedly applied to this model" (1949, 66). The therapist uses the energy of the patient's attachment to him or her to re-channel the energy trapped in the neurosis (1969, 347–89, 395). For Freud, only those neuroses—so-called transference neuroses—that allowed for this redirection of energy, at first concentrated on the therapist, were susceptible to cure. The importance of transference in the cure of the patient is clearly expressed in Freud's following statement:

> The doctor tries to compel him [the patient] to fit these emotional impulses [passions directed toward the analyst] into the nexus of the treatment and of his life-history, to submit them to intellectual consideration and to understand them in the light of their psychical value. This struggle between the doctor and the patient, between intellect and instinctual life, between understanding and seeking to act, is played out almost exclusively in the phenomena of transference. It is on that field that the victory must be won—the victory whose expression is the permanent cure of the neurosis. (1990, 34–35)

Thus, it was critical in Freud's view that the therapist take the feelings projected by the patient as information about the underlying conflicts, rather than as authentic interpersonal expressions. For example, the sudden outbreak of a positive transference, that is, the feelings of love, toward the male analyst by the female patient can be disconcerting, but Freud insists that the analyst maintain the "abstinence" of the scientific attitude. While all relations to others are partially driven by infantile sexual longings and reproduce infantile prototypes, this is especially manifest in the analytic situation. The analytic endeavor to trace back libidinal wishes, repressed memories, and ego defenses leads to resistance, and transference is an intense example of this. It is a neurotic symptom that is stronger in those who have other such neurotic symptoms. The analyst correctly takes the amorous feelings, in positive transference, of the patient as just more data to explore. He or she illuminates the libidinal origins and pathways of this behavior and aids the patient in strengthening the ego's hold on this material. Thus, for Freud, transference behavior is both a resistance or an obstacle to analysis and essential for successful treatment. Finally, it should be added that Freud's understanding of the significance of transference, both as a reflection of past attachment and as a manifestation of present attachment, opens the way for later theorists to reconsider the place of relationships to others in psychopathology and therapy, and, overall, in human life.

Erikson's understanding of the nature of psychoanalytic therapy demonstrates both his profound ties to Freud as well as his departures from him. In the essay "The Nature of Clinical Evidence" (1964, 47–80), Erikson follows the classic medical model in taking up the topics: complaint, anamnesis (historical reconstruction of the illness), and interpretation. He acknowledges his agreement with Freud's guiding conceptions of repression, regression, transference, and libido. Overall, the view of the analyst as offering interpretations of the data supplied by the patient, while carefully screening for her or his own projections, fully fits in with Freud's views. Further, Erikson's understanding of the "proof" of an interpretation and of analytic intervention, while very rich, could have been taken directly from Freud: "the way in which the communication between therapist and patient 'keeps moving,' leading to new and surprising insights and to the patient's greater assumption of responsibility for himself" (1964, 75). However, a hint of a break with the psychoanalytic founder is seen in Erikson's admission that the two subjectivities of the patient and analyst play a greater role in the psychoanalytic encounter than is usual in medicine. He writes in this context: "How the two subjectivities join in the kind of disciplined understanding and shared insight which we think are operative in a cure—that is the question" (1964, 53). Erikson's own contribution to the literature about transference consists in his taking into account not only the patient's earlier history, but her or his present life-stage, social position, and even cultural and historical setting.

Klein's portrayal of analysis and transference reveals continuities with Freud as well as revolutionary departures. There is room in her view of analysis for the Freudian staple of interpreting the symbolic meanings of the patient's dreams and free associations. While she includes the analyst's work on the patient's transferred projections, she also notes the importance of non-verbal and non-symbolic transactions with the patient. Further, Klein insisted that the patient must relive and rework his or her earlier infantile experiences. She writes:

> In taking analysis back to earliest infancy, we enable the patient to revive fundamental situations—a revival which I have often spoken of as "memories in feeling." In the course of this revival, it becomes possible for the patient to develop a different attitude to his early frustrations. (1997, 234)

This process focuses on the patient's witnessing to, and acceptance of, those impulses such as envy, greed, and jealously of the first (paranoid-schizoid) position.

Klein's commitment to object relations, that is, her belief that libidinal and destructive drives are never autonomous, but are always tied to images of persons and to persons themselves, is reflected in the very active role that is taken up by the analyst. She gave more prominence to the phenomenon of counter-transference, that is, the therapist's projections upon the patient. In a total break from Freud, Klein also believed that the analyst must play the role of the good object or the good breast. Ultimately, by taking back the good object (the image of the analyst) into the self, the patient supplements the dormant primal good object of the earliest infantile period. Klein writes, for example: "However, the introjection of the analyst as a good object, if not based on idealization has, to some extent, the effect of providing an internal good object where it has been largely lacking" (1997, 234). Through this process of introjection, the patient's ego is strengthened, guilt and depression (of the second stage) are re-experienced, and the overall sense of reality and responsibility is enhanced.

Fairbairn's understanding of analysis and transference continues Klein's theme of the centrality of relationships in the patient's transformation. Analysis provides the occasion to rework the first failures in relationships. The analyst offers herself or himself as a "good object." In relating to the analyst, the patient gains the confidence and security to overcome resistance, releasing the inner prosecutory objects. In Fairbairn's words: "resistance can only be really overcome when the transference situation has developed to a point at which the analyst has become such a good object that the latter [i.e., the patient] is prepared to risk the release of bad objects from the unconscious" (1986, 110). Analysis is not, of course, easy. There is deep resistance on the part of the patient to the release of bad objects. This appears as partially due to the security that comes with familiarity with the older inner identifications and compensations. Resistance also arises from the fear that losing the bad objects would cause the earliest relationships, of which they were residues, to similarly disappear. Still, with the release of bad objects, the patient can achieve the ultimate goal of analysis, which is fuller and more intimate relationships with actual persons.

Winnicott again directly connects what goes on in analysis between analyst and patient with what went on in infancy between the mother and infant. He begins his paper of 1969, "The Theory of the Parent-Infant Relationship," with this statement: "The main point of this paper can perhaps best be brought out through a comparison of the study of infancy with the study of the psychoanalytic transference" (1986, 233). The analyst goes over the terrain that the mother failed to satisfactorily cover. This includes offering a holding environment, intuition of the patient's unformed inner self, and, later, reading the patient's needs through signs. In all, the connection between the analytic situation—especially in transference—and the infant's life with the mother is so strong in Winnicott's view that he believed that one could learn about the latter from the former. In a compelling, almost audacious, statement, Winnicott wrote: "Indeed it is not from direct observation of infants so much as from the study of the transference in the analytic setting that it is possible to gain a clear view of what takes place in infancy itself" (1986, 251).

For Winnicott, the analyst's most important function is just to be there. It is the care and concern of human interaction, repeating what was first seen in the mother-infant relationship, that the therapist offers and that allows the undeveloped elements of the patient's ego to form. His notions of the true and false selves also enter this discussion of analysis, especially concerning severe psychological disorders. In these cases, the failures in mothering have resulted in a situation in which the patient's true self has been covered over by the false self. The false self allows superficial interactions with reality, but the deep interactions between the ego and the world have been forestalled. However, through the analyst's reparative efforts, her or his good enough mothering, the true self now has the opportunity to become a primary site of activity. Winnicott writes: "The behavior of the analyst . . . by being good enough in the matter of adaptation to need, is gradually perceived by the patient as something that raises a hope that the true self may at least be able to take the risks involved in starting to experience living" (1990, 248). The category of the true self introduces one other dynamic into analysis. Winnicott's belief in the true self's innate drive for realization is reflected in his view that the analyst must be very careful not to interfere too much in the patient's struggle to find his or her personal center. In this connection he writes: "The principle is that it is the patient and only the patient who has the answers" (1971, 87).

How do the three modern Jewish philosophers, Rosenzweig, Buber, and Levinas, portray the dynamics of significant personal transformation? While describing it in different ways, they see alienation in relations among persons as pervasive, but they also insist that a *transcendent* break with that situation is always possible. Rosenzweig's portrayal of the alienation of the interhuman is the most unequivocal. The individual by himself or herself is isolated from others and does not possess the resources to overcome this condition. Only a transcendent actor can rend the hold of the fear of death, which paralyzes the single, the dual, and the communal. In *The Star*, Rosenzweig presents a love scene between God and the soul to choreograph the incursion of the transcendent. God's call to the soul, issued out of love, breaks the shell of isolation. Rosenzweig wrote: "The living soul, loved by God, triumphs over all that is mortal, and that is all that can be objectively stated about it" (1972, 202). Divine love provides the trust, security, humility, and purpose that allows the individual to face death, and therefore to live life. The response of the soul to God's love, to God's command, eventually leads to the love of the neighbor. This love, in turn, has God's transforming call hidden within it, and thus extends the divine process. The movement from soul to soul, that is, from the individual who has been recast to the neighbor who is to be transformed, Rosenzweig designates as ensouling (*beseelung*).

For Buber alienation within the interhuman is neither endemic nor quite epidemic. The I-Thou relation is at hand—in the hand that reaches out—from the beginning. Still, both ontogenetically and phylogenetically, he speaks of the growth of the objectifying I-It realm. A transcendent catalyst is needed to overcome alienation, because of the two processes—as one gets older and as civilization develops—mentioned above. Yet, there is also another reason. What does the divine provide that is missing from all other I-Thou relationships and completes them? The lacuna is something that has to do with what Buber enigmatically labels as meaning "the inexpressible confirmation of meaning" (1970, 158). Buber's treatment of revelation focuses on a sense of meaning concerning the individual and all of life. Buber believes that once this meaning has been given, it is never again a question. With a sense of meaning, the renewed or returned (*teshuvah*) person is plunged back with a sense of purpose into the world of others.

What is the impetus for change in Levinas' schematic? While there is no systematic chronology, either ontogenetic or phylogenetic, to account for alienation, Levinas equates the physical and natural with egoism, pleasure, satisfaction, and the treatment of the other as a means. What introduces the metaphysical, the ethical, is the proximity of the other who stands above oneself: which is the other as neighbor, stranger, widow, orphan, and poor. Their appearance arrests satisfaction; it devastates self-concern. Innocence is lost forever, because one knows that he or she is guilty and must respond, unlimitedly, to the need of the other. Put another way, this is the process through which one's own physical needs have been transformed into metaphysical desire. Levinas continually sees the appearance of the other as a transcendent assault, governed by the interdiction "Thou shalt not kill!"

How do the psychoanalytic and the philosophical discourses about transformation compare? Perhaps the most prominent feature that emerges in conceptualizing change in terms of psychoanalytic transference is the impact of past relationships on the present. This was, of course, the core of the original Freudian discovery that in the heat of analysis the patient's behavior began to mimic the patterns and powerful emotional intensity of much earlier interactions. While Erikson does not question this finding, he believes that to account for the specific dynamics of any particular transference, one must be more attentive to present determinants, such as the patient's present life-stage, social position, and even the cultural setting. Klein explored transference in terms of those objects/persons that dominated the past paranoid-schizoid and depressive positions. Interpretation ferrets out the dynamics of the good and bad breasts, and analysis seeks to enhance the power of the former. Fairbairn seeks a release of past bad objects, that is, the inner images as well as the emotions tied to them. Finally, Winnicott even more forcefully views analysis in terms of overcoming earlier maternal failures. Thus, for post-Freudian theorists, transference is still about the interrelation between past and present, but they define both of these poles in terms of objects.

The role of the analyst as the catalyst for change has been revised following Freud. A small step in this direction was taken by Erikson. He holds that the encounter between patient and therapist brings their entirety as persons into play. The therapist cannot pretend to be some type of blank screen. This insight is accelerated through Klein's theories. The analyst is now linked to the good breast, that inner object which is the source of hope and wholeness. Through active interventions, the analyst deepens the positive powers of the good breast within. For Fairbairn the analyst must also become a "good object," if the patient is to be able to release the inner bad objects. Satisfactory interactions with the analyst remedy the patient's reliance on inner objects. Finally, with Winnicott, the analyst by providing a "good enough" environment, that is, by adapting to the patient's deepest needs, allows the center of the personality, the true self, to emerge. In these ways, the post-Freudian theorists have brought to the fore an understanding that another person—the therapist as person—is the primary factor in change. Presence itself, an open and supportive presence, provides a truly transformative healing.

The treatments of transformation by the three Jewish philosophers indicated that revolutionary change in the personal and interpersonal required a transcendent catalyst. The movement from isolation, or the I-It realm, or egoism, comes only through a foray from the outside. They have different names for the carrier of the transcendent: love, meaning, responsibility. Why does Rosenzweig make love the incitement for change, for the new? Why is it the vehicle for the transcendent? Rosenzweig's presentation of love is not just metaphoric: it is phenomenological. Love is chosen because while its source is enigmatic, its tremendous strength or powers to transform are well known. It is human. Yet, nothing else human is similar. It also is not in one's own hands, for it cannot be willed. Thus, Rosenzweig can suggest that at its foundation love has a divine origin. Additionally, love is connected to God—the commander—for Rosenzweig believes that love can be commanded. The lover may command the beloved, which is how Rosenzweig looks at the first stage of the relation between God and the soul, and from whence he finds the command to love the neighbor. The transformative powers at a minimum keep open the option of love's divine derivation, and nothing is the same afterward. In all of this, the biblical "Song of Songs" is the imprimatur for Rosenzweig's treatment.

Why is "meaning" the carrier of the transcendent for Buber? As was the case with Rosenzweig's treatment of love, Buber is perhaps suggesting that the giving and receiving of a sense of meaning is only properly described as something human and more than human. Meaning can be communicated by the presence of another. Mahatma Gandhi, Martin Luther King, and Nelson Mandela are examples of persons who conveyed a sense of meaning. One sees a life of commitment to others, and feels that a model has been affirmed that can withstand all tests. While meaning can be conveyed by the presence of someone, its origin seems to be more than human. This does not denigrate the human, but suggests that there is some transcendent point of reference or "secret."

For Levinas, it is the quality of "responsibility" that appears in response to the presence of another, but which points to a more than human origin. Levinas is insistent that the other *is* a human being. He defers from speaking of an immediate divine-human encounter, because, for him, there is no direct relationship to God. Yet, God's presence is elliptically there, as a "trace," in the face-to-face relationship. Why does Levinas resort to this language of trace in his phenomenology of responsibility? Is it because responsibility describes a response that transcends any calculation of mutuality and reciprocity? Is the religious language of the trace of the divine the only resource that allows one to say that, once again, nothing, not even death, overturns a life of responsibility?

One's fear of death has been subdued by the all-consuming concern for the other's death—established once and for all by the divine commandment.

In summation, the power of transference language is that it speaks about the continuity between past and present. It underscores the lesson of the difficulty of change by speaking of the powerful presence of inner objects, and of the patient's fear of losing connection to significant early figures. It recounts, additionally, that past relations not only stifle present and future ones, but that they must be worked through, the energy taken from them, to bring about significant change in the present. Further, working through is by working on new relations—to the analyst—and in a sense, making the old new through the new. Yet, to further complicate this, the analyst's own experiences and reactions are also understood to be deeply tied to past relations through countertransference.

The language of the Jewish philosophers reinforces the insight that change is miraculous. The past is not the only force pressing on the present, and people are not just dependent on it. Radical change, the unexpected, where there is no precedent, is possible. New things are possible that are not calculable, because the promise of the present is unlimited. The Jewish philosophers tie this promise to the one truly transcendent power. This power works from the other to the self, and the significant consequences affect the self with others.

The differences in the psychoanalytic and Jewish philosophical discourses about change may also be explored by differentiating the analytic from the phenomenological. The analytic in this sense explores the possibilities of the present through analysis of the past. It asks, how did we get here and how can we move forward? It believes that progress requires an understanding of the history and constituents of the present, and this understanding is told through the developmental narrative. The post-Freudian psychoanalysts look to reworking past relationships. The Jewish discourses offer phenomenological examinations. Of course, the meaning of the phenomenological is highly contentious. Still, the three Jewish philosophers argue for love, meaning, and responsibility as primary factors for change by offering phenomenologies of these features of the human/interhuman. They are saying, in the case of a need for significant change, one must explore those features of life that offer the greatest potential. Additionally, among other things, they affirm that these qualities refer to the transcendent. In this sense, change is a radical break with both past and present.

Despite their differences, the two discourses continue to have in common an appreciation for the power of another's presence to generate change. Buber once spoke of such a presence, but in the context of this investigation, it seems equally applicable to psychoanalytic discourse.[9] He wrote: "What do we expect when we are in despair and yet go to a man? Surely a presence by means of which we are told that nevertheless there is meaning" (1965, 14). This notion of the redemptive possibility of another's presence is a central leitmotiv of the Jewish philosophers' work and a deepening insight of the post-Freudian psychoanalysts. Further, since transference is often seen to have a universal reference, to all significant relations, the analyst becomes a model for others, of what is possible even beyond the psychoanalytic encounter.

Health and the Interhuman

How do the two discourses depict health, particularly as it concerns human interactions in their fullness? This question has been addressed indirectly in a number of previous sections, but a summary view of the two discourses will be revealing. The two portrayals reflect different views of human relationships as well as the distinctive parameters of the psychoanalytic and Jewish philosophical approaches. Just as the psychoanalytic theorists constructed more elaborate portrayals of the dynamics of change, that is, of analysis and transference, the Jewish philosophers present a more lavish vision of the transformed interhuman.

How is the fullness of relationships narrated in psychoanalytic discourse? The resources available to answer this question include statements about the goals of analysis and descriptions of the nature of mature relations with others. Freud had two ways of describing the goals of psychoanalysis. The first was in terms of the psychic structures id and ego, and the aim of bringing some limited consciousness, freedom, and control to our usually obscured and repressed impulses, feelings, and desires. The movement from id to ego was his way of explaining the effort to extend conscious control over unconscious contents. In a wider context, Freud spoke of health in terms of the "capacity for enjoyment and achievement in life" (1969, 398), or satisfaction in love and work (cited in Erikson 1963, 265). He saw the neurotic as one who was haunted by alien impulses. These restricted and shackled the possibilities for appreciating new things, interacting with others, and participating in creative cultural and scientific pursuits.

However, Freud's understanding of the nature of human relations is quite attenuated, as comes across in his discussions of love. As we saw, he believed that all significant relations, especially love, were to some extent driven by a sexual or libidinal motive. Love, once again, was discussed in terms of drives and objects. In addition, Freud held that the other as love object is a later development from the first such object, the self. While he recognized the power and importance of sexual love,[10] the idea that love of others is always a derivation of love of the self powerfully underscores Freud's account of human relations. In all, Freud offers a heroic ethic of singularity as the enlightened goal of human life. His two most philosophic books, *Civilization and Its Discontents* and *The Future of An Illusion*, indicate that reality is difficult and merciless. The highest life comes from honestly facing, without illusion, the inevitability of death, the real possibilities of disease and natural disaster, and the constraints of civilized life. His is a basically lonely vision, where the interhuman is very narrowly portrayed.

Erikson's view of fulfilling relationships does not appear in the context of his discussions of analysis. He described the fundamental goal of analysis much as Freud did, in terms of increasing the ego's hold over psychic material previously inaccessible to consciousness (1968, 74). Erikson demonstrates a more relational view of the human and offers some suggestive examples of the richness of relations in his discussions of the successful negotiation of the crises of intimacy and ego-integrity. One of the major factors that give rise to the issue of intimacy is sexual maturity. However, before this period the individual's sexual life was primarily oriented to self seeking, and the other was regarded almost as an opponent. With intimacy there is a moderating mutuality of satisfaction, what Erikson terms "mutual regulation of complicated [sexual] patterns" (1968, 137). Intimacy includes, as well, the willingness to partially share an identity through mutual trust and devotion. There are also significant roles for others in Erikson's characterization of integrity. He speaks of "[being] faithful to the image-bearers of the past," "a new and different love of one's parents," "a sense of comradeship with men and women of distant times and of different pursuits who have created orders and objects and sayings conveying human dignity and love," and of the link between one's integrity and "all human integrity" (1968, 139–40). Finally, the theme of responsibility to or for others is ubiquitous in Erikson's portrayal of the later psychosocial crises as well as in his discussion of analysis.

In what contexts does Klein's view of healthy relationships appear? The earlier discussion of Klein's description of transference has already explained her complex relation to the Freudian view of analysis. As with Freud, she seeks to expand the patient's awareness of infantile impulses and feelings, which, for her emphasize hate, envy, persecution, and guilt. Further, while she maintains the goal of aiding the ego in gaining "strength and coherence," she speaks of the way that "the unconscious phantasy life . . . can be better utilized in ego activities, with a consequent general enrichment of the personality" (1990, 244). As this statement indicates, she is more appreciative than Freud of phantasy/fantasy as a positive feature in human creativity. Further, Klein's description of the outcome of successful analysis in terms of relationships to others is quite telling. She speaks of "greater trust in constructive and reparative forces, actually in the capacity for love" and of "greater tolerance towards one's own limitations, as well as improved object relations and a clearer perception of internal and external reality" (1997, 232).

Klein's presentations of love/narcissism and the depressive position are diagnostic of her general relational stance. In harmony with her insistence that "object relations are operative from the beginning of post-natal life," she holds that "auto-erotism and narcissism are in the young infant contemporaneous with the first relation to objects—external and internalized" (1990, 239). Thus, Klein agrees that at least part of the infant's libido is indeed directed inward. However, turning Freud inside out, as it were, she finds that the attachment is not to the ego, but to inner objects. More or less ignoring the very terms she is discussing, she writes: "auto-eroticism and narcissism include the love for and relation with the internalized good object which in phantasy forms part of the loved body and self" (1990, 239). The subjects of the depressive position and gratitude, in particular, reveal characteristics of the fulfilled interhuman for Klein. The emergence of the depressive position proves that love is as innate in the infant as is hate and fear. The infant is able to turn to the m/other as a whole and for her own sake. Whenever the infant or later person addresses the other from this standpoint, an unselfish concern for the other, respect, trust, devotion, and love are the governing motivations. These abilities to give to the other draw upon (in gratitude) experiences of the richness and selflessness of the mother's original care (1997, 187–88).

Neither the treatment of the topic of analysis nor the discussion of the stage of mature dependence reveal a substantial description of the dynamics of the fulfilled interhuman in Fairbairn's work. The goal of analysis seems to be seen exclusively in terms of reversing the damage to the psyche that resulted from the failures in the earliest relationship to the mother. Although he believes that therapy can have only limited results, Fairbairn sees its aims as "to reduce the split of the original ego by restoring to the central ego a maximum of the territories ceded to the libidinal ego and the internal saboteur, and . . . to bring the exciting object and the rejecting object as far as possible together within the sphere of influence of the central ego" (1994, 129–30). At least the relational foundation of his work is reflected in the analyst's primary role of being a "good object." Fairbairn's characterization of mature dependence features the movement away from infantile identification, incorporation, and a one-sided taking from the other. He writes:

> it is characterized by a capacity on the part of a differentiated individual for co-operative relationships with differentiated objects . . . the relationship, is [in terms of physiology], of course, genital; but it is a relationship involving evenly matched giving and taking between two differentiated individuals who are mutually dependent, and between whom there is no disparity of dependence. (1994, 145)

Maturity means mutuality for him: a mutuality that grows out of the soil of dependence and deep interconnections.

Finally, as with Klein, love for Fairbairn is not reduced to either drive satisfaction or narcissism. We earlier saw that he made attachment to objects as the single explanatory feature of both development and psychopathology. Consequently, he defines narcissism totally in the currency of object relations. Primary narcissism is not self love, but "a state of identification with the object," here "the breast" (1986a, 91).

Much of Winnicott's discussion of the goals of analysis focuses on the inner self, rather than on relationships. Analysis allows the superficiality of the false self to be replaced by the inner self, with its ability to experience the depth of reality. A life of personal meaning and creativity is now possible.[11] While this approach to therapy is not very helpful for illuminating his portrait of the fulfilled interhuman, Winnicott is more forthcoming and relevant concerning the subject of the stage of independence. In addition to what this stage implies in terms of the individual's own development, in relations with others it marks the appearance of a real care for the other, and also love. He characterizes the latter through the vocabulary of "mutual object usage." In mature love persons express their desires and allow themselves to be used as the object of their partner's desire. Tellingly, Winnicott thought that one of the most important features of analysis was the analyst's willingness to be used by the patient in the ways that the mother had earlier not allowed (1971, 92–94). He thus combines the somewhat antithetical concepts, at least Buber would find it so, of mutuality and usage. Love is the acknowledgment of the separateness of the other, combined with the willingness to allow one's partner to also express his or her inner longings, fantasies, and desires.

Surprisingly, the presence of a relationship to others is especially prominent in Winnicott's treatment of narcissism. In his essay "The Capacity to be Alone," he corrects Freud's notion of narcissism by focusing on the idea of being alone. For Winnicott, while there are both early and later more sophisticated experiences of being alone, what the two share is the presence of another. Consequently, he writes: "the basis of the capacity to be alone is a paradox; it is the experience of being alone while someone else is present" (1965a, 30). The two constant poles in Winnicott's writing, the relational and the "personal," are well represented in a final quotation about health: "Being able to enjoy being alone along with another person who is also alone is in itself an experience of health" (1965a, 31).

The presentation of the transformed interhuman in the narratives of the three modern Jewish philosophers has been explored a number of times in this study, most extensively in the first chapter. This account will briefly summarize features in the previous descriptions and examine some of their implications. For Rosenzweig, the individual who first becomes a soul in the intense love relationship to God is commanded to turn to the neighbor and extend the divine word of love. Thus, the first element of the transformed interhuman is that it is lived as obligation. Responsibility for the other through command permeates all relations and is continually operative, for everyone becomes the neighbor merely by being the next or near one. In *The Star*, Rosenzweig actually places his portrayal of the fullness of relations between persons under the category of redemption. Revelation is the realm of the dual, while redemption corresponds to the communal. Thus, a second characteristic of the interhuman is that it includes a very wide circle of people. In fact, in Rosenzweig's conception, even the singular community must ultimately have the goal of including everyone in its "we." As we saw, only religious communities satisfied this element of being true communities. Such communities grow under the auspices of the command to love the neighbor.

In the first chapter it was suggested that Rosenzweig's narrative about the powers of speech or language best illustrated what could be found in the fullness of human relations.[12] The powers of speech are second to none. Not even love is its rival, for, according to Rosenzweig, speech and love are in many ways synonymous. In each case, the initiator and the recipient are brought out through the interchange. The word of calling and answering, of speech and response, binds together, but also demonstrates that the deepest human relationships can never be characterized in terms of merger. Speech performs at its highest level when each person is able to address the other out of his or her distinctiveness. Still, Rosenzweig held that it was specifically the communal prayer for the coming of God's kingdom that anticipated the highest, redemptive relations. Here the "we" speaks as one. It addresses God, eventually in the name of all persons for the sake of all persons. Further, it invites, or more precisely exhorts, a divine intervention that will end all strife.

The main characteristic of the transformed interhuman for Buber is responsibility, which he explores in the language of "calling and mission." We saw that the relationship to God bestowed the individual with a sense of her or his meaning and the meaning of all of life. With this assurance, one is commanded to turn back into the world. Buber writes that the "encounter with God" comes to a person "in order that he may prove its meaning in action in the world. All revelation is a calling and a mission" (1970, 164). What is one called to do? There is no singular or universal formula for this, for each person listens in the uniqueness of her being and the uniqueness of her history. One can only attend to what God asks in the life lived intensely, in each hour and each day.

Perhaps two characteristics of this calling and mission can be gleaned from *I and Thou*, as well as from other pieces of Buber's oeuvre. The first, is, obviously, that one remains open to the life of I and Thou. The individual must not allow the world of things, and his own desires and needs, to objectify and shield him from the other. Responsibility is to be present for the other. Secondly, one's responsibilities to others cannot be fulfilled exclusively through the I and Thou exchange. As Buber argued in his critique of Søren Kierkegaard's "single one," God ultimately asks that even the dual be supplemented by the communal.[13] Buber insisted that political life was not to be excluded from the realms of ethics and religion. Power must always be guided by responsibility. No areas of life are exempted from divine imperatives, and thus, expediency, nationalism, xenophobia, and violence must ceaselessly be exposed and critiqued.

The "face-to-face" relation or, alternatively, "proximity" are the ways that Levinas designates the transformed interhuman. As an ethical relationship, the face-to-face transcends both sympathy and mutuality. It is not some natural feeling, but a being shattered and taken hostage that initiates the relation to the other. The relation is one-way, or, put in other terms, the other stands in her height. It is a question of my duties and the other's rights. While I am responsible "for everything and for everyone" (1981, 114), the other's possible obligations to me are not within my horizon of concern. If the command not to kill marks the farthest parameter of the relationship, the demand to stand with open hands in welcome characterizes the nearest.

The communal is addressed by Levinas under the rubric of justice. As we have seen earlier, justice concerns both my obligations to all the "thirds," outside of the "face-to-face," as well as to the other's obligations to others. Unlike the face-to-face, this realm calls for calculation. Here a concern for "the color of his eyes,"[14] that is, noticing the specifics of the other and the situation, is required. One must ask: What would be a fair resolution for everyone concerned? What are the specific resources and the needs? And, perhaps, What are the present conditions and what has led to them? However, Levinas appears more skeptical than either Rosenzweig or Buber about the reality of a transformed communal life. While neither of the latter are unrealistic or utopian, they do include a notion of some movement toward deeper relations in the context of a community. There is no equivalent element in Levinas' writings. He is suspicious of the ways that the pursuit of justice mutates into violence against the other: the poor, weak, and stranger. Therefore, he makes proximity the ever-watchful guardian over justice.

Language, once again, is a key to the fullness of the interhuman with Levinas. It confirms that the other is separate, for words are not thoughts, and the new in dialogue transcends that which could be thought by oneself. It affirms that the other is outside of one's powers, to be respected in his or her integrity. Further, language is never just the transfer of information or communication. It is based upon the principle of being at the other's disposal. In Levinas' words: "Saying is communication, to be sure, but as a condition for all communication, as exposure" (1981, 48). Speech is predicated on being answerable to another. True speech requires that one both welcomes and awaits.

Two striking differences are initially apparent in the ways that the psychoanalysts and the philosophers address the question of healthy relations between persons or the fullness of the interhuman. First, there is a lack of balance between the two discourses in terms of the prominence of this issue. While this topic arises in psychoanalysis in two contexts, the goals of analysis and the later stages within the narrative of human development, in neither case is there an abundance of detail. For example, in the context of analysis the focus remains on the health of the single person, rather than the fullness of the interhuman, even though the need for therapy is given a relational explanation. In contrast, the three Jewish philosophers' discussions of responsibility, language, and community are especially fertile. This conclusion is in harmony with the examination of the earlier topics in this chapter. The psychoanalysts provide an elaborate and technical schematic of psychopathology and therapy, while the philosophical treatments are more metaphoric and reveal a detailed language about the mature dynamics of the interhuman.

The preeminent feature assigned to the highest human relations constitutes a second differential. Within the discourse of many of the post-Freudian psychoanalysts this quality is designated as mutuality. What defines mature interactions for Erikson and Fairbairn is the give-and-take of relations, while for Winnicott it is mutual object usage—the confidence to explore one's own fantasies through the other and the willingness to allow the same opportunity to one's partner. This mutuality is seen to develop and depart from the more one-sided infantile ways of relating. Equally important, the appreciation for mutuality is diagnostic of the importance of the other in every feature of experience, even in what would seem to be the most singular, that is, narcissism.

The language of responsibility that dominates the Jewish philosophical narratives signifies a major difference with the discourse of mutuality. This primacy is obvious in the cases of Rosenzweig and Levinas, but also accurately reflects the perspective of Buber. For all three, the highest relations are characterized by responsibility for the other. The transcendent command is that additional dimension, that third, that seems to transform mutuality into the asymmetrical relation of obligation. This is the language of what must be given without recompense: of what is owed to the other, without concern for what is due to oneself.

Conclusion: "Fettered Surprise"

In a chapter titled "Multiples," Jane Flax evaluates two contemporary discourses on subjectivity, the psychoanalytic and the postmodern, and then finds that neither can fully capture the depth and allusiveness of this significant Western topic. She writes:

> Each highlights some aspects of subjectivity while obscuring or denying others. . . . Each discourse tries to order the heterogeneous components of subjectivity with one master narrative or category. It would be more fruitful to treat contradictory elements of subjectivity as evidence for its multiplicity. We will need multiple stories in a variety of styles to appreciate its complexity. (1993, 98)

Flax's call for "multiple stories in a variety of styles" conveys the spirit behind the whole present study. The examination of post-Freudian psychoanalytic and modern Jewish philosophical narratives seeks to identify how each adds to our understanding of the interhuman. It recognizes that neither could possibly capture the fullness of their common subject, but that each illuminates some areas while overlooking, minimizing, or obscuring others. This conclusion will explore the strengths and weaknesses of the two discourses.

What are the strengths of the psychoanalytic accounts in narrating the human and the interhuman? The psychoanalytic narratives demonstrate how the mother-infant relationship or even unit is the basis for psychic organization, psychosocial development, and future patterns of relationship. Winnicott has the mother teaching the infant about both the inside/itself and the outside world, and for Fairbairn the whole endopsychic structure of ego parts and inner objects has its origin in (the inevitable failures of) maternal care. The mother is the focus in describing early developmental tasks, whether these are understood in terms of Erikson's basic trust, Klein's emergence of gratitude, Fairbairn's integration of the ego, or the flowering of the true self in Winnicott's portrayal. One of the most important perspectives of the post-Freudians is the lasting effect of early patterns of relationship. No new relationships begin or unfold ex nihilo, that is, these patterns influence whom one chooses to relate to and which types of relationships surface. Images and paradigms from the past constantly intervene. For example, the inner objects that are the residue of unsatisfactory initial relations in Fairbairn's thought make it difficult to give up the first patterns and determine what later types of relations are seen as natural and comfortable.

The topic of transference extends the psychoanalytic focus on the first caretakers. Especially in the work of Fairbairn and Winnicott, but also in Klein, the model for the relationship between patient and analyst is the mother-infant pair. While some have criticized the view that analysis makes up the deficiencies of that earlier, primal relationship, seeing analysis in this light has important implications. The great possibilities and responsibilities of the mother are at best reproduced by the analyst. Relationships are thus seen as the central force in both establishing the self and in overcoming its most serious problems.

From the time of Freud's first work, psychoanalytic discourse has been dominated by the language of the unconscious and fantasy—the latter refers to both unconscious and conscious images and storylines. This focus on the hidden and irrational factors that deeply affect human life continued in the theorists whom we have examined. For Klein, behind the images/imagoes/objects are relentless, domineering passions, while for Fairbairn they are mere aftereffects of the primary relation to the mother. For Klein they initially express the death drive, while for Winnicott, fantasy is the progenitor of play, itself the forerunner of culture. The overall contribution of the post-Freudians whom we have examined is to see these factors, that is, the unconscious and fantasy, as intimately connected to other persons.

The language of inner objects brings together in a most astounding way the dual emphases on the unconscious and on the importance of others. The multiple and often conflicting instincts, wishes, and fantasies that pervade the self are here portrayed as pieces or images of others. While Freud's super-ego stands as the origin of this feature of psychoanalytic discourse, the full potential of this language only comes to the fore in the work of Klein, Fairbairn, and Winnicott. Their narratives express in the most powerful way the manner in which the self is hostaged, to use Levinas' language, to the other. Others are not just significant partners, they inhabit the deepest and most inaccessible recesses of the mind: the other in me. These theorists have turned away from the self-referential language of the self and its inner selves, in an effort to provide an interpersonal source for all drives, desires, and fantasies. Ultimately, through the language of inner objects, the very stability of the distinction between self and others is subverted.

The model of the psychoanalytic narrative of development also furnishes extensive resources for understanding the nature of the human. With many of the post-Freudian theorists the narrative starts with the intra-uterine. This point of departure reinforces the overall framework of relationship and underlines the contention that there is no such thing as an infant by itself. The narrative of development features a natural inclination for growth and maturity that pushes the individual through the stages that punctuate the life cycle. It organizes and describes the challenges and crises that must continually be met. Resolutions to the problems addressed in earlier periods are never final, but still are seen to have deep effects on later developments.

While the complete dependence of the fetus and infant on others is obviously not repeated in later stages, the prominence that the relationship of dependence has in the narratives is striking. Fairbairn's characterizations of the stages of development in terms of dependence, from absolute to mutual dependence, is representative of the insight common to the psychoanalysts, that all human relationships exhibit aspects of a very deep, often unconscious, need, interconnection, and reliance on the other. They indicate that a variety of important dimensions of relationships, including trust, security, and love, cannot be easily separated out from more primitive ties of dependency.

A final strength of the psychoanalytic narratives is to recognize the tensions within relationships themselves. The psychoanalytic discourse carefully narrates the complexity that all relationships exhibit. There are perennial tensions between the unconscious and the conscious; the instincts of thanatos and eros or, alternatively, of hate and persecution as against grief, regret, and gratitude; the needs for contact and for autonomy; and the loyalties to past and to present relationships. Thus, while the post-Freudians insist on the importance of relationships in every aspect of life, they underline the conflicts that pervade each instance of this truth.

Rather than emphasizing the origin of the self in the relations with others, the modern Jewish philosophers accentuate the ways that others bring the mature self to fruition. They find that the fullness of the person requires connections both with other humans and with God. Mere existence is possible bereft of the divine, although that way of living is equally missing significant relationships with other persons. The life of inauthenticity is portrayed by Buber in terms of the I-It, Rosenzweig as the fear of death, and Levinas as the ennui of the life of egoism. Through a transformative contact with God, the relation to other persons is opened: Buber's mutuality and reciprocity of the I-Thou, Rosenzweig's love of the neighbor, and Levinas' responsibility. The relationship with God leads to a life of meaning, purpose, and orientation. Both the fruit and the proof, the sole proof, of the authenticity of that connection is the change in relations with others. For all three philosophers there is a subtle systole and diastole between the relation to the divine and the relation to other persons. This fluctuation is often so discreet that its elements cannot be distinguished. In addition to providing a way to acknowledge astonishment, the term God reflects the transcendent possibilities of the human. Human life is more than a product of the past. Its possibilities for transformation, change, cannot be foreseen. They are incalculable. This way of speaking of the divine is not reductive of the human, but is an effort to formulate a language about human greatness.

The prominence of the term "dependence" in the narratives of the psychoanalysts is paralleled by the philosophers' discussions of responsibility. Responsibility is seen as a, or perhaps the, fundamental quality of authenticity. It points to the self's possibility of transcending itself and its own concerns. Their treatments of responsibility find that this type of connection to the other is not limiting or alienating. Through responsibility the self becomes a person who has direction, freedom from self-concern, and meaning. For the philosophers, when the self forgets itself—and most importantly they indicate that it can—then meaning is discovered or created. However, responsibility is not given by the self, as Kant saw it. Rather, responsibility, obligation, commandment are powerful and directive because they originate from the other. The Jewish philosophers insist upon two essential links between the other and responsibility: obligation follows from relationship, and obligations establish or deepen further relationships. This insight can be put another way, in terms of the connection between responsibility and love. For the philosophers, these two features of life are not in conflict, but continually interact with each other: obligation follows from love, and love (of the neighbor) can also be an obligation.

In one of his long essays on the nature of persons, Buber spoke of the human as fettered surprise, that is, in terms of the dialectic between the past which cannot be ignored and the future which cannot be calculated. He wrote: "That means that man's action is unforeseeable in its nature and extent, and that even if he were peripheral to the cosmos in everything else, he remains the centre of all surprise in the world. But he is fettered surprise . . ." (1965, 78). Buber's category provides a powerful lens to evaluate the two discourses.

The strength of the psychoanalytic discourse is seen in the ways it understands humans as fettered. It speaks of transformation and change always being in the context of, in some continuity with, past relationships. Relationships in the present must always work out from past dependencies and loyalties. The earliest relations live on in the unconscious and are vividly portrayed in the language of inner objects. However, the psychoanalysts do not have an eloquent language to speak of future possibilities. Is the notion of making up for the not good enough mothering adequate itself to open up the potentialities for health and fullness? Is return or renewal sufficient to speak of what is yet to come? Winnicott's notions of fantasy and play reveal the ways that humans can move beyond the past, can creatively interact with the future. Still, even phantasy may be as much of a limit as an opening, which is one of Klein's most significant insights.

Obviously, the strength of the Jewish philosophers is in terms of their detailed language of surprise. This surprise, the ability to transcend the past and limitations that are regarded as inescapable, is tied, as we have seen, to their understanding of humans' relationship to the transcendent. The fullness of love, speech, and responsibility requires the possibility of a transcending relationship. The corresponding weakness within this discourse revolves around the issue of human fetters. The philosophers do not have a well-developed language to explore the ways that the past, and past relationships, bind us or limit the possibilities in the present. Also, the tensions that pervade every relationship are not prominent in their narratives, even though, more generally, Buber can speak of the conflict of I-It and I-Thou, and Levinas of egoism and responsibility. Still, at most these tensions are seen as alternating for the Jewish philosophers, while the psychoanalysts see them as simultaneous. As insightful as are the philosophical narratives, there are important dimensions ignored in presentations that sometimes appear to be idealized. In all, Flax's insight of the need for multiple narratives to reveal the complexities of human subjectivity (and the interhuman) is confirmed through this evaluation of the psychoanalytic and the philosophical discourses of transference and transcendence.

Notes

1. Mitchell actually distinguishes three models, that of drive, developmental arrest, and relational-conflict (1988, 10). For the purposes of this discussion, the two, more general, opposing options of drive and relational models are being explored.

2. Schafer (1976, 243–44) and Mitchell operationalize features attributed to the unconscious by focusing on notions of self-deception and awareness. Mitchell provides a good overview of the efforts of a number of theorists to move in this direction (1988, 259–66).

3. See the author's article "The Meaning of Hasidut: Martin Buber and Gershom Scholem" (Oppenheim 1981).

4. The complex relationship between philosophy and Judaism in Levinas' writings is explored in Gibbs' *Correlations*, through the rubrics of "Greek" and "Jew" (1992, 158–75).

5. The most explicit treatment of the difficulties in introducing the term "God" into philosophic discourse is found in Levinas' essay "God and Philosophy" (1989, 166–89). Also see his *Ethics and Infinity*.

6. See the discussion of Fairbairn's endopsychic structure in chapter 2.

7. See endnote 16 in the introductory chapter of this book.

8. Schafer presents an important discussion of transference as a present phenomenon in his essay "The Interpretation of Transference and the Conditions for Loving" (in Esman, ed., 1990, 418–19).

9. Also see Levinas' statement "Meaning is the face of the Other, and all recourse to words takes place already within the primordial face to face of language" (1969, 206).

10. Freud wrote: "Sexual love is undoubtedly one of the chief things in life, and the union of mental and bodily satisfaction in the enjoyment of love is one of its culminating peaks" (1990, 46).

11. Mitchell has written: "Psychoanalysis, for Winnicott, is a treatment aimed at the texture of experience, its richness, its felt reality, rather than at functional capacity" (1993, 23).

12. See the discussion of Rosenzweig's view of the powers of speech in chapter 1.

13. Buber has a long critical essay on Kierkegaard, "The Question to the Single One," (1965, 40–82).

14. Levinas once said: "The best way of encountering the Other is not even to notice the color of his eyes" (1985, 85). He meant by this that nothing in the other should distract from or undermine the first feature of the encounter, the immensity of obligation.

5

Luce Irigaray: An/Other Fling with the Philosophers

> To put it another way; the option left to me was to have a fling with the philosophers . . . (Irigaray 1985, 150)

> Sexual difference is one of the important questions of our age, if not in fact the burning issue. (Irigaray 1991b, 165)

A CONSIDERATION OF THE WORK of Luce Irigaray adds a unique and important element to the examination of the two sets of narratives that we have been discussing. Irigaray is a philosopher and a psychoanalyst whose work weaves together these two strands to challenge both disciplines. She confronts them in the name of that sex/gender, woman, who has been left voiceless and faceless by the philosophic and psychoanalytic masters. She insists that ethics forbids philosophic or psychoanalytic works from continuing their dereliction of women. Irigaray is also salient here because her critical writings on Emmanuel Levinas constitute a direct intersection of the two fields. While her training and vocabulary reflect the post-Lacanian stream of psychoanalysis, which is not the heritage of any of the psychoanalytic theorists explored in the earlier chapters, there are certainly many common features between her work and, especially, that of Klein and the object relations thinkers. Thus, an examination of the thought of Irigaray offers an exceptional opportunity to assess and to creatively tease out new possibilities from the modern Jewish philosophers and, indirectly, the post-Freudian psychoanalysts.

This chapter will take its point of departure from two essays that Irigaray wrote on Levinas: "The Fecundity of the Caress" of 1983 and "Questions to Emmanuel Levinas: On the Divinity of Love" of 1987. The examination of these essays will constitute the body of this chapter, enumerating the particular objections she brings to her dialogue with Levinas as well as elucidating some of her principal philosophic themes. At the end, Irigaray's dialogue with Levinas will be extended to include Rosenzweig and Buber. Irigaray's probing albeit appreciative attitude brings out important deficiencies as well as perspicacious features in the work of the other two Jewish philosophers. The chapter will conclude with an overview of what the introduction of Irigaray has added to the narration of the interhuman.

The full title of Irigaray's first essay, "The Fecundity of the Caress: A Reading of Levinas, *Totality and Infinity*, section IV, B, 'The Phenomenology of Eros,'" places it among her other careful readings and probings of specific fragments by such influential thinkers as Plato, Hegel, Nietzsche, and Freud. It is helpful to first portray what Levinas is doing in that section, before turning to Irigaray's detailed critique. Levinas' treatment of the erotic in *Totality and Infinity* is one of the major topics in the fourth and last part of the book, which he titles "Beyond the Face." The title indicates one of the central interests of the treatment, which is to compare and differentiate the erotic relation from the relation to the ethical, that is, to "the face." As we have seen, Levinas insists that the ethical relation is foundational both for every other relation and to what constitutes the essence of a person, that is, to subjectivity. In this context, the erotic does not "precede" or appear "before" the face, but is depicted as "beyond the face." In the ethical relation the subject is hostaged in responsibility to the other. The other stands in his or her height—in this sense stands as transcendent, and obligates or commands. The face of the other also reminds one of her or his vulnerability, which again translates into the necessity of the subject's absolute concern for the other. This concern, this obsession with the other, shatters the self-interest that also defines the human. Levinas sees self-interest and ethics as diametrically opposed, which he reminds us in the "Phenomenology of Eros," through this statement: "The fact that in existing for another I exist otherwise than in existing for me is morality itself" (1961, 261). However, for Levinas, while the erotic relationship is with another who is different from the self, beyond or above the self, erotic love obviously refers back to the self. It contains the element of pleasure: the self's pleasure. The pleasure is located not just in the physical sensations but also in the fact that one is loved by the other. One loves the other and also loves "the love the Beloved bears me" (1961, 266). In this sense, erotic love is "dual egoism" (1961, 266), according to Levinas. Unlike the clarity of the differentiation between self-interest and the ethical, Levinas finds that the erotic is "*the equivocal* par excellence." He writes: "this simultaneity of [egotistic] need and [transcendent] desire, of concupiscence and transcendence, tangency of the avowable and the unavowable, constitutes the originality of the erotic which, in this sense, is *the equivocal* par excellence" (1961, 255).[1]

Levinas' second interest, beyond the comparison between the ethical and the erotic, in this section of the text is to present an accurate account, a phenomenology, of the erotic, in-itself. Levinas speaks of the texture of the erotic in terms of the materiality, even "ultramateriality," of the body. The body reveals itself, in nudity, and, at the same time, keeps something hidden. Yet, even the partial revealing exhibits too much. It is immodest and profaning. He writes: "Ultramateriality . . . designates the exhibitionist nudity of an exorbitant presence coming . . . already profaning and wholly profaned, as if it had forced the interdiction of a secret" (1961, 256). For Levinas, the caress also expresses the ambiguous erotic contact with the other. It is a seeking that is never fulfilled: a touch with something that is tender, vulnerable, a presence that in its passivity does not seem to be fully there. Further, voluptuosity plays an important role in Levinas' phenomenology. He sees it as a hunger for the secret still behind nudity. The voluptuous points to the lover reveling in this passion and in the passion of the other.

A pervasive feature of Levinas' examination of the erotic is that the other, and not the self or subject, is gendered as "the feminine," or in terms of "femininity." In its first appearance the term "femininity" is defined as "the simultaneity or the equivocation of this fragility and this weight of non-signifyingness" (1961, 257). Non-signifyingness means that the body presents itself in the erotic as material and raw, not symbolizing or pointing to anything beyond itself. The treatment of the feminine continually reinforces the theme of the equivocation of the erotic. For example, Levinas writes: "In the feminine face the purity of expression is already troubled by the equivocation of the voluptuous. Expression is inverted into indecency, already close on to the equivocal which says less than nothing, already laughter and raillery" (1961, 260). In the course of the analysis of the other in the erotic, femininity, the feminine, or what is tied to "her," is presented or depicted in the following ways:

> The feminine essentially violable and inviolable, the "Eternal Feminine" . . . the untouchable in the very contact of voluptuosity. (1961, 258)

> The virgin remains ungraspable, dying without murder, swooning, withdrawing into her future. (1961, 258)

> The frailty of femininity invites pity for what, in a sense, is not yet, disrespect for what exhibits itself in immodesty and is not discovered despite the exhibition, that is, is profaned. (1961, 262)

> Where the chastity and decency of the face abides at the limit of the obscene yet repelled but already close at hand and promising—is the primordial event of feminine beauty. (1961, 263)

> The beloved, returned to the stage of infancy without responsibility—this coquettish head, this youth, this pure life "a bit silly"—has quit her status as a person. The face fades . . . in ambiguity, into animality. (1961, 263)

> The face, all straightforwardness and frankness, in its feminine epiphany dissimulates allusions, innuendos. It laughs under the cloak of its own expression, without leading to any specific meaning, hinting in the empty air, signaling the less than nothing. (1961, 264)

Irigaray's Critique

Irigaray's "The Fecundity of the Caress" is a philosophic and poetic commentary on Levinas' approach and presentation featured above. It has two major components that are combined, sometimes even in the same sentence. Irigaray contests the overall treatment of eros, and also offers her own insights into the tremendously creative powers of erotic love. The first component connects this text with many of her other essays and book chapters that carefully explore the images, especially the direct and indirect sexual and gender images, that philosophers have utilized to convey their ideas. In examinations of Aristotle, Hegel, a host of modern philosophers, as well as a classic reflection on Plato's myth of the cave,[2] she seeks to reveal, in the words of one commentator, "the imaginary body of philosophy, to show the sexual dynamics at work in the theoretical constructions of philosophy" (Whitford 1991, 103). In these writings, which constitute her flings "with the philosophers," as expressed in the quotation at the beginning of this chapter, Irigaray turns psychoanalysis upon philosophy, illuminating the underside of the writings of the philosophers, where hierarchical tensions, exclusions, and sexual images prop up the edifice of rational discourse.

The second component in Irigaray's essay is the poetic vision of the fullness of love between lovers, and of the caress as love's quintessential vehicle, its preliminary albeit perfecting "gesture" (1986, 232). This element is uncommon in her treatment of other philosophers. As counter-testimony it stands as a critique, but it is also more than that. It is a choreographed dance with someone she clearly appreciates. It is part of Irigaray's fling with Levinas, as well as her plea. Levinas' analysis of fecundity, in *Totality and Infinity*, follows the section that examines the caress. The title of Irigaray's essay, "The Fecundity of the Caress," encapsulates her view that erotic love, especially through its expression in the caress, is fecund in-itself.

In this adventure with Levinas, Irigaray exhibits many qualities found throughout her work, and thus the essay provides a good introduction to her more general standpoint and themes. The essay displays moments of stylistic flourish and heights, along with subtle varied repetitions. Allusions to Levinas and connections to her own overall oeuvre are often very oblique. For example, while there are continual references to Levinas' exposition, there is only one direct quotation. This example of criticism by way of absence is part of her unique style, which is partially explained at the end of her magnum opus, *Speculum*, in these words:

> Precise references in the form of notes or punctuation indicating quotation have often been omitted. Because in relation to the working of theory, the/a woman fulfills a twofold function—as mute outside that sustains all systematicity; as a maternal and still silent ground that nourishes all foundations—she does not have to conform to the codes theory has set up for itself. (1985a, 365)[3]

The ensuing pages will at best unravel only a few of the allusions and provide only a hint of the poetic power that her essay conveys. It will begin by exploring Irigaray's contention that Levinas' presentation reinforces the dereliction or abandonment of women, a situation that, moreover, pervades Western philosophy and culture. Following this will be an examination of her ode to the potentialities of love, its fecundity.

Irigaray writes: "The voice of she who sings and calls to the lover is still missing here" (1986, 249). This is one of the major themes in her essay. While Levinas illuminates the beauty of the caress and the access to the other through the body and touch, that other, which he continually engenders as female, is never, herself, an active subject, according to Irigaray. She has no voice, can neither call nor sing to her lover. Starting at an early part of her essay, Irigaray makes the distinction between the loved one (*l'aimée*) and the beloved (*l'amante*). This is not an insignificant differentiation for Irigaray. She reports and repeats that the active lover for Levinas is male, while the passive loved one is female. Levinas speaks, as she finds it, of the female as "The loved one. Not the beloved. Necessarily an object, not a subject in touch, like him . . ." (1986, 238). Since the loved one in Levinas' presentation is not a subject, she is frozen (1986, 238), without responsibilities (1986, 242), and powerless (1986, 245). Despite his best intentions, Levinas abandons women as passive, even in the purportedly mutual exchange that constitutes eros. This dismissal of women's subjectivity and power allows her to place Levinas in a list of philosophic thinkers, best exemplified by Aristotle, who equate women with passivity.[4]

In the context of what should be a mutual, amorous exchange, this portrayal of women's passivity translates the woman into a figure without desire. She writes: "Forgetting that I exist as a desiring subject. . . . Desire for nothing—the abolition of the other's willing, which would become a nonwilling" (1986, 253). According to Irigaray, nowhere does Levinas explore, or even consider, what female desire might be: how it might be similar and different from male desire. Irigaray alludes to what might be characteristic of female desire: "tuned differently to the rhythm of the earth and the stars" (1986, 238); "intimately tied to universal motions and vibrations" (1986, 238); perhaps, the celebration of the caress itself ?[5]—which, again, at least makes the point that this interest in specifically female desire is lacking in Levinas' treatment. In the wider arena of philosophy, this topic broadens into Irigaray's contention that unless sexual difference is recognized, unless women are seen in their specificity, speaking, acting, desiring in their own right, they are betrayed.[6]

Without desire, women are left to the theater of the feminine, that is, femininity, and celebrated as the guardians, the protectress, of "modesty." Femininity thus refers to the woman's submissive role in the arena of masculine desire. Women are not granted the right to express their desire, only allowed to entice, seduce, beckon, thrill those who are the actors in the male game of eros. They put on evocative clothes, masks (1986, 234), all of which indicates that they are only for the other and never in the least for themselves. In Irigaray's words, the loved one, "deprived of the suppleness of her amorous mobility," dressed in "the brilliance of her finery," is ultimately frozen "into the shapes that separate her from herself" (1986, 238). Irigaray regards the discourse about modesty as another subterfuge for insisting on women's erotic passivity. Women are made to appear too modest to express their own desire, to act as agents of their own passions (1986, 246).

In her wider work, Irigaray refers to Freud's psychoanalytic narrative of the development of women as making normative this relinquishment of desire. While Freud portrays the infant girl as having the same libido as the boy, later, following the Oedipal complex, she takes up her "normal," sanctioned role, which consists of the masquerade of femininity (1985, 36). In *This Sex Which Is Not One*, Irigaray contends: "In the last analysis, the female Oedipus complex is woman's entry into a system of values that is not hers, and in which she can 'appear' and circulate only when enveloped in the needs/desires/fantasies of others, namely, men" (1985, 134).

Irigaray's examination of Levinas' withdrawal of agency from women extends to the (Lacanian) topic of the gaze. Men's attitude, "gaze" (1986, 236), toward women as objects and not subjects of erotic love, reflects women's wider status as possessions in the patriarchal linguistic, social, and political economies of the West. In this "male territory" of possession and "consumption," the woman is not an active subject, but "remains without an identity or a passport" (1986, 239). This political critique of Levinas' presentation represents a broad feature within Irigaray's extensive corpus. In a number of texts she examines such diverse thinkers as Freud and Levi-Strauss, who proffer founding social myths about the establishment of society.[7] Both believe that society is first established by agreements between men about how women should be distributed. Women thus become the central objects of circulation, that currency, which permits the closed system of patriarchal civilization to embark. In *The Sex Which is Not One*, Irigaray writes, for example, that it is "women's bodies—through their use, consumption, and circulation—[that] provide for the condition of making social life and culture possible" (1985, 171). In contrast to this, Irigaray envisions the situation where feminine desire is allowed to bloom, enriching the amorous exchange between couples, as destabilizing this exclusionary compact with its deadly economy.

A second theme of Irigaray's analysis, in addition to that of the dismissal of women as subjects and agents, concerns her contention that with Levinas the erotic is reduced to masculine self-love. She brings together her critique of the lack of agency of the woman who is loved, with the idea of man's love for himself, in her comments following the solitary direct reference that she provides to Levinas. Irigaray quotes Levinas about the "frailty," "her *regime* of tenderness," of the "loved one" (1986, 245). She then introduces this statement: "The loved one's frailty and weakness are the means for the lover to experience self-love, as a loved one who is powerless" (1986, 245). Women's enforced passivity clears the field for "a subject who wishes himself to be the sole master of desire" (1986, 247). Since the male lover has divested the loved woman of her desire, whose desire could he be experiencing? As we saw, through her feminine costume the woman exhibits *his* desire. The "brilliance of her finery" is the "mirror"[8] (1986, 238) for or "screen" upon which male desire is reflected. This love which "encounters only self as object" (1986, 246) certainly fails to acknowledge difference or respect the "irreducible strangeness of the one and the other" (1986, 251).

In some of her other texts, Irigaray labels this self-reflective love "homosexual" (1985, 193).[9] She, again, links it to woman's role as the passive "occasion for mediation, transaction, transition, transference, between man and his fellow man, indeed between man and himself" (1985, 193). In contrast to this, she believes that only women can represent the true other for men. Sexual difference is for her the ultimate and quintessential difference that humans experience. When it is forgotten, ignored, or overshadowed, one sex, the male, is left without any other, without limits. She writes in *Sexes et Parentes*: "the community of men needs people, who are people in every way to enable them to understand themselves and find their limits. Only women can play this role" (quoted in Whitford 1991, 36).

The topic of the "son" reinforces Irigaray's view that Levinas' treatment of the erotic is circumscribed by masculine sameness. While Levinas sees the son as representing the father's future that does not lead back to himself, Irigaray is not convinced that the son introduces substantial difference or a real other.

She writes: "The aspect of fecundity that is only witnessed in the son obliterates the secret of difference. As the lover's means of return to himself outside himself, the son closes the circle" (1986, 245). As the most important product of erotic love, given the way that fecundity follows eros for Levinas, Irigaray believes that the son detracts from the female other as well as the significance of erotic love as an event in-itself. The loved one becomes "a bridge between the Father and the son," important only "for the shelter that she gives to the son—prior to his birth" (1986, 245). Additionally, the "fecundity, in the here and now, of lovemaking" (1986, 244), is abandoned for the father's "future as a man, his horizon, society, and security" (1986, 245).

In other works, Irigaray develops further her critique of the role of the son in accounts of the erotic. She sees it as a particularly male concern, part of the male economy, that the erotic must be productive in terms of children, especially of the male sex. Freud, for example, centers his developmental narrative and the treatment of sexuality solely on the reproductive organs (1985a, 18). For him, woman's sexuality is concentrated exclusively in the vagina. In addition, she quotes Freud in his insistence that "a mother is brought only unlimited satisfaction by her relation to a son" (1985, 42). Irigaray's view of "the fecundity of the caress" will respond to the first problem, of devaluing the importance of the erotic in-itself, and her query "but why a son and not a daughter, her other self?" (1986, 240) echoes the second.

Irigaray sees masculine sameness as deadly and destructive, especially of the erotic. In responding to Levinas, she writes, for example: "Sameness, quantitatively polemical when it comes to its place, occupies my flesh, demarcates and subdivides my space, lays siege to and sets up camp on my horizon—making it uninhabitable for me and inaccessible for the lover" (1986, 235). In the larger context, her examination of the domination of masculine sameness has often focused on what she designates as the imaginary and the symbolic. This conception of the imaginary is influenced by Lacanian psychoanalysis and by modern French philosophy. For Lacan the imaginary is that pre-Oedipal stage, before the access to language and culture, when the infant's identity is being pieced together by way of its bodily images. The imaginary becomes unconscious with the Oedipal stage, and refers also to life and death, and family relations. At times, the imaginary is interpreted more widely as including what in everyday language is described as the imagination and imaginary images. The symbolic represents the social arena. Here language, and symbols more widely, expresses unconscious features of the imaginary as well as the regnant social realities.[10]

Irigaray's overall approach to philosophy often draws upon her understanding of the symbolic. She insists that the rational discourse of philosophy both reflects and hides the domination of the male morphology of the symbolic.

Such philosophic expressions of "rationality" as the principles of identity and non-contradiction, and the focus on the singleness of truth, on strict demarcations and on polemical divisions, prop up the reign of the male morphology.[11] Commenting on Plato's story of the cave, she writes: "Thus, to state everything quite clearly, only the effigies of men's bodies, the words of men, the gaze of men . . . will be available to decide what is true and false" (1985a, 264).

Irigaray's concern for the otherness of sexual difference is expressed in two ways in her essay on Levinas. First, as we have seen, it is manifested in her effort to uncover and contest the power of masculine images and symbols. Second, it is reflected by the pervasive use of female metaphors and images that ground the possibilities for women's own identities and for an eros of full partnership. Exemplifying this second direction, in speaking of the erotic she refers to "a mucous shelter that extends from the depth to the heights" (1986, 233); to the lover: "Beneath her veils, she keeps secret watch over a threshold. A slight opening onto the depths or abysses of all language, of all birth and generation" (1986, 241); and, on (almost any) one page, to "porosity that moves from the inside to the outside of the body," "a protective veil," "crossing . . . like a threshold," "touching, touching each other, retouching," "invisible" (1986, 236).[12]

Irigaray's essay is pervaded by an important theme that combines theoretical and methodological concerns. She exposes and challenges the dualism of abyss and transcendence that finds multiple expressions in Levinas' discourse. Sometimes this dualism is played out in the relative positions of the female loved one and the male lover. Repeatedly she writes that "The loved one would be relegated to the abyss so that the lover might be sent back to the heights" (1986, 241); or, alternately, "The lover sent back to the transcendental, the loved one plunged into the abyss" (1986, 233). Metaphorically, the "subterranean, the submarine" may substitute for abyss, while "light and fire" may stand for the transcendental (1986, 239). Of utmost importance, this dualism is conceptually represented in the initial separation of eros and ethics.

Levinas' dualistic separation of eros from ethics leads to a host of consequences and is tied to multiple allusions. According to Irigaray, this division is enacted by assigning the female, in "her nudity" (1986, 236), to the former, and the male to the latter. A first result of this is that the woman is left out of the site of the ethical. In Irigaray's words: "She quits the locus of all responsibilities, her own ethical site" (1986, 241), and becomes "the irresponsible woman, the loved one" (1986, 245). Further, it appears that it is through the very action of rejecting or at least stepping beyond the erotic and the woman, that the male enters into the height and the future of the ethical. In transcending the erotic and woman, "the lover goes beyond love and voluptuousness, towards the ethical" (1986, 245). Irigaray repeats her understanding of this process in these statements: "For the lover, the transcendence of the other justifies this infidelity of love. Returning to his God in a discontinuity of *eros*" (1986, 242), and "Dragging the lover down into the abyss so that, from these nocturnal depths, he lets himself be carried off into the absolute future [of ethics]" (1986, 238).

The dualism extends further, with woman characterized by or identified with the child or animal, and again, the male with the ethical and transcendental. Irigaray writes that "the loved one is relegated to infancy and animality" (1986, 252) and of "The loved one relegated to the inwardness that is not one because it is abysmal, animal, infantile, prenuptial; and the lover, to a solitary call to his God" (1986, 244). She contends that the dualisms that infect Levinas' language, and philosophy more widely, are the result, from a psychoanalytic perspective, of male splitting and projection. This is the point of her question "Does the lover not lay upon the loved one what he cannot see in himself?" (1986, 253). The separation of eros and ethics at the same time expresses and masks the male splitting off of erotic and passionate elements. These "lower" attributes, sometimes seen as childlike and animallike, are then projected or wrapped upon women. Thus, we read: "Wrapping her up in what he cannot bear of his own identity . . . she surrenders as a child or animal" (1986, 253). The splitting and projection leave men as the illusionary masters of the "higher," the "divine," domains of ethics and reason (1986, 245).

The dualism and splitting have two other broad consequences. First, relegating woman to the realm of the child and the animal cuts men's ties to nature and the cosmos. She writes:

> When the lover relegates her to infancy, animality, or maternity, he leaves unsolved, in part, this mystery of a relation to the cosmos. What is lacking is participation in the construction of a world that does not forget natural generation and the human being's part in the preservation of its efflorescence. (1986, 239)

The quotation indicates that as a result of the dualism between the erotic, matter, and nature on the one side, and ethics, the transcendent, and the divine on the other, men fail to recognize their connection to nature and ignore their responsibility for its preservation. They become unable to see the importance of nature's rhythms, such as birth, growth, and death. Not placing themselves within the natural, of which the body is a microcosm, they distance and objectify nature as something out there. Nature (and woman) is seen as an object, something to be possessed, consumed, mastered: something "to be exploited endlessly, carelessly, irretrievably" (1986, 239).

A second consequence of the male splitting and projection is that men refuse to acknowledge death and the innate human death drives. These are identified with the other who is woman. Irigaray writes: "Touching that which is not contained within the limits of his flesh, of his body, the lover risks an infinite outpouring in dead being. He who has no connection to his own death puts the other at a permanent risk of loss of self in the wrong infinity" (1986, 245–46). The death drives, first labeled as such by Freud, are the self-destructive impulses such as the drives to repeat, to return to stasis, immobility or even non-existence.[13] According to Irigaray, they have been allocated to women, along with the body, nature, and death. Touching "the female sex" becomes symbolic of touching death (1986, 253), and creativity and generation—the opposite of the death drives—are made synonymous with male transcendence.

An Ode to Eros

The focus, which initially has isolated the critical constituents in Irigaray's treatment of Levinas, will now shift to her alternative portrayal of eros. This exciting, exuberant feature of the writing actually constitutes the major chord in her song. Often the critical dimension only arises out of Irigaray's singing of the nature of an eros that reinvests the beloved with subjectivity and desire. Of this love she serenades:

> The loving act is neither an explosion nor an implosion but an indwelling. Dwelling with the self, and with the other—while letting him/her/it go. Remembering, while letting be, and with the world. Remembering the act, not as a simple discharge of energy but as a quality of intensity, sensation, color, rhythm. The intensity would be, or would constitute, the dimensions of the dwelling, always in becoming. Never finished. Unfolding itself during and between the terms of encounters. (1986, 252)

And of the caress:

> This caress would start off from a distant point. A tact that informs the sense of touch, attracts, and comes to rest on the threshold of the approach. Neither paralyzing nor breaking in, the lovers would beckon to each other, at first from far away. A salutation that means the cross of a threshold. Pointing out the space of a love that has not yet been profaned. The entrance into the dwelling, or the temple, where each one would invite the other, and themselves, to enter in, also into the divine. (1986, 248)

The hallmark of Irigaray's ode to erotic love is the portrayal of eros' creative powers. This fecundity of the caress and of erotic love is, of course, in contrast to Levinas' seeing these powers in terms of progeny, especially the birth of the son. Concerning love's potency, she writes: "Searching for what has not yet come into being, for himself, he invites me to become what I have not yet become. To realize a birth still in the future" (1986, 233); and of the powers of the caress: "The caress seeks out the not yet of the beloved's blossoming" (1986, 251). For Irigaray, love's fecundity is "a future coming . . . the call to birth of the self and the other" (1986, 232). It occurs through the activity of each, and demands the taking of risk, the opening to new possibilities of identity and life, by both (1986, 247). Passionately dual, Irigaray's descriptions of eros alternate between his hands (1986, 233) and her greeting (1986, 248), and together: "Each one welcoming the birth of the other" (1986, 235).

Still, how can the caress lead to a second birth "of the self and the other"? What can it bring forth that was not there earlier? The touch of the other gives one a new sense of their skin, it gives birth to an active awareness of the borders of his or her body. Irigaray writes: "these palms with which he approaches without going through me, give me back the borders of my body" (1986, 233). The love of the other brings forth a confirmation of the self in its difference and its specific identity (1986, 235, 248). It gives a revitalized sense of life. Irigaray concludes, simply: "Prior to any procreation, the lovers bestow on each other—life" (1986, 235).

One way Irigaray indicates the fertile powers of love is to view it as itself constituting a new creation. Love is a third in addition to the two lovers. Alternately, she sees it as a new covering or even dwelling that is built by the two. She writes: "Dressing the one and the other without-within, within-without, in a garment that neither evokes, invokes . . . but contemplates and adorns it, always for a first time, with in-finite, un-finished flesh" (1986, 232). At another point we find: "The house of flesh, which allows them to remember each other, to call to each other—even from a distance" (1986, 254). As with many other features of Irigaray's panegyric to eros, love as a dwelling or house is an indirect response to Levinas. In *Totality and Infinity*, Levinas spoke of the home as a comforting dwelling, featuring a feminine face, where the active male took refuge from the world (Levinas 1969, 154–56).[14]

An important characteristic of Irigaray's account of erotic love is its capacity to unbind and make free the partners. Love itself unbound—"*Eros* prior to any *eros* defined or measured as such" (1986, 231)—could not be creative, if it were constrained by all of the limits, the assigned roles, forces of domination, dualisms, and hierarchies of the patriarchal social order. These realities might pervade the lovers' lives prior to coming to each other, but eros has the power to release them. Love's capacities are not even limited by what appears as the most intransigent of structures, space and time (1986, 248). Overall, she writes:

> Voluptuousness can reopen and reverse this conception and construction of the world. It can return to the evanescence of subject and object. To the lifting of all

> schemas by which the other is defined. . . . *Eros* can arrive at the innocence that never took place with the other as other. At the nonregressive in-finity of pathetic feeling for the other. (1986, 231–32)

How is this possible? Is this merely a utopian desire? For Irigaray, touch corresponds to the realm of the imaginary, while it is the symbolic, language and all the other types of exchange, that reflect and constitute orders of domination. There is cross influence between the imaginary and the symbolic, and it is possible for the imaginary to escape the strictures of the symbolic as well as to have an impact upon it. Thus, earlier and prior to the institutes of the symbolic, touch, the caress, promises another approach. In her words:

> Prior to and following any positioning of the subject, this touch binds and unbinds two others in flesh that is still, and always, untouched by mastery. . . . Life always open to what happens. To the fleeting touch of what has not yet found a setting. To the grace of a future that none can control. (1986, 232)

Of course, not all expressions of eros exhibit the creative and liberating, even redemptive, features that Irigaray describes in this essay. As she writes in *Passions Elementaires*: "Love may be the becoming which appropriates the other for itself by consuming it, introjecting it into itself, until the other disappears. Or love may be the motor of becoming which allows each its own growth" (cited in Whitford 1991, 61). Much of her essay details the requirements of the redemptive eros. It must respect the differences and otherness of the two partners, remember the original "house of flesh," as well as humans' relation to nature, and overcome such dualisms such as those between pleasure and reproduction, the material/sensible and the divine, the aesthetic and the ethical, and, of course, the erotic and the ethical.

An eros that can be transformative demands, first of all, that the two subjects be allowed to stand in their autonomy and difference. The beloved's subjectivity and desire cannot be merged, submerged, or identified with that of the lover. Irigaray speaks of the caress as that "gesture" that "perfects while abiding by the outlines of the other" (1986, 232). More than even respecting difference, it "seeks out and affirms otherness, while protecting it" (1986, 232). While erotic love may destabilize prior structures, and ties the two bodies together "within and without," it still acknowledges sexual difference. In her words, love recognizes that "the lover and the beloved's horizons" are "irreducible" (1986, 248).

In speaking of the creativity of eros to awaken an "amorous" birth (1986, 233), Irigaray insists that the new life would be stillborn unless the first birth out of the maternal womb is remembered. Only the lover who recalls the central place of the mother has the power to evoke the creativity of the beloved.

Thus, we find: "As he caresses me, he bids me neither to disappear nor to forget but, rather, to remember the place where, for me, the most intimate life holds itself in reserve" (1986, 233). The parallelism is seen in the line, again in terms of the woman lover: "Without respect for the one who gave me my body and without enthusiasm for the one who gives it back to me in his amorous awakening" (1986, 233). The voice of the beloved's welcome cannot be heard, if the mother's voice has been silenced. Profanation, a term recurrent in Levinas' description and echoed, if not mimicked, in Irigaray's, refers for her especially to the forgetting of the person/place of the first birth. Profanation is a betrayal of the fullness of love and, for Irigaray, "always designates . . . the presentiment of the first dwelling place" (1986, 233–34).

This refrain about the respect for both the mother and the other woman plays a significant role in many of Irigaray's writings. The abolishment of women as subjects in their own right begins by obscuring mothers' active role in the gestation and birth of children. Irigaray's many references to the history of this covering over begins with her examinations of Plato and Aristotle. Plato's narrative of the cave is an inverted birth story that disparages the cave/womb in favor of the "truly" creative power of the (male) sun. For Aristotle, man's seed is the only active element in birth, the woman is merely a receptacle.[15]

In the essay, Irigaray often introjects the term "substitution." She warns that the beloved of the erotic relationship cannot be substituted for by any other, and also forbids the substitution of the beloved for the mother. She writes: "When the lovers substitute for, occupy, or possess the site that conceived them, they founder in the unethical, in profanation" (1986, 233), and, "Wrapping her up . . . he places her, secretly, in the maternal position" (1986, 253). In addition to questioning Levinas' description of the ethical relationship where the self in its responsibility substitutes for the other, Irigaray's use of the term substitution refers to the unconscious process by which the woman/wife is sought as a substitution for the repressed or erased mother. An ethics that includes eros, on the other hand, acknowledges the original creative power of the mother and the maternal line. It also respects the uniqueness of the beloved, and has no need to replace her.

The tie to nature, what Irigaray exclaims as "this mystery of a relation to the cosmos" (1986, 239) is another feature of the human that must be recalled if eros is to fully enliven. The erotic dies as a giving and receiving if humans are not appreciated as natural creatures. As we saw, when solely women are identified with nature, a host of repercussions follows. Among these are men's estrangement from the rhythms of nature—including death—and the denial of their responsibility for their own death drives. Further, ignoring human's connection to nature allows men to treat nature as an exploitable commodity. Irigaray's vision of eros, on the other hand, "does not forget natural generation and the human being's part in the preservation of its efflorescence" (1986, 239). Finally, the reaffirmation of the place of nature within a conception of the erotic reclaims the terminology of "infancy" and "animality." When no longer split off and projected upon women--and thus also allowed to stand as opposed to the human, the infant and animal come to represent the passion and innocence of love. Not allowing these words to be denigrated, Irigaray illuminates that fecund love in terms of "a childlike trust, an animal exuberance" (1986, 235).

Irigaray's counter-testimony to erotic love overrides many of the oppositions that she discovered in Levinas' work. Among these are the aesthetic and the ethical, the sensible/material and the transcendental, and, of course, the erotic and the ethical. Irigaray takes a number of approaches to overturn the dualism between the aesthetic and the ethical. In one instance, she focuses on the face of the loved one aglow after the act of love. Irigaray speaks of the "beauty" of this face, unlike the masked face in all its feminine finery.[16] In her description: "The loved one's beauty announces the fulfillment of the flesh. More beautiful, or differently beautiful, after lovemaking than in all her shows and finery . . ." (1986, 235). This beauty indicates the fulfillment of the intimacy and creativity of eros, and also illuminates "the aesthetics and ethics" of love (1986, 235). Continuing the effort to repossess the significance of the aesthetic, Irigaray compares the creators of love to sculptors and architects. She writes: "Like sculptors who are going to introduce themselves, entrust themselves to one another for a new delivery into the world" (1986, 237), and: "Architects of beauty who fashion enjoyment—a very subtle material. Letting it be and building with it, while respecting the approach, the threshold, the intensity" (1986, 254). Irigaray's criticism of Levinas' opposition between pleasure and the ethical may be placed under this rubric of the aesthetic/ethical dualism. The critique of the way pleasure is usually disparaged is a recurrent theme in her work,[17] which is referred to in the essay when she writes: "Pleasure . . . is presented as an amputation of being's ecstasy and not as a fulfillment. . . . Never up to what is expected. Never ethical" (1986, 252).

The division between the sensible/material and the transcendental is at the heart of Irigaray's argument with Levinas. Many of her writings collapse the two sides, through the notion of the sensible transcendental.[18] She holds that when the two sides are opposed, as they are by Levinas, this indicates that the highest realm—the ethical, divine—can only be reached when the everyday, sensible, material is forsaken. Since women are often seen as representatives of the latter, men's approach to the transcendent comes at the cost of thrusting women into the abyss, as we have seen. Irigaray insists that the transcendent permeates the sensible and material, or, said in another way, that the divine inheres in the flesh.

We find: "Her attraction for the divine that becomes incarnate—in the light, in the contemplation of the universe and the other. The divine revealed in its also sensible dimensions" (1986, 250). From another angle, it is the caress and love that bridge the sensible and the transcendent. For example, she asks whether the caress should not be seen to "attain that most intimate dwelling place. . . . In and through a mucous shelter that extends from the depths to the heights? From the most subterranean to the most celestial?" (1986, 233). Additionally, the notion of threshold, which appears throughout her essay, also represents the concrete tie between material and transcendent.

Irigaray's essay is filled with references to the divine and to God. Levinas uses the term "God" in key sections of his philosophic works, and, thus, through her use of the term, Irigaray concurs with Levinas' position that the word has an appropriate place in philosophic discourse. Whereas for some feminist critiques the word "God" is highly suspect, Irigaray believes that it cannot just be discarded. While her conception of the divine appears to be very close to that of the nineteenth century "atheistic theologian" Ludwig Feuerbach, and his understanding of God as a projection of the highest human attributes, she holds that the term still has important psychological and cultural meanings.

Irigaray contests the material/divine polarity and affirms the divine dimensions of the body, flesh, and the gestures of eros. She speaks of the need to perceive God in the beloved's acts of love. She writes: "in the here and now, he [God] is already held out/withheld: in the beloved's sensibility. In the creation that she perpetuates. . . . God of the universe, God of the fecundity of a future coming, which is also preserved in the beloved" (1986, 240). Together the lovers evoke God: "The one for the other, the mediators of a secret, a force, and an order that touches also on the divine" (1986, 242). God is witnessed in that risking of one's present identity that the giving of the self in love requires: "The fecundity of God would be witnessed in the uncalculating generosity with which I love, up to the point of risking myself with the other" (1986, 247). Irigaray speaks of the divine in terms of the new creation, that third or dwelling that is love: "The entrance into the dwelling, or the temple, where each would invite the other, and themselves, to enter in, also into the divine" (1986, 248). Additionally, the figure of the angel briefly appears in her text to bring together passion and the divine. She defines the role of that figure in this way: "This simultaneousness of concupiscence and transcendence is traditionally represented by the angel—the divine messenger" (1986, 242).[19] And, finally, Irigaray points to women's association with God, through her question, "But what of her call to the divine?" (1986, 239).

The crescendo of Irigaray's essay is found in the concluding lines, which also summarize the main theses of her text: "this memory of the flesh as the place of approach is ethical fidelity to incarnation. To destroy it risks suppressing alterity, both God's and the other's. Thus dissolving all possibility of access to transcendence" (1986, 256). Irigaray affirms that unless sexual difference is respected—in fact, celebrated as it appears in love—there can be no recognition of the other. If the loved (woman) is collapsed into man's identity, no other or alterity can possibly remain. Even God then becomes merely a justification or adornment for male sameness. Transcendence, true otherness, is not found by casting eros, the body, and the loved into an abyss. Transcendence can only be approached by way of that caress which awakens and listens for the song of the beloved.

"Questions to Emmanuel Levinas"

"Questions to Emmanuel Levinas: On the Divinity of Love" is Irigaray's second provocative essay on Levinas. Its style is much different than that of "The Fecundity of the Caress." The more direct and explicit prose of "Questions," follows and explains some of the more indirect, allusive, and passionate reflections of "Fecundity." This order of treatments and change in style mirrors the authorship of Irigaray's two major books, *Speculum of the Other Woman* (1974) and its heir, *This Sex Which Is Not One* (1977). In less than nine full pages, "Questions" braids together suggestive queries with terse arguments. The examination of this essay will be give prominence to assessing what new features it adds to Irigaray's specific considerations of Levinas and philosophy. "Questions," is, once again, an intriguing and complicated production, and only a few of its myriad of associations and suggestions can be touched upon here.[20]

Many of Irigaray's earlier objections to Levinas' discussions of the caress, erotic love, and the role of the woman lover are important features of the later essay. She begins "Questions" with the query "Is there otherness outside of sexual difference?" (1991, 109). Irigaray argues that there is no real other in Levinas' phenomenology of erotic love, because the woman lover "is left without her own specific face" (1991, 113). Stripped of identity, subjectivity, of any desire of her own, she becomes the passive recipient or object of man's desire. Labeled as the "feminine other," the woman lover loses respect and responsibility. She is transformed into the other side or underside of man's desire: identified with "animality, perversity, childhood" (1991, 113, 116).

Irigaray offers two reasons that Levinas fails to articulate an ethics where the woman is separate from and "irreducible to" oneself, that is, the man (1991, 110). This departs somewhat from her earlier treatment, in that it includes a few new criticisms as well as grouping elements together in a different manner.

First, Levinas does not know of that "communion in pleasure" (1991, 110), that immediate ecstasy of the flesh where the other is experienced inside and outside of oneself. Here the boundaries between self and other remain, but are also overwhelmed, and through the two partners a new creation is produced. The "third" is not the child, but the reality of that ecstasy itself. Additionally, Irigaray wonders whether sexual difference might account for why Levinas does not seem to have experienced the waves of this particular love that she knows so intimately. She asks: "Is what I am describing here only my pleasure as a woman?" (1991, 111).

The second reason that the feminine other is left unknown is that Levinas "substitutes the son for the feminine" (1991, 111). The father uses the son to confer "being or existence on himself," and to "return to himself" (1991, 111). Irigaray finds that this fails to recognize two types of otherness. It does not respect the feminine other, and it subsumes the son into the project of the father. The son, the person in himself, is appropriated from out of "his own generation" (1991, 112) to be included within the father's identity.

The loss of woman's subjectivity is part of the reason that Levinas' phenomenology of the caress is hollow. When the beloved is only allowed to sustain man's desire, pleasure or voluptuosity has neither concreteness nor delight. Levinas seems satisfied with a caress that never touches the other, that does not break out of its solipsistic mold. Irigaray cites Levinas when she argues that he allows the caress to be remembered as a "fundamental disorder," "something elusive, a play absolutely without aim or plan" (1991, 110). Pleasure then becomes sacrificed to what is hoped will appear in the future. In this way, Levinas transforms "the flesh of the other into his own temporality" (1991, 110).

According to Irigaray, her earlier use of the term "woman lover" (l'amante), rather than "beloved" (l'aimée), was to "signify that the woman can be a subject in love" (1991, 115).[21] For a woman to be this lover, much is required. Among other needs, there must be, at the individual and cultural level, the recognition of the place of mothers. Mothers as physical beings and also in terms of their spiritual heritage have to be inscribed in memory (1991, 115). Further, man's incarnation, that is, his life as a body, as well as his tie to the natural universe, has to be recognized (1991, 113). Men must be seen as more than inhabitants of the social world. Persons have their "roots also in the natural universe" (1991, 113). It is as incarnated, as bodies, that one has a human identity and is, in actuality, able to contribute to the creation of culture.

Irigaray is more explicit in this essay in avowing her respect for Levinas' intention and work. She writes: "After having been so far—or so close—in the approach to the other sex" (1991, 113), and: "He certainly aspires to something else and to the Other" (1991, 116). However, she finds that especially the stereotyped presentation of the feminine other and the eclipsing of pleasure in the caress and erotic love, result in a lack of recognition of woman's existence. His treatment is shipwrecked on "this rock of patriarchy in the very place of carnal love" (1991, 113). Thus, despite his promise, Levinas fails at the most crucial point, for "his philosophy falls radically short of ethics" (1991, 113).

The distinctly new in the essay coalesces around the topic of the biblical "Song of Solomon" ("The Song of Songs"). Irigaray's treatment of this love poem brings together the persistent theme of women's desire along with her understandings of the historical development of gendered images of the divine, the cultural and individual functions of the divine, and her critique of Western, and especially Jewish, monotheism. Irigaray is ambivalent about the "Song of Solomon." At times, it speaks equally of two passionate lovers who give themselves with erotic abandon to each other. She writes that it "tells of the complexity of the nuptials between two loves, the two beloveds . . . who wed each other with all of their senses, with their whole body" (1991, 110). However, the figure of woman as lover is not unambiguous, for the poem equally expresses and represents the clouding of her desire through the eclipsing of her genealogy and her gods.

Irigaray alludes to the homologous fit between the social understanding and position of women, and society's images of the divine. She maintains that at an early period in "the history of women" (1991, 109) when there were goddesses, female sexual organs were indicated in the depiction of women's bodies and the bodies of the goddesses. As goddesses later became solely associated with motherhood and, especially, "mothers of sons" (1991, 109), the sexual organs—and the acknowledgment of women's sexual desire—gave way to representations of the womb. This development corresponds to the rise of male, patriarchal culture, and to "the monopoly of divine power by male gods" (1991, 109). The culture of male gods and of "men-amongst-themselves" (1991, 109) thus buried the earlier social representation of active female gods and matrilineal lines of descent. For Irigaray, the "Song of Solomon," with its hint of female desire, illustrates a transitional stage in this history. It does not express the full coming to fruition of the love between the lovers, because the female lover's desire, genealogy, and divine representations have been taken from her.

Irigaray's more pointed interrogation of monotheism begins with the striking query "Is monotheism wisdom or a patriarchal and masculine passion?" (1991, 114). She elaborates this question through her insistence that there be an ethical interrogation of the "monotheistic religions." This would include an examination of "the sexual attribution of their paradigms, whether these be of God, the ways in which God is referred to (in particular the masculine gender used by language, when he is not represented pictorially), God's commandments, etc." (1991, 114). Following her view of the centrality of images of the divine in the ways that social reality is structured and individual development is understood, Irigaray wonders whether "the peoples of monotheism" are prepared to "assert that their God is a woman?" (1991, 115). The question implies that a true ethical concern for a realignment in the "entire socioreligious economy" would bring people to advocate such an "upheaval in the symbolic order" (1991, 115).

Irigaray's challenge to the notion of God's commandments focuses on the possible relationships between an invisible male God who commands and the appreciation of the divinity of the flesh, especially the other's flesh. She believes that when God's presence is known primarily by means of an abstract law that is enforced upon the body, the importance of the flesh or the carnal is diminished. She, thus, writes: "The law creates invisibility, so that God (in his glory?) cannot be looked upon. What happens to seeing, to flesh, in this disappearance of God?" (1991, 117). Further, Irigaray wonders about the importance of the change from seeing God as one who nourishes the flesh and the senses, to a God of law, of "an inscription which is not immediately legible" (1991, 117). Does this not block the possibility of looking upon "the other's flesh as divine, as the locus of a divine to be shared?" (1991, 117). Finally, the invisible God is still imagined as male. Does not this mean the total social and religious domination of the male image, that "He imposes forms on a nation of men as he might have given forms to a man's body"? (1991, 117).

Irigaray finds it troubling that Levinas does not address the issue of mysticism. She raises the question of whether his "lack of interest" in mysticism mirrors his neglect of "sexual difference?" (1991, 116). More specifically she queries whether mysticism is "not linked to the flesh in its sexual dimension?" (1991, 116). If the answer is affirmative, then the absence of mysticism in Levinas' thought is a symptom of the same philosophic tendencies through which the body and sexuality are excluded. Irigaray follows this observation with her usual refrain that without a sense of the importance of sex, sexual difference, and the divinity of the flesh, the female becomes "reduced to animality, perversity, or a kind of pseudochildhood." (1991, 116).

There are a final group of features in "Questions" that are important to present. These concern relationships in Levinas' work between the phenomenological and the metaphysical, and between philosophy and theology. The first pair, phenomenological/metaphysical, represents a dualism, or in Irigaray's words, reveals the "two levels" of his discourse (1991, 113). The phenomenological is descriptive, and includes the caress, sexual love, and the "alterity" of the feminine. The metaphysical situates the other with the father, and speaks of the "father-son, man-God relation" and of ethics (1991, 113).

This division results in the feminine being separated from the divine and from ethics. In addition, since the phenomenological is ultimately subordinated to the metaphysical, the feminine other is jettisoned from the realm of human identity, freedom and ethics, to be "submerged in animality, perversity, childhood" (1991, 113). The second pair, philosophy/theology, leads Irigaray to a reference to the philosopher Martin Heidegger. She comments that unlike the latter, Levinas "fails to distinguish between the foundations of philosophy and the foundations of theology" (1991, 114). This brings him to hold that "Being is the other or he points to the other as Being" (1991, 114). Irigaray believes that Heidegger's distinction between being(s), that is, specific things that exist, and Being as "an operation of thought" can be said to "respect the other" since it means that the other is considered "within the horizon of Being" (1991, 114).[22]

"Questions" concludes with another reference to the "Song of Solomon," which, actually, ends up framing the whole essay. She uses this poem to reinforce one of her overriding concerns, as well as to close on a note of hope, writing: "But the Song of Solomon bears the trace of the woman as lover, for it says, and repeats: 'do not awaken (my) love until *she* please.' She, the lover, remains a subject in the act of love" (1991, 117).

Recapitulation

The questions Irigaray raises about Levinas' work are profound. A familiarity with her distinct vocabulary, intent, and overall philosophic project, which was one of the major goals of the present excursus, is required to understand the significance of her queries. The essays that we have just examined contain a broad range of topics and interests, which coalesce into two streams. At the outset there stands her insistence on the importance of sexual difference, including her critique of Levinas' positioning and characterization of women and the feminine. The other stream encompasses her views about the nature of and relationships between the erotic and the ethical, and the issues that ensue in terms of Levinas' writings.

As we saw, Irigaray finds that Levinas' work stands in a long line of philosophic systems that ignore sexual difference. In her view, unless this theme is explicit, women are in one way or other dispossessed of their subjectivity. They appear or are implicitly cast as the shadow, underside, supplement, or complement of men's domain. The male then is taken to be synonymous with the whole, real, or rational, and the female with the lacking, illusory, or irrational. Thus, according to Irigaray, the autonomy of women, or better, their reality as persons in-themselves, is dependent on the fundamental acknowledgment that there are two distinct sexes. Irigaray's characteristic designation of women as "this sex which is not one" reiterates the dual claim that the two sexes must not be just elided into a singular human and that women's integrity is tied to an understanding of their uniqueness.

According to Irigaray, Levinas' failure to recognize sexual difference means that women cannot appear in his work as autonomous subjects. Their role as the quintessential "other," reveals that subjectivity arises in his philosophy as exclusively male. In relation to men's desire, women are passive recipients. At most, the feminine is given the role of eliciting/evoking masculine passion through a crafted masquerade. In the wider context of Levinas' treatment of the erotic, women and the feminine are characterized as the underside of men. Thus, for example, the feminine "loved one" is identified with infancy, animality, or perversity and described in terms of the coquettish, silly, and one who dissimulates allusions. The subservience and inferiority of women are also seen in that dualism in which ethics and the male stand for transcendence, while the erotic and the female represent the abyss. She believes that this particular dualism reflects the wider horizon of monotheism, in which the divine is portrayed in exclusively masculine images and metaphors.

The second stream of her inquiry focuses on the nature of the ethical and the erotic. This itself has two tributaries, in keeping with the metaphor, one critical and one constructive. The first includes her analysis of Levinas' description of the ethical and the erotic. For him, the ethical is the highest dimension of the human. It is the place where subjectivity is established through the relation to the other and to the divine. It is, thus, the domain of authenticity and transcendence. Despite Levinas' sensitive phenomenology of the caress, the erotic is not fundamentally a substantive domain. It is where the subject seeks and searches, but never reaches, the other. Eros is the world of the unsubstantial, the shadow, and illusion, as well as the profane and the perverse. This is the realm of the mask and not the face, of finery and nudity, but not fulfillment. Fecundity begins in but transcends eros, an understanding that is represented in the way that Levinas places the figure of the son in the domain of ethics. In light of this hierarchical dualism and the sexate language of ethics/subject/male and eros/other/female women's dereliction is inevitable.

The critical becomes constructive in Irigaray's discussion of what Levinas—or is this typical of males in general? (1991, 111)—fails to recognize in the erotic. For her, it is fecund and liberating. Nothing can be compared to the creativity of the erotic meeting between persons. It allows the two partners to become what they have not been and could not be without the other: opening new possibilities of identity. The powers of the caress and eros can only be likened to birth, a second, amorous birth, because life is given to the one and to the other. Or is the new creation a house of flesh, a home that is built from the respectful touching and intermingling of skin, fluids, and sensations? Erotic love's creative potential is linked to its ability to liberate. Even though the lovers may approach each other in the shackles of symbolic and cultural categories and economies, since eros reaches to the imaginary, it can overturn the false barriers between them. Liberation may also come in the guise of new insight: into the pleasure of the body, the processes of nature, as well as every person's maternal debts.

Fashioning a new view of the erotic leads Irigaray to reconsider the divine and the human. The category of the material or sensible transcendental emerges from her collapsing the dualism of ethics and eros. God is no longer restricted to the "out there" and the beyond, but is found in the here and now of a redeemed pleasure. Eros reveals the divine in its sensible dimension, and divine creation is perpetuated in the forces of love. Through her portrayal of the erotic, Irigaray offers a significant model of human relationship. As that communion in pleasure, eros points to the centrality of the body, the redemption of pleasure, as well as the possibilities of human relationships of respect and mutuality.

Response/Assessment

The matter of assessing Irigaray's critique of Levinas is complex. It must consider Levinas' overall intention, his specific references to women and the feminine, his approach to ethics and the erotic, possible developments in his writings, as well as Irigaray's general approach and specific contentions. This response will follow the two tracks—sexual difference and views of women; ethics and the erotic—laid out in the summary of Irigaray's analysis, and then offer a few closing statements.

An evaluation of Levinas' statements about women and the feminine should begin with at least a few brief remarks about the evolution of his writings.[23] Usually four works are cited in reviewing the development of Levinas' language about this topic: the two books of 1947, *Existence and Existents* and *Time and the Other*; and then *Totality and Infinity* of 1961, and *Otherwise Than Being or Beyond Essence* of 1974.[24] A central concern within Levinas' work has been to describe human relationships in such a way that the absolute integrity of the other is secured. From this perspective, Levinas protests a cardinal line of thought within Western philosophy, especially in the modern period, as well as launches his own revolution. In the first two works, while he saw features of the incommensurability of time between persons as pointing to the other's independence, it was primarily the erotic relation that he analyzed as demonstrating the other's transcendence of the self. Eros is founded on the fact that humans are sexual beings and that there are two different sexes. In this context, he designates the other par excellence as the feminine, or alternately, that alterity is the very essence of the feminine. Levinas sees the feminine as other, not conceptually related as in the feminine in opposition to the masculine, but as, in its own essence, positively other. He tries to describe the way that the feminine is not included in the consciousness of the self/same through defining it, for example, in terms of a "withdrawal into mystery," and as a "hiding" and "modesty."[25] In the later two works, the phenomenology of the ethical relation replaces the erotic relation as demonstrating the infinite alterity of the other. In *Totality and Infinity*, as we saw, the erotic is relegated to the ambivalent as against the clear otherness of the face in the ethical relation. This work still ties the feminine to the erotic, as well as to the dwelling, and also puts forward the relationship of the father to his son as the highest model of ethics. *Otherwise Than Being* does not feature the caress and the erotic, but language and the saying. Also germane in this regard is the appearance of maternity, rather than paternity, as the paramount illustration of the ethical.

The controversy between Irigaray and Levinas has become an important topic in feminist philosophical literature, and references to that literature will help guide this discussion. Just as Irigaray's comments reveal both an appreciation for and criticisms of Levinas, the large literature by feminist thinkers on Levinas includes positive and also critical judgments. Tina Chanter's position stands as a good representative of the ambivalence that careful feminist readings of Levinas often, almost inevitably, exhibit. She holds that the preeminence of the other in Levinas' philosophy is an extremely valuable model and resource for feminist thought, perhaps actually influencing Irigaray's own project of giving voice to the otherness of women. However, Chanter can neither ignore nor trivialize the traditional cultural stereotypes concerning women that Levinas repeats and, by repeating, reinforces. His portrait of women is not just a stylistic problem, but calls into question, and may even undermine, central elements of his extensive philosophy. In the end, she believes that the promise of his work exceeds its execution, which mirrors his own understanding of the relation between the saying (the infinite, redemptive possibilities of human relationships) and the said (the concrete expressions of such relationships, which are always limited by linguistic, cultural, and political structures) (Chanter, ed., 2001, 5). Chanter concludes: "Perhaps in keeping with the vacillation of the saying and the said, a more ambivalent reading is called for, one that is both too generous, perhaps infinitely so, and one that is less generous, perhaps necessarily so" (Chanter, ed., 2001, 25).[26]

An assessment about how literally Levinas means the citations about the feminine that punctuate his work is always an important part of feminist examinations.[27] There is a divide among the critics concerning how Levinas' statements about the feminine should be taken, that is, whether he is consistently using the feminine as a metaphor to speak of otherness or whether he is designating women concretely at times with that term. Usually the conclusion is that his language is metaphorical, but also sometimes concrete and explicit. While presenting a style that sexualizes his notions (Chanter, ed., 2001, 5), one commentator finds that he "simultaneously denies and suggests the connection" of the feminine "to empirical sex or gender" (Brody in Chanter, ed., 2001, 59). As an illustration of the latter, in the context of explaining the appearance of the feminine, Levinas has written: "at the same time interlocutor, collaborator, and master superiorly intelligent, so often dominating men in the masculine civilizations it has entered, and woman having to be treated as a woman, in accordance with rules imprescriptible by civil society" (cited by Brody in Chanter, ed., 2001, 60).

The basic thrust of Levinas' philosophy is what is so appealing to feminists and many other commentators. Insisting on the other's infinity and transcendence unequivocally rejects all those standpoints that see the other as a mere appendage of the self, consciousness, and reason. Describing the other in its ethical height entails that the other and not the self commands. The self's concern must be for one's responsibility and not one's rights. Finally, in arguing that only the ethical relation to the other redeems the self, Levinas repudiates all those views where the other is an obstacle, or at the best neutral, in terms of the question of the authentic life. Through these features of the ethical relation, Levinas renounces philosophic and political theories that justify individual and state mastery and domination over others. In biblical terms these others are the poor, orphan, widow, and stranger, and in today's political terminology, the foreigner, sick, weak, poor, and dispossessed, who are frequently women and children.

In my view, there are good, that is, ethical, reasons for Levinas' choice of identifying the other as feminine.[28] Elevating the other as feminine above the self is part of Levinas' design to contest philosophies and systems that collaborate with, if not celebrate, the self's mastery—of existence, nature, and other persons. As Chanter states it: "Levinas's understanding of the feminine as a disruption of the virile categories of mastery, domination, and self-possession opens up the possibility of another way of (non)being, a different mode of existence" (Chanter, ed., 2001, 16).[29] In this setting, his statements about the feminine as mystery and escaping the light are ways of speaking of the limits of consciousness, and his allusions to feminine silence and weakness play an essential role in his effort to uproot those usual ways of thinking that highlight power. In his system that identifies the other as feminine, the other clearly takes precedence over the masculine, virile same.

However, there is danger in having women stand for alterity and the other. Irigaray's ability to place Levinas' thought—almost seamlessly—in the roll call of Western philosophers who equate women with the other, the outside and underside, demonstrates the way it submits to and buttresses reigning stereotypes of women and the feminine. This judgment is reinforced by Susan Shapiro, who finds a disturbing continuity between classic philosophic associations of the feminine with the despised "rhetoric" as well as deception, and Levinas' portrayals (2003, 174–76). The danger in equating women and alterity remains despite any and all "good" reasons that one can offer. For example, Derrida has suggested that the feminine is identified with the other in the context of eros, because Levinas' phenomenology is positioned from a male (heterosexual) perspective (Derrida 1999, 39). This interpretation is insightful, even if it would be more convincing coming from Levinas himself. However, does it mitigate statements about the feminine that reinforce negative stereotypes as in the following?

> In the feminine face the purity of expression is already troubled by the equivocation of the voluptuous. Expression is inverted into indecency, already close on to the equivocal which says less than nothing, already laughter and raillery. (1969, 260)

> Where the chastity and decency of the face abides at the limit of the obscene yet repelled but already close at hand and promising—is the primordial event of feminine beauty. (1969, 263)

The movement from the topic of paternity in *Totality and Infinity* to maternity in *Otherwise Than Being* is significant although, once again, not unambiguous. Irigaray has shown that, in the first book, the place of the feminine is deeply troubling. Not only is the feminine face identified with the erotic, as against the higher realm of the ethical, but the father's relationship to his son emerges as the paradigm of ethics. It is not difficult to concede Irigaray's claim that it appears that man's transcendence is thus dependent on leaving women or the feminine behind in the abyss. However, the critic Kelly Oliver has elaborated the corrective features, as it were, in Levinas' "alternative notion of paternity" (Chanter, ed., 2001, 225). She contrasts Levinas' description of the father-son relation with that of Freud, for whom the son enters into patriarchal society by acceding to the father's authority. Oliver finds that for Levinas "the promise of paternity is not a promise of authority or repetition, but a promise of nonrecognition, of strangeness, of an open future, of what he calls infinity" (Chanter, ed., 2001, 226). Still, once again, there is no convincing rejoinder to Irigaray's suggestion that the substitution of the father's relationship to his *daughter* rather than to the son would have more powerfully, and unambiguously, reinforced many of the more positive elements in Levinas' account of ethics.

In Levinas' second major work, maternity is the very model for ethics. The mother's sacrifice of herself—including even the substitution of her infant's or child's welfare for her own, her obsession with the child—including even her voluntary persecution by its demands, and the physicality of her giving with her own body—in birth, in her nourishment of this other, all are utilized by Levinas to exemplify what responsibility to the other means. Thus he writes:

> It is being torn up from oneself, being less than nothing, a rejection into the negative, behind nothingness; it is maternity, gestation of the other in the same. Is not the restlessness of someone persecuted but a modification of maternity, the groaning of the wounded entrails by those it will bear or has borne? In maternity what signifies is a responsibility for others, to the point of substitution for others and suffering both from the effect of persecution and from the persecuting itself in which the persecutor sinks. Maternity, which is bearing par excellence, bears even responsibility for the persecuting by the persecutor. (1981, 75)

> Signification signifies, consequently, in nourishing, clothing, lodging, in maternal relations, in which matter shows itself for the first time in its materiality. (1981, 77)

> The evocation of maternity in this metaphor suggests to us the proper sense of oneself. The oneself cannot form itself; it is already formed with absolute passivity. (1981, 104)

> Maternity in the complete being "for the other" which characterizes it, which is the very signifyingness of signification, is the ultimate sense of this vulnerability. (1981, 108)

Some have seen the progression from paternity to maternity as a response to Irigaray, or at least to feminist concerns.[30] Chanter's question underscores this development in Levinas' work, asking whether *Otherwise Than Being* then unsays what is said in *Totality and Infinity*, and thus representing a "retraction" of the "thematization of women as silent, discreet, marginal presences, and portrays maternity as a resource for an ethic of infinite demands?" (Chanter, ed., 2001, 18). Further, it is clear that while Levinas' language of "the feminine" may be essentially metaphoric, maternity ultimately is an example that is fully open only to women. However, there are also problems with this use of maternity. Is it really helpful that women's relationship to the erotic has been followed/corrected by their identification with maternity? Is women's essence now to be identified with maternity, as opposed to the erotic? Additionally, in what way should the example of maternity be considered a break with and an undermining of philosophy? As one critic indicated, there is a long history of philosophy's utilization of maternity to "appeal to the legitimacy of the true order," which has not affected its overall negative approach to the images, role, and integrity of women (Ainley in Chanter, ed., 2001, 203).[31]

Finally, serious objections, reiterating issues voiced by Irigaray, have also been raised even about the laudable direction of Levinas' oeuvre overall. While it seeks to overturn (male) mastery and feature the responsibility due to the (female) other, what message does it have for the present situation of women or for women for their own sake? In terms of the former, what are the consequences for women's liberation, when the notion of priority of the other over the self may undermine the pursuit of women's equality and arguments for philosophies of mutuality? In light of the latter, critics have asked, should women sacrifice themselves for the other, when this is exactly what they have been acculturated to do, when they have never been allowed to master even their own voices and desires? This question is well put by Chanter: "If women have not yet been granted the full status of their subjectivity, then what effect does the call to circumvent the model of reciprocity as untenable have on us?" (Chanter, ed., 2001, 3). Overall, does the radicality of Levinas' position actually work against it?

Irigaray's question about the exclusive use of male images and metaphors to speak of the divine is significant and persuasive. Female metaphors for God would certainly reinforce Levinas' effort to break the link between the (male, virile, masterful) self and the transcendent. In our culture, an exclusively male God only substantiates the "*Gott mit uns*" of all of the reigning powers. Thus, it is important that the other is (at times) conceived in terms of female metaphors, and it is also fully in keeping with Levinas' own principles.[32]

The preceding discussion of Levinas' language concerning women and the feminine returns us back to Irigaray's starting principle, the importance of sexual difference. Many of the difficulties and ambiguities within Levinas' language and philosophic position would be resolved if he gave prominence to the issue of sexual difference. Levinas' intention is to affirm the infinity of the other, that is, the absolute integrity of the other above and beyond all the conceptual, social, and political reaches of the self; the ethical height of the other above the rights and interests of the self; and the cause of the widow, orphan, poor, and stranger. However, this intention—Levinas' own "saying"—is undercut by the serious flaws—his "said," that leave women derelict, that is, without any place of their own. With no distinctive voice or desire—at times no face—as the underside of the male, thrust down into the abyss of the infantile, the carnal, and the animal, the identity and integrity of women is not furthered in the ways that they could be by Levinas' philosophy.

Two Models

The second constellation of issues that Irigaray explores concerns the erotic and the ethical. In the end, Irigaray and Levinas offer two different models of what constitutes the highest human relationship. For Levinas this is the ethical, as portrayed in the face-to-face relation or, later, through the terminology of proximity. It is the ethical that establishes subjectivity, brings authenticity and meaning to life, and is ultimately the only path to a relationship to the divine. As we have seen, Levinas is definitive about the nature of this relationship. The other person is infinite, in the sense that she or he is totally separate from the self, not a continuation, supplement, or expansion of the self's same. The other stands in his or her height, which means that the concern for the other's well-being has absolute priority over one's self-interest. In his words: "The fact that in existing for another I exist otherwise than in existing for me is morality itself" (1969, 261). Further, in relation to the other, one is deeply aware of the other's vulnerability or fragility as over against one's power, so that the injunction not to kill is continually present, haunting all of one's designs and actions. While, at a later point, the ethical relation includes considerations of justice and equality, the paradigm of the absolute demands of the face-to-face are never left behind and are the basis for those concerns. Finally, the relationship to God is never direct, but emerges in the context of responsibility for the poor, orphan, widow, and stranger.

For Levinas the erotic relationship falls short of the supreme qualities of the ethical. The main reason for this is that in the erotic relation there is not an exclusive interest in the other. The erotic relationship reveals a desire for something for the self and, thus, it results in some return to the self. However, this concern with oneself is, in Levinas' view, egoism, the opposite of ethics. While there may be many ways that egoism or self-interest is exhibited in the erotic—for example, through power—it is primarily pleasure which seems to be Levinas' focus. One gains pleasure from the tactile contact, voluptuosity, as well as from the love that the other gives to the self. For him, erotic love is, thus "pleasure and dual egoism" (1969, 266). Finally, the other is not transcendent in the erotic relationship, because one is also loving the self, that is, loving the love that the other gives to the self (1969, 266).[33]

Levinas, of course, does not see the erotic as evil. It is an important human relationship between one person and another, even if it does not reach to the height of the ethical. Also, in opposition to the clarity of the lines between self and other of the ethical relationship, the erotic comes to be labeled as "equivocal." The relationship to the other respects some difference between the self and other, but not completely. In the erotic, one cares for the other, but not to the exclusivity of the self. In *Totality and Infinity*, the movement to the higher human relationship only appears when fecundity and the son arise out of the erotic.

For Irigaray, the erotic, at least when it is not undermined or desecrated, represents the loftiest relationship between persons. It is a relation where one is able to give pleasure to the other. In one's own pleasure, the other is given pleasure. Giving to another is an important feature of the highest relationship for Irigaray. It is a relationship where difference is respected, but also there are instants of comfort in the other and of merger of the one in the other. The erotic relationship is creative, a rebirth for the other and the self. For example, one teaches the other about the contours of the other's body and learns about one's own body. The erotic relationship has power to overturn all of the ways that patriarchy, and the political, social, and economic powers that are tied to it, have of corrupting, restricting, and perverting persons. In particular, the erotic brings sexual difference to prominence, and with that, it gives women their lives as subjects, with desires and voices of their own. Through the erotic, persons are reminded of the importance of themselves as embodied, of their relationship to nature, and of the reality of death. Finally, through the erotic one gets in touch with the dimension of the divine. Awareness of the transcendent, but a transcendent within the material and the here and now—the sensible transcendental—awakens through the erotic.

In effect, each thinker poses serious questions for the other. Obviously, Irigaray interrogates Levinas about sexual difference and about the dualisms that pervade his understanding of ethics. She endeavors to demonstrate that unless, at the very beginning of one's philosophic work, the principle that women and men are both different and distinct is affirmed, the heritage of male domination will continue. For her, every other difference, the very respect for difference, evaporates unless that fundamental sexual difference is upheld. Further, sexual difference is the determining element for whether all of the possible fecundity and meaning of relationships will be forthcoming. She also asks about the oppositions that put the erotic, pleasure, the aesthetic, the body, the material, and woman on one side, and ethics, transcendence, and man on the other.[34] Must the erotic and the ethical, and the host of elements that follow on each side, be set in opposition? Is it necessary that self-interest be completely abolished from the ethical? Must there be a suspicion about giving pleasure to the other because one also gets pleasure back? Cannot the giving to the other of the highest, also include a receiving? Following this, can the body, being embodied, sexuality, sensuality, the caress, be either acknowledged or understood if pleasure is abolished from the most important human relationships? Finally, Irigaray queries whether it is ethical to remove women's subjectivity and desire, plunging them into the wrong side of Levinas' oppositions and into the abyss.

In assessing these issues, one might look at Levinas' paradigm of maternity. Maternity is a powerful model to show the features of the ethical that Levinas values. It concretely speaks of giving to the other with and out of one's own body. It evokes images of absolute sacrifice of the self for the other, of placing the other's needs above one's own, and of being obsessed with the other. It should be seen as a corrective to the one-sidedness of paternity and the son, and also to the place and images of the feminine/woman in Levinas' overall work. Yet, many of the same, deep problems still remain. Women are tied to maternity, but now their contact with the erotic is jettisoned. Does this leave the negative connotations about the feminine and the erotic in place? Do women, or our images of women, have to decide for one or the other? Further, as Irigaray wonders, if ethics and eros are separated so clearly, does that mean that the erotic is bereft of ethical concerns? As erotic relationships are extremely open to all kinds of domination over the other, must there not be a thorough discourse of the ethics required within the erotic, of the "ethics of eros"?[35]

As great a model as is maternity, in reality it also speaks of a return to self and of pleasure. The mother who gives to the infant or child certainly sees the child as part of herself. Winnicott in particular features this process of identification as integral to the mother's care for the infant. The mother's ego is extended to include her child, as is the father's to his child. Giving to the other is then also receiving something back. Even further, in many ways, caring for the infant brings tactile pleasure. There is the pleasure for the mother in breast-feeding, for example. In light of these considerations, can or should a philosophy of ethics that highlights the paradigm of maternity insist that there be no return to the self? An answer to this might have significant ramifications for Levinas' philosophy because of the centrality of his view about the separation of self-interest and the concern for the other.

Levinas also poses questions for Irigaray. Is Irigaray sensitive enough to the way that self-interest can pervert relationships? Is her language about the union and merger of the two in the erotic wary enough of the possible dangers when the other is taken into the self? Is her portrait of the erotic thus too ideal and does the ethical suffer if it is too intertwined with it? Further, despite the positive features of the notion of the sensible transcendental, does the collapse of the divine into the human not threaten to apotheosize the human? Is not the language of the divine as transcendent a tremendous protection from allowing oneself or anyone to identify themselves, their interests, and their group with God—the *Gott mit uns*? Levinas maintains that the language of the divine must act as the most powerful guarantee against ignoring, dominating, excluding the other. This is why he insists that God is totally other and stands with the other. Levinas understands that this principle is not just philosophic, but has tremendous social and political ramifications. For him, the integrity of all relationships depends on the parallel separations between self and other, self (and even human) and divine.

This examination of Irigaray and Levinas will conclude by highlighting what views and concerns they share, what lessons they teach. The significance and intensity of their arguments can be accounted for not only by the areas of disagreement, but also by the important elements that they have in common. In the context of this project of narrating the interhuman, Irigaray and Levinas contribute, each in their own way, to understanding the primacy of relationships. They are philosophers of the dual or interhuman, and not of the solitary. For them, integrity, meaning, authenticity, and the new are not discovered or created alone; these are the fruits of relationship. While Irigaray values most the erotic and Levinas the ethical, both of these are types of relationship. They believe that these, the highest human relationships, are liberating and transcending. Also, their work on these relationships highlights the embodied and passionate nature of the human and the interhuman. Ethics and the erotic are passionate relationships. Their philosophies are eloquent about the caress, the skin, and breath. Further, for them the embodied and the passionate point to one's need for the other. In their thought, the skin is a symbol for the openness of the human, of the one for the other. Finally, they share the view that the integrity of relationships rests on the respect for difference. As we have seen, with Irigaray this is sexual difference, and for Levinas authenticity rests on the ethical difference between the self and other, and the religious language of the separation of the self and the divine. They recognize the dangers to the self and society when difference is eliminated. They are philosophers who demand the acknowledgment, even more, the welcoming, of difference.

Rosenzweig and Buber

Irigaray's dialogue with Levinas will now be extended to Rosenzweig and Buber. This treatment will not be as extensive as it was with Levinas and will not attempt to duplicate Irigaray's critique of Levinas. This is thus a somewhat different step in the ongoing dance/fling with the philosophers. In terms of Rosenzweig, the topics to be explored include his remarks about the deficiencies of philosophy, the differences between men's and women's development, the use of the "Song of Songs" in *The Star*, and his focus on love and language as the fundamental features of human relationships. With Buber, the examination will concentrate on the mutuality that he sees defining I and Thou relationships, his portrayal of the I and Thou relationship first manifested in the interaction between mother and infant, his depiction of marriage as a connection that equally respects difference and stands as a new creation, and, again, his focus on language and relationships. We will see confirmed here what was fundamental in Irigaray's earlier fling, the partners sharing the deepest of concerns for an ethics of relationship and believing that it begins with respect for the other.

Out of an insistence on the importance of difference for understanding the nature of the human and the interhuman, a parallel critique of philosophy appears in the works of Rosenzweig and Irigaray. For Rosenzweig, philosophy represents a continuous stream of thinkers who reduce the multiplicity of elements in experience to a one. Distinctive of the modern period is that this one is the self. A major objective of Rosenzweig's philosophy is to split apart philosophy's totality so that there will be room for real experiences of and relationships with multiplicity: God, other humans, and the world. Irigaray also characterizes philosophy in terms of totality and the search for (masculine) sameness (1985a, 322). She writes that the "domination of the philosophic logos stems in large part from its power *to reduce all others to the economy of the Same*" (1991a, 123). In addition, Rosenzweig and Irigaray see the philosophical endeavor as requiring the rejection of the body as well as death. Rosenzweig weaves together these two rejections, arguing that by denying the reality of the body "Philosophy takes it upon itself to . . . rob death of its poisonous sting" (1972, 3). Irigaray points to philosophy's gender division of the sensible, body, death, and woman, on the one hand, and the transcendent, mind, eternity, and man, on the other. However, while their remedies for these philosophic distortions focus on the need for plurality and difference, the specific levers they propose to pry apart philosophy's system diverge. Rosenzweig insists on the "and" of the three elements—humans, world, and God—and Irigaray argues that sexual difference grounds the respect for plurality.[36]

While the issue of sexual difference does not have a significant role in Rosenzweig's narrative, it is interesting to note, as was briefly discussed in Chapter 1, that in *The Star* he does speak of a difference in the development of men and women as persons. The crucial confrontations for this differentiation are the encounters with eros and thanatos. In Rosenzweig's view, a human being is just another member of the species, at most distinguished by her or his peculiar personality, until one day she or he awakens to being a unique self (1972, 71). This "day" occurs when the individual's character emerges in the encounter with eros. In the erotic encounter that has the goal of reproduction, the individual first glimmers the actuality of being replaced. He senses his unique death, and this hardens him in his uniqueness. The final stage in the development of character, or the self, occurs when, at the end of life, death is again faced, but even more starkly. Now what is special to a woman, according to Rosenzweig, is that "even Thanatos can approach her in the sweet guise of Eros. . . . Already in the tremors of love her heart has become firm. It no longer needs the tremor of death. A young woman can be as ready for eternity as a man only becomes when his threshold is crossed by Thanatos." (1972, 156). These lines are enigmatic, but they do provide some hints. It appears that for a woman, when she comes together with her lover, she is crystallized as a person in the way a man is not until the end of his life. Perhaps this insight should be connected to the opening lines of Rosenzweig's treatment in this section on "Revelation," the statement from the "Song of Songs" that "Love is strong as death" (1972, 156). The section describes the way that through the love of God, the person or self, transformed into loving soul, is able to stand up to the fear of death. Together these two insights might suggest that when a woman has an erotic love relationship with her partner, she is already possessed of soul and shielded against death. Of course, since Rosenzweig does not believe that human love is ever bereft of a divine dimension, his lines are not as out of harmony with the wider text as they may seem. Too much should not be drawn from these elusive lines. At the least, Rosenzweig can be seen to be saying that the erotic has more transformative power and meaning for women than it does for men, an issue that we have seen Irigaray address. Whatever Rosenzweig meant by this, or what can be made of it, at the least these lines testify to an acknowledgment of sexual difference.

Far less speculative is the interest that Rosenzweig and Irigaray have in the biblical "Song of Songs," which she characteristically denotes as the "Song of Solomon." Their ideas about this poem have been discussed before, so that some brief reflections will be sufficient here. In addition to seeing this exceptional song as an important artifact from the time of the beginning of patriarchy, Irigaray comments about its exaltation of the sensual abandonment of the two lovers, even if the woman's desire is at times eclipsed. It also does not hesitate to speak of the divinity of this bodily love, of these two lovers who "wed each other with all of their senses" (1991, 110). The "Song of Songs" has a more prominent function in Rosenzweig's writings. He places it at the center of *The Star*, and uses it as the template for his discussion of the love between God and the soul (1972, 202). In a lengthy excursus he unravels the sublime moments of this dialogue of love. He underscores its dual lessons about the appropriateness of love, especially erotic love, as a metaphor for the relationship between God and humans and, equally, of the divinity of human love. He writes:

> Love simply cannot be "purely human." It must speak, for there is simply no self-expression other than the speech of life. And by speaking, love already becomes superhuman, for the sensuality of the word is brimful with its divine supersense.

> Like speech itself, love is sensual—supersensual. . . . But love is not "but simile"; it is simile in its entirety and its essence; it is only apparently transitory: in truth, it is eternal. (1972, 201)

There cannot be a clearer celebration of the divinity of love, its bodily concreteness not an obstacle or even metaphor for the godly and eternal, but the royal path to experiencing God's love. This represents one of Rosenzweig's fundamental understandings of the interconnection between the divine and the human.

Two of the features of the interhuman that are especially significant in the work of Irigaray and Rosenzweig are language and love. For these philosophers, a relational view of the human translates into the understanding that language and love uniquely possess the powers of birth and creation. Without the gifts that come through linguistic and erotic intercourse there are no full persons. Language's powers, extending almost to life and death, are well expressed by Irigaray in this statement: "The subject may be masked, bogged down, buried, covered up, paralyzed, or may be engendered, generated, may become, and grow through speech" (1991a, 147). Irigaray also appreciates the tremendous reach or influence of language when she writes of its impact on "the preservation, organization, consciousness and creation of life, of the world" (1991a, 143). Through the full exchange of an I and a Thou, of persons who are alternately speaker and hearer, the subject comes to acquire an identity and a place in the social world. The study of language is thus a key to discovering the state of health of the individual and the world.

Sexual difference, of course, is a principal concern in Irigaray's discussion of language. For language to fulfill all of its promise, it must reflect the differences in the two sexes. The house(s) of language must have sufficient resources, of distinctive subterranean images and conscious symbols, for both men and women to draw upon. However, this requirement is not met today. Speech is not the dialogue between two equal partners, but the monologue of men with themselves. According to Irigaray, women do not have a language to speak of themselves as subjects. Women enter language as things spoken about, as objects of linguistic exchange. For many years Irigaray carefully examined the linguistic expressions of women and found that they were unable to speak the language of the subject as men did. Her studies of psychological pathology, religious language, and grammar also revealed the linguistic monopoly of men and the eclipse of the female sex.[37]

Irigaray's discussion of love parallels her insights into language. The ideal of an amorous exchange between the sexes is, thus, linguistic and erotic. She has a visionary discourse about love and the erotic. Only through the love of the other does one truly come to life. Love is a birth and creation of the self, fully as much as is the first birth. It gives identity and body to the other, through an exchange where two become a new one, but also remain authentically different. Love bridges the gap between sensible and transcendent, unveiling the divine within the passion and flesh of the human. Love's fertility, its power to heal, is stronger than even the reigning unconscious, social, and religious forces that repress women. Through love one comes to appreciate that humans are body, embodied, erotic, sexate, and part of nature. Love reminds us that we are part of the round of birth and death, but through this knowledge, as Rosenzweig would say, death loses much of its sting.

Once again, Rosenzweig's discourses about love and language are fully parallel to those of Irigaray. Just as love—God's love and the love of the neighbor—turn the enclosed self into a loving soul, he holds that the subject or "I" only appears when it has turned in answer to a "Thou" (1972, 174–75). Love and language are pivotal to humans' self-transformation. They point to the deepest of desires, but not of and for the self. Rosenzweig believed that the "Song of Songs" was the narrative of revelation, because it weaves together the themes of love, language, and the coming to be and turning to the other in a story that is both human and divine. He writes about the way this biblical love poem was viewed, before sophisticated moderns insisted on separating human and divine, body and spirit:

> The Song of Songs was recognized as a love lyric and precisely therewith simultaneously as "mystical" poem. One simply knew that the I and Thou of human discourse is without more ado also the I and Thou between God and man. One knew that the distinction between immanence and transcendence disappears in language. The Song of Songs was an "authentic," that is, a "worldly" love lyric; precisely for this reason, not in spite of it, it was a genuinely "spiritual" song of the love of God for man. Man loves because God loves and as God loves. (1972, 199)

Rosenzweig says little of the possibilities of the distortion of love or language. Among other things, he seems to be answering those who see these features as intrinsically dangerous and alienating. His answer is that if these overlapping realms cannot be trusted, nothing can.

Martin Buber's work exhibits many similarities with basic themes of Irigaray. Along with Irigaray, Levinas, and Rosenzweig, Buber affirms that humans are fundamentally relational. There is no human being by herself or himself. The longing for the other is not a matter of what the other can provide.[38] It is *sui generis*: the presence of the other has meaning in itself. As with the other three philosophers, Buber is eloquent about the powers of language and convinced of its centrality for human life. Human lives are permeated with language, or better: "in truth language does not reside in man but man stands in language and speaks out of it—so it is with all words, all spirit" (1970, 89). The two basic attitudes that humans take to the world are understood as word pairs: I-Thou and I-It (1970, 53). These two depict not just different experiences but different worlds. Further, while a person can be in an I-Thou relation with Thous that cannot speak—natural objects, animals, objects of art, or with humans through silence—language is the natural medium for this relation of address. The topics of language and speech lead Buber, as they did Rosenzweig and Levinas, to refer to the divine. For him, God addresses and calls upon each person through everyday events. Ultimately, this calling to the other in responsibility is not different from the address from person to person. In Buber's words: "speaking with God . . . is not something *toto genere* different from speaking with another human being. For in the latter case there is common the fact of being approached, grasped, addressed, which cannot be anticipated in any depth of the soul" (1965, 50).

In company with Irigaray, and unlike Levinas, Buber holds that a relation of mutuality is sufficient to guarantee the respect for difference. The I and Thou relationship features mutuality and reciprocity. In *I and Thou* Buber states: "Relation is reciprocity. My Thou works on me as I act on it. Our students teach us, our works form us" (1970, 67). In the I and Thou relation the two sides remain independent and distinct, and, for Buber, it is only in terms of this type of relation that each can address the other in respect to that other's uniqueness and fullness. He speaks of this as the "power of exclusiveness" (1970, 58). For Buber, the alternative to a relation of mutuality and reciprocity is one of domination and objectification, the I and It relation. A notable difference here between Irigaray and Buber is that Irigaray does not hesitate to speak of a moment of unity, in at least the erotic (and mystic?) encounter, while Buber conscientiously and systematically shuns this term, even in the mystic encounter (1970, 131–43). Also distinguishing them is the importance of the relation to God. While Irigaray recognizes that religious language may be vital to complete her project of liberating both women and men from the present deeply alienating situation, for Buber the term God is not a matter of philosophical supplement. In his work, the lines of relation to each Thou can only be completed and fulfilled in the relation to the "eternal Thou" (1970, 123).

There are two specific portraits of the I and Thou relation in Buber's work that are reminiscent of some of Irigaray's lines. The first occurs in his discussion of the mother-infant relation in *I and Thou*, which has been examined previously. Actually, the very fact that he utilizes this relationship is certainly important in the context of Irigaray's concerns. Buber finds the first glimmers of the life of relation in the experiences of the fetus. In the womb the life of association is thus presaged. He writes: "The prenatal life of the child is a pure natural association, a flowing toward each other, a bodily reciprocity; and the life horizon of the developing being appears uniquely inscribed, and yet also not inscribed, in that of the being that carries it" (1970, 76). The earliest developments of the infant continue along this line, proving to Buber the innateness of the longing for the other: a desire, once again, not reducible to any other need or design. Still, this presentation is not uncontaminated, as it were. As important as it is to remember the infant's mother, Buber also overwrites this recognition with statements such as "the womb in which it dwells is not solely that of the human mother" (1970, 76). He refers to notions of the "womb of the great mother" (1970, 76). It is difficult to determine whether this is an acknowledgment of a tie also to nature, or whether there is some type of transcending of the mother through a vision of being born in the "spirit" (1970, 76).

Less equivocal is Buber's fine discussion of marriage as a paradigmatic relation. In many ways, it resembles Irigaray's discussion of erotic love. Its context is equally impressive. Buber's essay "The Question to the Single One" is an answer to what he sees as one of Søren Kierkegaard's extremely lamentable positions, that he had to reject Regina, his fiancee, in order to serve God. Buber values many things in marriage. It is a relationship not of the moment but of a lifetime. It speaks of devotion and commitment. Even more importantly, it demonstrates that true relationship does not abolish, but confirms otherness. As Buber sees it:

> He who "has entered on marriage" . . . has been in earnest, in the intention of the sacrament, with the fact that the other *is*; with the fact that I cannot legitimately share in the Present Being without sharing in the being of the other; with the fact that I cannot answer the lifelong address of God to me without answering at the same time for the other; with the fact that I cannot be answerable without being at the same time answerable for the other as one who is entrusted to me. (1964, 60–61)

Marriage creates a new entity or unit of being. One is responsible not only for oneself, but for the two-fold marriage unit. One is oneself, and, at the same time, with another. In addition, Buber's understanding of marriage is a confirmation of his and Irigaray's view that a relation of mutuality sustains respect for difference. Finally, there are some similarities and differences between the way the two philosophers use religious language in their discussions of such significant relationships as those in the sphere of the erotic and in marriage. Irigaray and Buber could agree that these relations have a divine dimension. However, Irigaray would use the language of immanence and the sensible transcendental, while Buber utilizes the discourse of divine transcendence and one being entrusted by and answerable to God.[39]

The Last Step—In the Dance

> That place may only emerge if the feminine is granted its own "specificity" in its relation to language. Which implies a logic other than the one imposed by dis-

> cursive coherence . . . that it would entail a different relation to unity, to identity with self, to truth, to the same and thus to alterity, to repetition and thus to temporality; that it would retraverse "differently" the matter/form dyad, the power/act dyad, and so on. (Irigaray 1985, 153–54)

Irigaray argues that the issue of sexual difference has tremendous consequences.[40] It is the basis for respecting and understanding all differences. In regard to what it means to be a self, sexual difference affects how one relates to the other and to the transcendent, what the resources of language are, what being embodied and the erotic represent, and even what truth is. This litany of consequences could equally be cited in discussing Levinas, Rosenzweig, and Buber in terms of their understandings of difference. For Levinas this would be the difference between self and other that emerges in the ethical realm—in the face to face, while for Rosenzweig it might be the difference between the human and the divine or the soul and its neighbor. For Buber one may point to the difference between I and Thou, or, once again, the human and the divine. In each case these philosophers critique notions of totality or sameness, grounded in philosophic discourse and expressed in all the spheres of social life, by appealing to difference. The other's difference and distinctiveness give life its vitality and its integrity. Understanding and respecting that difference acts as a critique of language, notions of self and identity, society and truth.

Difference and otherness come to have the importance they do because of the relational notion of the human that pervades all of these philosophers' works. We have seen that Buber's declaration that "There is no I as such" is shared by Rosenzweig, Levinas, and Irigaray. Relationships are fecund. It is through relating to real others that the fullness of love, language, and life overall become available. For them, truth is hidden from the same, the one genre, the single one. Truth is one of the fruits that ripens through plurality and is achieved and verified in relationship. These thinkers stand against a major stream within the Western philosophic tradition in their arguing that self-consciousness, language, reason, justice, the aesthetic, and love do not emanate from the self by itself, but are engendered through relationship. Further, in emphasizing the relational character of the human, the topics of the body and the erotic move toward the center from the periphery of the discourses about persons.

The four philosophers include religious language in their narratives about the human, the other, and relationships. They find that the ways that the relationship between the divine and the human is expressed deeply affects the understanding of the interhuman. The language of the divine may affirm or undermine human differences and otherness. Still, Irigaray is distinctive here. She finds that concepts and images of the male divine have reflected, reinforced, and justified the history of women's dereliction: their lack of identity, subjectivity, and a place in language and society. For her, the remedy is to create concepts and images of a female divine. While the need for this, in my view, is indisputable, there are some problematic features in her endeavor. Does the discourse about the importance of difference suffer when the argument is in terms of supporting the one sex through its own images of the divine? Given, on the one hand, the consequences that have resulted from a history of the exclusively male image, and on the other hand, the lack of female images of the divine to support and stimulate women, the answer to this question is neither obvious nor simple. Irigaray also argues that female images are needed by men, for the sake of their relationships with women, their understandings of the other sex and of themselves. In my view, the ethical and philosophic principles of Rosenzweig, Levinas, and Buber would bring them to concur with Irigaray in this matter.[41]

Irigaray's concept of the sensible transcendental is important, but also ambiguous. It stands as a helpful corrective to the philosophic inclination to graft the opposition between the sensible and the transcendent onto those of body and soul, nature and society, women and men. Clearly, except possibly for Buber, there are few resources in the works of Rosenzweig and Levinas for bringing together ethics and nature into an environmental ethics. Is their notion of the transcendence of the divine implicated in their neglect? However, some of Irigaray's ways of presenting this idea again undermine the discourse about difference. The idea of the infinite difference between human and divine is a central part of the critique of sameness and power in the works of Rosenzweig, Buber, and Levinas. They maintain the integrity of the two partners, the distance between them, and, in different ways and to different extent, still affirm the body, the erotic, and the everyday.

Irigaray's critique of philosophy's dereliction of the relationship between mother and infant does pose a serious challenge to the three Jewish philosophers. She holds that the male hold on life and creativity is cemented by forgetting how and where human life begins. Philosophy substitutes the relation to the divine for this all-too-human relationship, and then portrays the divine in exclusively male terms. Buber's depiction of the infant's I-Thou exchange with the mother, and Levinas' elevating the ethical paradigm of maternity do represent acknowledgments of the significance of the mother/infant dyad. Still all three Jewish philosophers, or at least those today who find their work meaningful and resourceful, need to take heed of her call. Unless the significance of mothers is unambiguously affirmed, and the exclusive use of male language for the divine is explicitly rejected, the suspicion that the male divine has replaced the female mother will deeply haunt all philosophic narratives and interpretations.

Consideration of another question that Irigaray introduces, about the relationship between the divine and law, furthers the dialogue about religious language and difference. In her "Questions" Irigaray queries about the connection between God and his commandments in Levinas, as well as monotheism's overall treatment of "the God who makes his presence known in law" (1991, 116). She contrasts this with an understanding of a God who "gives himself, through his presence, as nourishment, including nourishment of the senses" (1991, 116), and also alludes to mysticism with its link "to the flesh in its sexual dimension" (1991, 116).

Do the Jewish philosophers have a response for this challenge? They might begin by indicating that Irigaray's language is reminiscent of traditional Christian views of Judaism, with its insistence on contrasting the commanding God of Judaism with the loving God of Christianity. Irigaray's allusion to the traditional Christian stereotype of Judaism does not further understanding and respect for religious difference. There is also more at stake in their response. All three Jewish philosophers find that God's dialogue with humans should be understood as an ethical call. For Levinas this is expressed in the face-to-face relationship, when the other's vulnerability declares the divine commandment not to kill. Even in Buber, who is antinomian in so many ways, God's revelation is understood as an ethical address to each individual in the uniqueness of her or his life and the singularity of each moment (1970, 159). However, it is with Rosenzweig that the portrait of the commanding God is presented so eloquently. God's revelation, that is, the relationship to humans, is expressed through the double commandments to love God and love the neighbor. For Rosenzweig, only the lover can command love from the beloved, which is how he sees, following the "Song of Songs," the initial dynamics of revelation. Nothing encompasses more fully the immediacy of the divine presence, and the nature of God as lover, than this command. The next step in this dialogue for Rosenzweig is God's commandment to love the neighbor. Rosenzweig's treatment of revelation illustrates the powers of a religious language built upon an understanding of a divine who is transcendent, yet also makes His or Her presence known through commandment, to affirm the connection to and otherness of the neighbor. In addition, the three Jewish philosophers are sensitive to the ways that love and obligation, passion and responsibility, are intertwined throughout life.

Finally, all four philosophers insist that their critiques are not exhausted within the realm of philosophy, nor their visions limited to erotic relationships or those of the face-to-face. Their strenuously won views of life with others have consequences for facing death, and their insights into relationships lead to new descriptions of community. The topics of authentic life and facing death, the singular, dual, and the communal will be welcomed in the next chapter: narrating life and death.

Notes

1. This quotation directly precedes the section "B. Phenomenology of Eros."

2. The long section on "Plato's *Hysteria*" is in *Speculum of the Other Woman* (1985a, 243–364).

3. Irigaray is saying here that since women do not have the "privilege" of being allotted a place in the system or in theory making, they are not obligated to conform to the usual codes of citation.

4. In the essay "Sexual Difference," Irigaray refers to Aristotle's belief that women's only role in the birth of a child was as an envelope (1991, 169).

5. In *This Sex Which is Not One*, she holds: "Woman takes pleasure more from touching than from looking, and her entry into the dominant scopic economy signifies, again, her consignment to passivity" (1985, 26).

6. As part of Irigaray's long examination/interrogation of Freud in *Speculum*, she alludes to his view that it makes no sense to speak of a feminine libido. She wonders if it might be important to pursue the issue of whether desire/libido is specific to each gender (1985a, 43, 93–94).

7. See the chapter "Women on the Market," (1985, 170–91).

8. Her use of the term "mirror" always has behind it allusions to Plato and Lacan: to Plato's cave/womb and to Lacan's mirror stage in his narrative of development.

9. There has been a critical examination of Irigaray's view of the erotic and the homosexual. Is homosexual love disparaged in her insistence on the importance of sexual difference, especially in understanding the "fecundity" of the erotic? Tina Chanter, in *Ethics of Eros*, believes that elements in Irigaray's critique of Levinas actually open the way to an appreciation of homosexuality (1995, 218).

10. See Whitford's discussion of the imaginary and the symbolic in *Luce Irigaray* (1991, 53–97).

11. Irigaray equates philosophy with sameness, as, when she writes: "this domination of the philosophic logos stems in large part from its power to *reduce all others to the economy of the Same*" (1985, 74).

12. Images of blood, milk, and other fluids are also important to her creation of a female imaginary. Images of fluids contest the static and definitive lines of solids. Irigaray has an exciting essay on this, "The 'Mechanics' of Fluids," in which she provocatively states that woman "speaks 'fluid'" (1985, 111).

13. This topic has been treated in earlier chapters. Also see the treatment of the death drive or thanatos in Freud in chapter two. In *Speculum* women are seen as representing death (1985a, 27). Whitford has a helpful discussion of this issue (1991, 95–97).

14. Irigaray has detailed the ways that many philosophers use women, rather than love, as a protective house of flesh. While, for example, women are left derelict, men live in "grottoes, huts, women, towns, language, concepts, theories, etc." (cited in Whitford 1991, 81). Women are always the building material, the ground, without subjectivity, for men's solitary creations.

15. Irigaray refers to this in *Speculum* (1985a, 167).

16. This can also be seen as a comparison with what is actually the abstract face—the face-to-face—of Levinas' ethical relation.

17. It is also tied to her critique of attempts to divide pleasure and reproduction. If the caress is fecund in the pleasure that it gives, and the erotic is important both in-itself and as a means for the birth of another, then the separation has been bridged.

18. See Whitford's discussion of the sensible transcendental (1991a, 144). Whitford indexes Irigaray's sensible transcendental under the heading "senile transcendental" (1991, 240). Given Irigaray's critique of the historical male images of the divine, this is a great *double entendre.*

19. Whitford speaks of the role of the angel in Irigaray's wider works (1991, 163–64).

20. I have discussed "Questions" at length in *Speaking/Writing of God*, in a chapter "To Notice the Color of Her Eyes," that uses Irigaray's questions as a foundation for exploring important features of the feminist Jewish critique of Judaism (1997, 53–82).

21. The way that the two French terms "l'aimée" and "l'amante" are translated into English differ in the two essays by Irigaray that we are examining. I have retained the particular English terms used in each translation. Still, in both cases, the distinction between the woman as a passive or as an active partner is the primary concern. See (1986, 238, and note 1 on 256), as well as (1991, 115).

22. I have difficulty following Irigaray's argument here, and am especially skeptical when she claims: "The philosophy of Heidegger is more ethical . . . than his philosophy itself says explicitly" (1991, 114).

23. Feminist Jewish philosophers have made significant contributions to the critique of Levinas by noting the influence of his Jewish writings on his philosophic works. Levinas' Talmudic essays and other articles on Judaism seem to reveal sources for some of his enigmatic ideas and references about women and the feminine. See Claire Katz's *Levinas, Judaism, and the Feminine*, and Susan Shapiro's "And God Created Woman."

24. Three essays in *Feminist Interpretations of Levinas* are especially helpful here: Chanter's introduction and the chapters by Perpich and Brody.

25. These quotations from *Time and the Other* are cited in Diane Perpich's review of the place of the feminine in Levinas' early works (Chanter, ed., 2001, 32).

26. The ambivalence to Levinas' treatment, (in his treatment?), is also reflected in Jacques Derrida's considerations. In *Adieu to Emmanuel Levinas*, Derrida provides two different readings of Levinas' approach to the feminine, and then queries whether one must really choose between them. He writes, beautifully as always: "Need one choose between two incompatible readings, between an androcentric hyperbole and a feminist one? Is there any place for such a choice in ethics? And in justice? In law? In politics? Nothing is less certain" (1999, 44).

27. The examination of Levinas' Jewish writings by Claire Katz and Susan Shapiro also shed light on this issue.

28. In *Levinas, Judaism, and the Feminine*, Katz argues that themes tied to the feminine, such as sexual difference and the erotic, elicit: the overall experience of alterity, the initial experience of present and future, the condition for the possibility of the face-to-face relation, the possibility for asymmetrical intersubjectivity, the interruption of male virility, and the highest model—as maternity—for ethics.

29. A similar point is made by Ewa Ziarek (Chanter, ed., 2001, 94).

30. Levinas' 1979 preface to *Time and the Other* also appears to respond to criticisms of his treatment of the feminine in that text. He states that femininity was used to argue for or illustrate the fundamental differences in the sexes, and thus "as the very quality of difference" (1987, 36). He also seeks to clarify his understanding of paternity and the son.

31. Maternity is also a category of excess that often belies an attempt to attribute self-interest to all human endeavors. For example, in Kierkegaard's *Works of Love*, only the relation of the mother to the child seems to contest his main thesis that all human love, as against Christian love, is motivated by self-interest (Kierkegaard 1995, 214, 221). However, in a supplemental text Kierkegaard does identify maternal love as self-love (183).

32. This argument is made in *Speaking/Writing of God*, for both Levinas and Rosenzweig (Oppenheim 1997, 83–93). However, there is a place in one of Levinas' essays, "Judaism and the Feminine," in which his own words about this are deeply disappointing. He writes: "The feminine will never take on the aspect of the divine. . . . The dimension of intimacy is opened by woman, not the dimension of loftiness" (cited in Chanter, ed., 2001, 76).

33. Levinas' separation of ethics from self-interest and from pleasure certainly reinforces determinate features of Kant's treatment of ethics.

34. Shapiro forcefully argues that Levinas' removal of the feminine/women from the ethical is pervasive. She writes, for example: "This exclusion of the feminine from the public domain in which justice pertains problematically registers the exclusion from principles of justice of the feminine, of Woman defined through and in relation to the feminine, and, perhaps, even of women" (188). On the whole, I find her essay to be compelling, but I believe that Levinas' portrayal of eschatology is more radical, and thus possibly more redemptive, than she does. See the concluding chapter of this book.

35. This is the title of Tina Chanter's book on Irigaray (1995).

36. Along with philosophy, Irigaray finds that the discipline of psychoanalysis is also based upon a rejection of sexual difference. In her long examination of Freud in *Speculum*, she uncovers all of the ways that Freud sees the little girl as just a little man. Despite this, as with all of the critiques that she offers, there is also a deep respect for his intent and contribution. As convoluted and injurious as his discussion of women is, at least it allows women some distinctive experiences and relationships.

37. See her essay "The Three Genres" (1991a).

38. This point, that the desire for relation is not just a derivative from other basic human needs, so important to object relations thinkers and the Jewish philosophers, is also clearly expressed by Irigaray. She writes: "Before orality comes to be, touch is already in existence. No nourishment can compensate for the grace, or the work, of touching" (1986, 232).

39. A major theme in Buber's extensive literature on the Jewish mystical movement, Hasidism, does offer a parallel to Irigaray's notion of the sensible transcendental. The Hasidic idea of the "hallowing of the everyday" is one of the most important features that Buber identifies. In his view, Hasidism recognizes that the divine can be met in or introduced through every action with the material world. The erotic relation

between the husband and wife—this is from the husband's point of reference—is one of the privileged arenas for such hallowing. In explaining his view of Hasidism, Buber has written of the "devotion to the divine and the hallowing of lived life through this devotion . . . the hallowing extends fundamentally to the natural and social life" (in Schilpp and Friedman, eds., 1967, 732).

40. Reading Irigaray has given me a new appreciation for Erikson's essay "Womanhood and Inner Space." The essay insists that the issue of sexual difference is salient in each of the psycho-social stages. He writes, for example: "the fact that a woman, whatever else she may also be, never is not-a-woman creates unique relations between her individuality, her somatic existence, and her social potentials and demands that the feminine identity be studied and defined in its own right" (1968, 290) Further, Erikson rejects Freud's portrait of the feminine in terms of lack, and ponders the emerging impact of women's voices on all areas of culture, including science. Despite some problematic features, this is an insightful attempt to explore the meaning of sexual difference.

41. Again, I make this argument in chapter 4 of *Speaking/Writing of God.* See note 32 above.

Conclusion

Narrating Life and Death

THE MODERN JEWISH PHILOSOPHERS and the post-Freudian psychoanalysts whom we have studied feature the relationship to others in their exceptional view of the human. They narrate birth, growth, and maturity in terms of those essential gifts, such as identity, trust, integrity, and purpose that are received from others or that are cultivated through the interactions between persons. These narratives also include, sometimes in great detail and other times only suggestively, accounts of society, history, and the encounter with death. The point of departure for the last stage of our investigation are the questions: How does this distinctive perspective on the human affect the understandings of what communal life is or should be, of what one can expect from history, and of how one goes on living in the face of death? These issues have been touched upon previously, but it is fitting that this conclusion brings them into prominence. Each group of thinkers uses a distinctive language and has available particular resources to address these concerns. In the main, these questions about the social order, history, and death have a more central role in the narratives of the Jewish philosophers and that is why this treatment will begin with their reflections. Despite some important differences, the Jewish philosophers provide a very harmonious vision. The presentations of Rosenzweig, Levinas, and Buber feature such terms as community, history, and messianism in deliberating upon these dimensions of life, and the term meaning in discussing the issue of death. While the psychoanalysts do not consistently address these issues, they offer important and sometimes startling insights. The expositions of Erikson, Klein, Fairbairn, Winnicott, and Irigaray explore the social dimension in terms of group and society, and, paradoxically, the challenge of death through the language of health. Many of the particular narratives of the Jewish philosophers and the psychoanalysts join together treatments of the two issues, death and society. They see a relationship between inauthentic ways of facing death and destructive forms of individual and communal life.

History and Society

Rosenzweig's discussion of the state, history, true community, and God's kingdom are sometimes in the background or implicit, and at other times in the foreground and explicit in *The Star*. The topics appear in many of its sections and in some ways are the allusive bedrock for his unique narrative. Rosenzweig's treatment of history and communal life parallels his discussion of the human and the interhuman. History is the domain of the state. As with the unredeemed individuals, states antagonistically face each other as independent and sovereign wills and also crave some escape from the inevitability of their disappearance from history. However, that time and history in which states live makes their efforts ultimately futile. This time is always finite, despite protests and pretensions. Internally, they seek to stop up the rush of time through laws that violently force the ever-changing lives of its citizens into frozen paths. Externally, states seek to defend themselves against the self-affirmation and growth of other states. These two patterns of behavior dominate history, or in Rosenzweig's words: "Thus war [against other states] and revolution [when citizens themselves violently overthrow the state's outworn laws] is the only reality known to the state" (1972, 333). History is the record of transient victories floating in a stream of violence and blood. There is no overall meaning, direction, or permanence to be found in this dimension.[1]

Eternity, that meeting of the above and below, is stitched into time through the interhuman and the communal. Wherever the individual has forgotten the battle with death to turn to the neighbor with love, there a moment of eternity has arisen. Here a piece of soul has been planted in history, a process which Rosenzweig characterizes as ensouling. Loving the other, the neighbor, is only possible for Rosenzweig, because she or he has experienced God's love and trusts in the direction that love imparted. Loving the neighbor transfers and extends this love to the other, the next one, who stands on one's destined path.

Participation in God's kingdom, another dimension of eternity, brings the individual into the wider community. True community, as against the state, achieves actual permanence. Rosenzweig spoke of two such communities, of

Judaism and Christianity. In each of these, individuals and groups are not isolated and in confrontation with each other. These communities represent two different, peaceful ways that each group's particularity is expanded into the universal. The Jewish community sees itself as ultimately including everyone, and at every moment, through prayer, takes up the burden of responsibility for all humanity. The Christian community lives by continually adding new members and looks toward the day when it also includes everyone. Both testify to the imperceptible growth of God's kingdom.[2]

In essence, Rosenzweig is saying that meaning is only found in authentic relations between individuals and within communities. These are communities that do not separate persons from other persons. Their religious experience and vision allow them to envision a transformed communal life where all are represented and responsible for each other. They live and grow not through the expansion of the self/same, but through respect and responsibility for the other. Rosenzweig believes that it is, once again, the encounter with the divine that provides communities with the trust and hope requisite for such openness.

Thus, Rosenzweig is very clear about what he expects from history. The answer is nothing: nothing but fear, evasion, illusion, and violence. One cannot look to history for the good cause to be victorious. Victory and the good are not on the same plane. Still, the individual is not permitted to bypass life. Through loving the neighbor, the pluralist, peaceful, and all-inclusive "we" of the community's meaning appears. In Rosenzweig's narrative eternity and the kingdom, which stand opposed to history, are often synonymous. In truth, they are existential terms, not referents to everyday time, history, and reality. They speak of another reality. As Rosenzweig writes:

> Eternity is a Today which is, however, conscious of being more than Today. If then the kingdom is eternally coming, this means that, while its growth is essential, the tempo of this growth is not fixed, nay, more exactly: *the growth has no relationship at all to time.* An existence which has once merged into the kingdom cannot drop out again; it has entered the once-for-all; it has become eternal. (my emphasis, 1972, 224)

Thus stands Rosenzweig's distinctive religious narrative about the way that the interhuman naturally evolves into a story of a redemption above history.

Buber's views about community, politics, history, and eternity directly grow out of his presentations of the two-fold attitude of humans and the redemptive quality of meetings, particularly between persons. We have seen that humans are intentional, that is, they are always turning toward the world, either with the basic word I-It or the basic word I-Thou. Both attitudes are needed, that of getting things done where the world is basically an object, and meeting the other in mutuality and reciprocity where each partner speaks out of her or his wholeness and actuality. Of course, in the judgment of the everyday world, both public and private, success is measured in terms of the achievements in the realm of I-It. Buber sees an increase of this attitude in all corners, so that the realm of It dominates modern life as never before. Still, it is only through the dialogue with another, whether the other be nature, artistic objects, or persons, that humans emerge in their fullness. Saying "Thou" to another is not only a transformative event for the participants, but ultimately addresses the Eternal Thou, the One who can never become an it. Human lives are thus formed in the deepest ways by moments where this dual address is realized. At its highest, the human is a response to a word continually available, giving direction and a sense of mission in the world. As with Rosenzweig, Buber notes that there is no worldly ledger to record and document these events of meeting. Buber writes in *I and Thou*:

> These moments are immortal; none are more evanescent. They leave no content that could be preserved, but their force enters into the creation and into man's knowledge, and the radiation of its force penetrates the ordered world and thaws it again and again. Thus the history of the individual, thus the history of the race. (1970, 82)

From his earliest days, Buber had an abiding interest in communal life, social movements, and politics, and his writings on these subjects are extensive. The duplex character of the basic attitudes is reflected in his understanding of these phenomena. This is seen through such distinctions as those between true community and collectivity or society, and between the social principle and the political principle. Yet, these distinctions also reveal that Buber thought that there was an obligation, and here the Kantian maxim of ought implying can does apply, to re-direct communal and political life. There are many discussions of the nature of true community. For example, in *I and Thou*, he holds that persons "have to stand in a living, reciprocal relationship to a single living center, and they have to stand in a living, reciprocal relationship to one another" (1970, 94). Other treatments are less epigrammatic than this dialogic formulation. He has compared community to marriage. In all, he finds that community must be grounded in such elements as the acknowledgment that the individual is now part of a group that as a unit lives its purpose and mission before God, the respect and celebration of the "otherness" of those in the group, the insistence that group life not be immune to ethical judgment about "right and wrong" or "truth and lies," and the recognition that there may be times when the individual must stand apart and speak out against what is happening in the community.[3]

Buber concedes that communal life is not usually assessed in such terms. The political arena is always defined in terms of power and success. It often is the raw expression of a group egoism that rejects internal otherness and is willing to go to all lengths to defend or extend its security and sovereignty. However, Buber would not just concede the political domain to those who were committed to this viewpoint. He spoke of a Hebrew humanism that recognized the legitimate need for security but also did not forswear judgments about right and wrong. He writes:

> The *humanitas* which speaks from this Book [the Bible] today, as it has always done, is the unity of human life under one divine direction which divides right from wrong and truth from lies as unconditionally as the words of the Creator divided light from darkness. (1973, 458)

> Israel is chosen to enable it to ascend from the biological law of power, which the nations glorify in their wishful thinking, to the sphere of truth and righteousness. (1973, 461)

For him, the people of Israel was constituted to be a model community—and thus, that its "election is completely a demand" (1973, 461), where justice guided both the means and end of public policy.

Still, Buber was not naive about history. As we saw above, moments of redemption, of true I and Thou meetings, whether with single partners or in group life, were fleeting. He rejected the Hegelian perspective that believed that meaning resided in history, actualized through the inevitable accumulative outcome of an all-encompassing dialectical process. Buber hinted that there was a secret pattern or meaning to history, but this was neither incremental nor manifest. At one point he wrote about "the history of the created world" as a "journey." This is not marked by outward signs, but by "the very soft, very slow, very roundabout, not at all successful step of the deity through history" (cited in Schilpp and Friedman, eds., 1967, 441).

Perhaps the earlier, but continually reaffirmed, concluding panoramic of history in *I and Thou* should be added as the ultimate statement by Buber about history. Burdened by the increase of the I-It world, he fights for a model to describe his faith in history's meaning. History does not uncoil through empty cycles of eternal recurrence nor through secure stages of progress. Even in the darkness of the present he finds hope, but it is deeply marked by the apocalyptic. He writes:

> But the path is not a circle. It is the way. Doom becomes more oppressive in every new eon, and the return more explosive. . . . Every spiral of its path leads us into

> deeper corruption and at the same time into more fundamental return. But the God-side of the event whose world-side is called return is called redemption. (1970, 168)

While ethics is the heading under which all of Levinas' later work resides, the topics of history, war, politics, the state, messianism, and eschatology are frequently addressed. His major books testify to their importance in his philosophic project. The second sentence in *Totality and Infinity* asks: "Does not lucidity, the mind's openness upon the true, consist in catching sight of the permanent possibility of war?," and he continues: "The state of war suspends morality" (1969, 21). The dedication for *Otherwise Than Being* is "To the memory of those who were closest among the six million assassinated by the National Socialists, and of the millions on millions of all confessions and all nations, victims of the same hatred of the other man, the same anti-semitism" (1981, iv).

Levinas' discussion of life in the world follows upon his analysis of the twofold character of the human. On the one hand, there is the self which is for itself and jealous of its freedom and rights, in Pascal's words, its "place in the sun."[4] This is the natural creature who reluctantly joins together with others in the state, to guard against a war of all against all. Thus, the state is the extension of the self's purely egotistical being. It erases all that is different, by either appropriating what can be taken in and made into itself, or repressing and destroying all that stands for otherness. Levinas depicts this political entity as the State of Caesar or of Hobbes: "jealous of its sovereignty . . . in search of hegemony, the conquering, imperialist, totalitarian, oppressive State, attached to realist egoism" (1994, 184). Politics is the terrain of states, where they stand in hostile opposition to each other. War is the default position, peace only a respite.

As with Rosenzweig, Levinas sees history as the record of this life of politics and states. It covers over the weak and the good, to tell the story of survivors, usurpers, and conquerors. Sometimes another vision of history is offered, but one that is not essentially different. This is a vision that somehow at the end, through some teleology, theodicy, or afterlife, evil is vanquished and good prevails. However, Levinas distrusts such a deus ex machina as much as history itself. For this divination is still based on a concern for the self, its goals, and its ultimate permanence.[5]

What would a vision born of an otherwise or a beyond being provide? It would arise out of conscience, out of one's apology for this place in the sun. In the face of the other, the self, every self, stands accused. As we know, ethics is the language of this proximity or priority of the other one. This second dimension of the portrait of the human, but from another perspective both prior and primary, provides a way of seeing, a prophetic eschatology, that subverts the verdict of history. One looks in vain for its "victories" to be recorded, now or even at some all-inclusive end time. In Levinas' words: "The eschatological, as the 'beyond' of history, draws beings out of the jurisdiction of history and the future; it arouses them in and calls them forth to their full responsibility" (1969, 23). Eschatology or messianism refers to the obligation to judge the present from the perspective of ethics. It also alludes to a standpoint that perceives instants of the good or flashes of truth as they intersect the seemingly impenetrable tight-stitched material of history. Such instants that are dedicated to the other's time, constitute time in its fullest reality. Their meaning endures. As Levinas writes: "The eschatological . . . restores to each instant its full signification in that very instant . . . it is the judgment of all the instants in time, when the living are judged" (1969, 23).

Levinas comments about what might be termed true community are much less cohesive than those of Rosenzweig and Buber. He does speak of a politics that is "beyond politics." This is the possibility of a community rising above the usual rules of its own self-interest. This "Messianic City" would have to adopt a prophetic attitude. In some essays Levinas has a very guarded optimism about the state of Israel, and also recognizes messianic acts in the lives of some political figures, such as President Sadat's visit to Jerusalem. However, such terms as Israel and messianism also have an explicitly universal reference in his texts. Following his understanding of rabbinic exegesis, Israel always, equally, stands for certain ethical potentials in every person. For, in his words: "One belongs to the Messianic order when one has been able to admit others among one's own" (1994a, 98).

Thus, Levinas is saying that the only meaning available is when the self is hostaged to the other. That this meaning cannot be inscribed through a syllogism, a bill of rights, or a historical text is inevitable. How could a rationality of being and identity or even of mutual obligations identify infinite responsibility, and what place could the prophetic have in the magisterial record of victors? Just as the other interrupts the self in its satisfaction, morality/ethics interrupts politics. The dimension of meaning is otherwise, its sign is found in the evanescence evoked by the religious term "glory."

The themes of community, society, and history in somewhat analogous ways to the treatments by Rosenzweig, Buber, and Levinas appear with varying frequency in the main narratives and subsidiary writings of the post-Freudian psychoanalysts. How does the relational view of the human affect the understanding of society for these theorists? We have looked at the narrative of Erik Erikson primarily as a transitional statement, between Freud himself, and Klein and the object relations theorists. Erikson's narrative of the eight psychosocial stages emphasizes the theme that human development must always be examined in terms of the interaction of the individual with an ever-widening social environment, from mother to the history of generations. Still, as the label "ego psychoanalyst" accurately notes, he does not provide a fully interhuman account. While his examination of society has been a major pole in his work, much of that does not therefore necessarily fall within the parameters of our treatment.

Erikson's early book, *Childhood and Society*, provides a good indication of his approach to the social environment. He is interested in the ways that communities, societies, and cultures either enhance or undermine the ego development of the child. In his words:

> to understand either childhood or society, we must expand our scope to include the study of the way in which societies lighten the inescapable conflicts of childhood with a promise of some security, identity, and integrity. In thus reinforcing the values by which the ego exists societies create the only condition under which human growth is possible. (1963, 277)

For example, in the earliest stage, the mother is only able to convey an elemental sense of trust if she is herself sustained through the resources of a positive, supportive community and culture. The identity stage also demonstrates this interaction of ego and society. The sense of identity requires a social order that provides possible roles or careers for the adolescent in order for her or him to begin to coalesce a sense of who she or he is. Society also furnishes values, ideologies, rituals, creeds, and programs that provide further foundation and direction to the budding adolescent. However, Erikson equally documents the ways that social orders, from religious groups to whole societies and civilizations, undermine ego growth. They often exploit the fears and failures of infantile development, in order to sustain their precarious cohesion or to vilify an external enemy. Erikson is particularly helpful concerning the way that groups stave off the fear of disintegration and death. In the next section we will explore these insights.

Klein offered little directly upon the topics here, but there are features of her provocative narrative that are promising. There has been some examination of Klein's meaning for social theory,[6] which has concentrated on her most important innovation, the paranoid-schizoid and depressive positions. As related earlier, Klein replaced Freud's narrative about drives with an account of passions and their objects. The time of infancy is divided by the two positions, but these are more than just infantile stages. The paranoid-schizoid and depressive positions are attitudes or relationships, which express distinctive constellations of emotions, fantasies, anxieties, and defenses, and their related inner and outer objects. In addition, they continue to stand as a foundation for later life, since the individual is always in the midst of one or the other of these attitudes. Ultimately, the positions tell the tale of two basic emotions, hate and love. They relate how human life is lived, through the struggle between, and permutations of, these emotions. As critics have noted: "The central conflict in human experience, for Klein, is between love and hate, between the caring preservation and the malicious destruction of others" (Greenberg and Mitchell 1983, 142).

The paranoid-schizoid position emerges from the infant's efforts to defend against a primitive aggression that overwhelms her or him. It is not clear to what extent the relationship to the mother affects the first expression of violence, but the inevitable frustrations in the relationship between infant and mother further fuels it. The infant experiences this violence as threatening in the deepest way and defends against it through such techniques as projection, projective identification, splitting, and idealization. The governing emotions of this stage are envy, jealously, and greed, all of which incite hoarding the good and undermining and poisoning that which cannot be appropriated to the self. These techniques and emotions can be generally correlated with a wider viewpoint about society and the world. The paranoid-schizoid position is driven by fear. In later life, those caught in this stage project their own aggression onto the world, which, in typical paranoid fashion, they invariably see as threatening. Other persons are placed into two camps, some idealized and some demonized. The actual views and actions of these others have little impact upon the dominating fantasies. Momentary safety is achieved through manipulation and control. Instrumental reason is valued, because it allows one to achieve his or her ends. This is also the morality of the *lex talionis*, where a definition of justice vindicates perceived aggression and violence from others being responded to by equally destructive acts.

The infant moves to the depressive position as her or his cognitive skills mature and in reaction (gratitude) to positive experiences with the mother. Motivated by guilt about the violence of phantasies concerning the mother, the infant seeks reparation. He or she fears that this is too late: that the aggression against the mother has proved totally destructive to the only person and world that is known. However, recognizing and identifying with the good in the primary object, the infant has some faith in her or his own powers to heal. The emotions that govern this stage are care, concern, mercy, and gratitude. The infant is more sensitive to the nature of the other and to reality overall. Thus, there is a more realistic and integrative understanding, recognizing that good and bad features reside together, both in the self and in others. One critic sees a significant dynamic being worked out in the depressive position. He writes: "Through reparation [with the other] we begin to integrate those parts of the self devoted to love and hate. In so doing, we make ourselves as whole and complete as possible, while gaining confidence in our own goodness" (Alford 1989, 172).

The depressive position may be seen to generate its own distinctive worldview. In this scenario, others are important for themselves, and persons are capable of care and concern, which is not motivated, or primarily motivated, by self-interest. This attitude recognizes the possibility of individuals making sacrifices for the well-being of others. Its guiding rationality is reparation, which is concern for others, for their own sake. In this light, the world is more nuanced, and reality is allowed to have an impact on fantasy, through reality-testing. The integrated standpoint of the depressive position should not, however, lead to splitting good and bad. The self and other persons are seen to have both positive and negative features; and fears, anxieties, defensive positions, and guilt also have a place here. The lesson of the depressive position is that hate and aggression can never be eliminated or fully subdued. They can be integrated into a wider attitude of understanding, love, and care.

Thus, it is possible to draw important lessons about social theory from Klein's insights. She suggests that there are two distinctive ways of viewing the world, and that both emerge from equally deep human attitudes. The first approaches the world in terms of power and self-interest: a Hobbesian universe? It would see that the violence of persons can be contained through a social order that sought to lessen and reconcile conflict through a system of strict justice. Klein seems to think that at the group level this is the usual modus operandi. However, she also finds that care and concern for others is as equally as innate, equally as realistic, as the attitudes of aggression and self-interest. Humans are capable of addressing others in their own light and for their own sake. This position, actually less dominated by phantasy and more open to reality, provides a fruitful standpoint for thinking about the possibilities of the social order.

Winnicott and Fairbairn do not offer expansive resources, at least as far as I have seen, in their discussions of history and society. Winnicott's thinking about society follows upon his presentation of infantile stages and transitional phenomena, and again demonstrates his modified relational paradigm that sees the mother and infant as a single unit, but also focuses on the true self. For Winnicott, the mother must protect the child from the impingement from the outside world as well as help it cope with and shape the forces of its inner world. If these tasks have been accomplished in satisfactory ways, then the sense of self and its meaning are allowed to develop. In commenting upon the "social sense" in individuals, Winnicott characteristically has written: "Here it is implied that the individual can identify with adults and with a social group, or with society, without too great a loss of personal impulse and originality" (1965a, 66–67). Beyond the mother, father, and family, individuals interact with the world through other groups. If there is identity and security within the group, the individual is able to explore wider horizons. Creativity and acceptance of difference are based on the dynamics of the transitional object. This object is both me and not-me. Through the fantasy of the transitional object, the self is able to encounter what is new and accept and play with difference. When the individual has the security and freedom to be in touch with its secret self and to also expand its horizons to what lies beyond, she or he establishes a life of creativity and meaning.

Fairbairn has offered a number of ideas that extend his narrative about the stages of infantile and mature dependence to speak of the social world. He believed that societies could foster either immature and deeply dependent individuals or mature persons. In societies where the majority of persons have not firmly arrived at the ability to live in mutuality, or where there is great deprivation and persons are not given the resources to have some independence and integrity, then the potential of its members will be greatly stunted. In these cases, reflecting the stage of infantile dependence, individuals will treat others as part objects or things, and quickly react to frustration through violence. However, societies also have the possibility of actually furthering the psychological development of their members.[7]

It may prove to be more helpful to take a wider angle on the question of the social implications of the relational narratives of Fairbairn, Winnicott and similar psychoanalytic theorists. The writers Greenberg and Mitchell close their classic treatment, *Object Relations in Psychoanalytic Theory*, by examining the distinctive views of society that correspond to drive theorists—especially Freud—and to these relational theorists.[8] For the former, the individual is primarily an autonomous unit. The innate drives punctuate development: their expression and structuring define each person. The authors correlate this with the theories of society by such British thinkers as Hobbes and Locke. From this perspective individuals have their own goals, which often conflict with those of other persons. The social contract tries to minimize conflict while maximizing individual liberty. Some individual sacrifice is thus necessary, in order to pursue life and pleasure, and to protect property. The other model of human nature with roots in Rousseau, Hegel, and additional Continental thinkers sees humans as intrinsically relational and social. Persons are structured to desire contact and to feel mutual concern. Humans require others in order to develop, since there is no self outside of relationships. The important point here is that if persons are seen as requiring others, then society is neither a secondary concern, nor can its telos be understood primarily in terms of security. Ultimately, a supportive social order is needed for the highest human experiences and expressions to occur. In outlining this viewpoint, Greenberg and Mitchell conclude with a quotation from Rousseau: "Through the social contract, the individual transcends his private, isolated existence to become part of something broader and more meaningful, 'a larger whole, from which he in a sense draws life and being'" (1983, 402). The relational psychoanalysts may be seen to suggest that a sense of "life and being" can only be achieved through a society that is based on an understanding of persons' attachment to, dependence upon, and respect for others.

The philosophic and psychoanalytic streams that make up Irigaray's work are clearly brought together in her critique and recasting of the social order. This is evident in an explosive quotation from *This Sex Which Is Not One*:

> When women want to escape from exploitation, they do not merely destroy a few "prejudices," they disrupt the entire order of dominant values, economic, social, moral, and sexual. They call into question all existing theory, all thought, all language, inasmuch as these are monopolized by men and men alone. They challenge *the very foundation of our social and cultural order*, whose organization has been prescribed by the patriarchal system. (1985, 165)

Irigaray has also tried to suggest what types of community, as both means and end, follow upon her critique and revisioning.

As we have seen, the various ways that women have been denied a place in society as well as turned into imagoes, reflecting the rejected aspects of the male psyche, have brought society to a dangerous standstill, a warring standoff. Women are made into objects reflecting male desire, circulating things, whose exchange among men cements society together. The image of the female or the feminine, through male splitting and projection, has come to represent difference, the body, sexuality, nature, and death. Society now is monological and monolithic, where men are the only subjects in the male God's kingdom. All of this has lead to a rejection of real difference and a refusal to acknowledge the limits of life or the inevitability of death. Lives of endless repetition, hollowness, desperation, and illusory hope have made violence and destruction inescapable.

Irigaray's notion of "amorous exchange," represents the requisite corrective to this situation.[9] Based upon the acknowledgment of the reality and differences of the two sexes, such an exchange between equals would embrace psychic, bodily, linguistic, cultural, and political dimensions. Women would need to be full subjects, with their own desire, phantasies, and linguistic forms. Men would come to acknowledge their limits, including their dependence upon their mothers, and understand that difference, both within and without, fuels creativity and life. This exchange is no panacea. Humans will also be alternately propelled and torn by drives, phantasies, and fears. However, the fullness of life is only open to those who find some joy in its differences and limits. The excessive, transformative logic of sexual love is the paradigm for the amorous exchange. In this bodily love, the two partners become one yet remain two; find their own body and integrity through exploring and respecting that of their lover; and in being reminded of their past/birth, create new possibilities for the present and future.

What types of social form follow Irigaray's analysis and vision? Certainly there would have to be plural communities. Among these, some would be constituted by women among themselves, where their own relationships to their mothers, sisters, and daughters could be explored. There would also be communities of the two sexes. Here not only the issues of equality would be addressed, but also the particular duties and rights of each sex would have to be thought/lived through and negotiated. Finally, there would be new expressions of the imaginary, symbolic, and linguistic orders, expressions that cannot be foreseen.

What can we conclude from these reflections on community, society, and history, which are sometimes embedded in and at other times emerge from the two narratives about the interhuman? In their own ways and through their particular vocabularies, these narratives portray how the self hungers for, emerges from, and develops through relationships. They recount that through relationship to the other, the self is constituted, brought into maturity, and led to meaning and health.

Consequently, one can infer from the above that the richness of communal life requires an acknowledgment of what is owed to others, a trust in the other, and an appreciation for difference. Maturity, meaning, and health cannot occur, or cannot fully occur, if the self forgets its reliance on others, or rejects the essential otherness of its neighbors. In fact, such a forgetting and rejection inevitably converge. The vision of an autonomous self requires that others be similar to oneself, independent and self-sufficient, containing all that is real and true. However, meaning and health, new opportunities and new openings, require that the other be welcomed, in gratitude, for the sake of her or his otherness and difference.

Perhaps we can tentatively connect the Jewish philosophers' language about responsibility to the other with the view of society that was seen to be implied in the positions of the post-Freudian psychoanalysts. Together the narratives envision communities brought together in respect for the debts that each person owes to all the others. This language is manifest in the Jewish philosophers, who see, for example, love of the neighbor and concern for the widow, stranger, orphan, and poor as commands. Debt is experienced as an asymmetrical command for them. In terms of the psychoanalysts, debt may be said to flow as a repayment to what has been given. If the self becomes and matures only through the other, then the self is in debt to those others. Who are these others? They are first of all, obviously and following Irigaray, mothers. Further, explicitly following Erikson, they would be the whole societies that provide the resources that allow parents to nourish the trust of their infants, families to give direction to their children, communities to provide meaning and opportunities for their adolescents, and adults to pass on their legacy to the next generation. For both the philosophers and the psychoanalysts, the debt extends from the neighbor, whom everyone potentially is, to communities and societies, eventually including all the world.

What might a society based on this viewpoint look like? There is a discussion of some alternative views of society in the eighteenth century that might offer a clue in this direction. In an acclaimed biography of the Jewish philosopher Moses Mendelssohn, Alexander Altmann attempted to differentiate Mendelssohn's reflections on society from that of his influential contemporary, Thomas Hobbes. This reference to Hobbes thus repeats and extends the remarks of Greenberg and Mitchell introduced above. As we saw, Hobbes represents a perspective that understands humans as basically autonomous and antagonistic. Individuals enter society only with the most reluctance, motivated by their fear of violence from the other. The role of government is to maximize individual freedom and minimize the conflict between persons. Mendelssohn presented a very different view of humans and society. As Altmann explained: "Mendelssohn thus considered the origin of society to lie in a moral necessity or sense of duty inherent in the very nature of man" (1973, 521). He held that persons come together to form communities because they cannot fulfill their responsibilities to others as isolated individuals. Mendelssohn wrote: "Man cannot be happy without beneficence, whether it be passive, through receiving it, or active, through extending it. He cannot attain perfection except through mutual assistance, through reciprocity of service, through active and passive connection with his fellowman" (cited in Altmann 1973, 524). Just as Hobbes' understanding of human nature led to a specific vision of the nature of society, the relational understanding of human life leads to its own, very different one. In this case the purpose of society would be to help persons, individually and in communities, fulfill those fundamental debts that are owed to others. To fulfill this purpose of society, communities would be judged on whether they provided adequate levels of health care, shelter, wages, and schooling; furnished opportunities for advancement in social, political, and cultural life; and welcomed the dispossessed and refugee. In these ways, communities would help to meet the obligations of all members to the sick, poor, orphan, widow, and stranger. There is a rabbinic midrash that presumes this understanding of society, where each member begins not in innocence but in obligation, and where failure to act is considered a crime. As recounted by a recent commentator:

> "How," it is asked in the midrash, "can one rob from the poor?" The answer is given that one robs from the poor when we do not give them what we are obligated to give them—gleanings, the forgotten sheaves, the corner of the field, and the poor man's tithe. We rob them when we fail in our obligations. (cited in Chanter, ed., 2001, 170)

Death

The major place that the theme of death takes up in Rosenzweig's principal narrative has been noted many times earlier. *The Star* begins with the words "from death," and concludes with "into life." Death enters into discussions about the individual, the soul and the other, and community. Rosenzweig starts by criticizing the inauthentic response to death given by philosophic Idealism, which features the proposition that "only" the body dies while the essence of the individual lives on. Rosenzweig insisted on taking death seriously, which was probably reinforced by the fact that he was writing while dug in at the Balkan front, in the midst of the horrendous carnage that was World War I. He replied that the Idealistic evasion did not constitute a realistic answer for the actual, living human being. Still, the fear of death had to be honestly quieted, or else the individual would not be able to creatively turn to life and the world of others.[10] This cannot be done by the solitary individual, but only with the help of others. Ultimately, it requires an encounter with the divine. The experience of divine love provides trust and meaning. This love is, as the Bible proclaims, "as strong as death." It reassures the transformed soul that the created world does not conclude with death, for the Creator is also the Revealer and Redeemer. The soul, fortified by love, trusts in the meaning of her or his life, and is now able to extend this love to the neighbor. This reiterates a message we have seen before: authentic relation to the other requires resources beyond those of the isolated individual, resources that follow upon another's gift.

Death also looms large as a presence in Rosenzweig's understanding of communal life. As we saw, the political life of states is dedicated to trying to create islands of eternity while struggling with the constant flow of time. However, these efforts are not effective, and they inevitably lead to divisions among groups and the violence of war and revolution. Ultimate meaning only corresponds to a transcendent dimension. Put another way, states can only fabricate artificial eternity. Religious communities, on the other hand, which Rosenzweig characterizes in terms of inclusiveness and diversity, provide true experiences of eternity. Judaism and Christianity are able to "wrest their eternity from time" (1999, 94).

In all, for Rosenzweig, neither the individual's life nor life itself is eternal. All life "flows from birth toward death" (1999a, 101). Even the two communities of Judaism and Christianity will not prevail when at the very end, God becomes "All in All." Death cannot be evaded, but it also is not allowed the final word. The life lived with others has transcendent meaning. As Rosenzweig writes: "The living soul, loved by God, triumphs over all that is mortal, and that is all that can be *objectively* stated about it" (my emphasis, 1972, 202). In another text, he expresses this in terms of health: "There is no remedy for death; not even health. A healthy man, however, has the strength to continue towards the grave. The sick man invokes death and lets himself be carried away in mortal fear. . . . In health, even death comes at the 'proper' time. Health is on good terms with Death" (1999a, 103). Rosenzweig, whose own life was weakened and cut short by a debilitating paralysis, is not referring here to physical health. Health that is "on good terms with Death" is a health nurtured by trust, meaning, and a sense of direction that point beyond death. Strengthened by these gifts, a person can affirm that death, whenever and however it arrives, comes at the "proper" time. For despair, which in Rosenzweig's narrative would characterize a life cut off from others, there is no proper time.

The term death rarely appears in *I and Thou* or other major works of Buber. One critic argues that "the between," that is, the narration of life lived between birth and death, eclipses all speculation about beginning and end (Kepnes 1992, 98). *I and Thou* does contain an elusive reference to "mankind's craving to take the edge off the mystery of death" (56). This is written in the context of Buber's discussion of the way that individuals often seek, without success, to establish a depth and meaning in their lives by differentiating between inner and outer experiences, hoping to find in the former some key to existence. Buber, of course, was as critical of this process of splitting as was Rosenzweig of Idealism's endeavor to escape death by distinguishing an inner essence from the outer body. For both, meaning only appears in the between, that is, in the life with others.

For Buber, the meaning that accrues to life out of the double dialogue, with beings in the world and with the eternal Thou, provides the only possible response to the question of death. The mystery of life cannot be solved, but in living in the world with a sense of purpose and mission, one transforms its evanescence into an answer to God's call. The life of dialogue recognizes the reality of death and the other terrors of existence. Buber believes that all of this, life and death, mystery and direction, terror and fulfillment, exist together and must be embraced together (1970, 143). He has expressed this enigmatic insight in various forms, including through the following statement: "You need God in order to be, and God needs you—for that which is the meaning of your life. . . . The world is not divine play, it is divine fate. That there are world, man, the human person, you and I, has divine meaning" (1970, 130).

How does the optics of ethics affect one's perspective on death? The approach to death in Levinas' narrative exhibits characteristic stances and the unsettling but profound insights that often accompany his distinctive viewpoint. His narrative of relation and responsibility refuses to turn away or forget this daunting fear and threat, but takes it up again and again. Levinas' friend and critic, Jacques Derrida, writes: "And yet all of Levinas's thought, from the beginning to the end, was a meditation on death, a meditation that diverted, disconcerted, and set beside itself everything in philosophy, from Plato to Hegel and Heidegger" (1999, 120).

Typically, Levinas' reflections on death are obsessed with the other person's death, and not one's own. Death enters into one's consciousness from the face of the other. Many of the lessons found in the vulnerability of the other's face touch upon death. The neighbor's face communicates its susceptibility to suffering and death. It reminds the self of its own potential to violence, to the possibility of murder. This, in turn, evokes that universal feature of ethical conscience that is expressed in the biblical command "Thou shalt not kill!" The face that suffers the possibility of death also calls to me not to leave the other alone to her or his fate. In all, death shakes the self out of its self-satisfaction, its pretensions to innocence and indifference, at the thought of the other's death. Once again, the self is put into question and reminded of those responsibilities that point toward infinity. Yet, it is precisely, and only, that by being for the other, one is taking a stand "against death" (1969, 224).

For Levinas, the theme of death never returns the self to itself. In his words: "Fear for the other person does not come back to anguish over *my* death" (1998, 131). Ethics brings an interruption to the concern about my death and the possibilities that somehow the self can continue. It does not speak of an escape from death or allude to the perseverance of the self in another life. Still, ethics opens the way for a meaning despite death. Levinas writes: "No one is so hypocritical as to claim that he has taken from death its sting, not even the promisers of religion. But we can have responsibilities and attachments through which death takes on a meaning" (1981, 129). Being for the other, thus, witnesses to a belief that responding to the other builds up, in an incalculable way, a dowry for the future. But, whose dowry? This is a future that is real, but one that is not mine: "a future *without-me*" (1998, 228). Levinas also describes it as "an awaiting, where nothing is awaited" (cited in Derrida 1999, 122).[11]

Putting this in another way, being for the other testifies to an understanding of life's meaning that transcends thinking about power, success, reward, whether these are taken in an everyday or "sophisticated" way. In giving to the other, one affirms that to be human requires a surpassing of mere existence. Levinas often utilizes the word "glory" to allude to this fugitive meaning. For him, glory, which is also an evocation of God's elusive presence, is immune to death, because it is "beyond [both] being and death" (1998, 147).

Erikson's statements about death contribute to this examination in two ways. They reflect his view of human development that recognizes the importance of the social component, but still takes the individual ego as central. They also delineate an important connection between communal violence and the refusal to face death. For Erikson, the serious encounter with the inevitability of one's own death is an essential criterion of authenticity. For example, the confrontation with death is a prominent feature of his definition of ego integrity, the last of the eight stages of psychosocial development. This integrity includes "the acceptance of one's one and only life cycle" and its absence is "signified by fear of death: the one and only life cycle is not accepted as the ultimate of life" (1963, 268–69). Erikson often finds that the lives of great religious persons illuminate the nature of ego integrity. Following this, he defines "religiosity" as the "consciousness of death, the love of all men as equally mortal" (1969, 194), and emphasizes the importance of Mahatma Gandhi's "conscious nothingness" in the face of death (1969, 397). However, Erikson does not believe that integrity necessarily requires some heroic struggle with the consciousness of death. He speaks favorably of a "practical religiosity," which can "experience death as an intrinsic part of a boundless and boundlessly recreative life" (1969, 400).[12] Still, it is diagnostic of Erikson's non-relational narrative that the confrontation with death, rather than with the other, plays such a fundamental role in the definition of authenticity.

Erikson's reflections on the relationship between the failure to accept death and the individual's conceits about the permanence of his or her community center around his term "pseudo-species." When persons despair of the meaning of their lives and seek to escape from the terrifying judgment that death issues, they often turn to a faith in the ultimate or infinite meaning of their group. They believe that their community is fundamentally and ontologically different from all others, and this requires that they defend its interests with everything, including their lives. Erikson writes that in these cases "men hate other men 'mortally' in the hope of gaining a sense of immortality out of the vaingloriousness of their own pseudo-species" (1969, 194). In the book *Gandhi's Truth*, he contrasted the dangers of such perennial conceits to Gandhi's acceptance of the universal fact of death and thus the ultimate equality of all persons.

As has been evident throughout the various presentations of Klein's thought, death, as depicted in the death drive or instinct, is the initiating force and paramount factor in her narrative of psychological development. The death instinct expressed as an initial violence and aggression directed against the self engenders a fear of the death or annihilation of the organism. The response to this fear and its anxieties includes the processes and phantasies that have been discussed earlier. Klein's movement beyond Freud consists in the tremendous elaboration of the importance of the death drive and also in her insistence that it is tied to objects. Fear of death becomes fear of persecution. Initially it is experienced as the threat of persecution and destruction from the mother, both as outside object and as partial object, the bad breast within. Klein summarizes her insight in this way: "I hold that anxiety arises from the operation of the death instinct within the organism, is felt as fear of annihilation (death) and takes the form of fear of persecution" (1997, 4). In light of this understanding, the paradoxical conclusion by one critic that in Klein's narrative "the death instinct brings the child to life" appears justified.[13]

While the status of the infant's actual interaction with other persons, as against the phantasies tied to objects, remains open in Klein's account, it still can be said that the response to the death drive is also consistently relational. As long as a person is alive, this drive and its consequences continue to be extremely important factors in psychic life as well as in relations to others. It is partially eclipsed when the infant is able to mitigate its hate and fear with love and gratitude, the "life instinct," starting with the depressive position. Thus, relationships to others, in part stemming from experiences of others, provide the only possibility for reconciliation with death. As the self comes to integrate the death and life instincts, its hate and its love, it comes to accept death (1997, 245). Klein believes that this integration of the instincts and of the self heralds in a life of health and creativity.

Fairbairn's rejection of Freud's theory of the death instinct is diagnostic of his strong relational standpoint. He held that "What Freud describes under the category of 'death instincts' are for the most part masochistic relationships with internalized bad objects" (1986, 79). For Fairbairn, there was no constitutional instinct for violence or death, because bad objects and the parallel pieces of the ego related to them were caused by failures in the infant's earliest relationships. Unfulfilled desires for meaningful contact, which Fairbairn did see as intrinsic, led to split-off portions of the ego. What he terms the "internal saboteur" takes up some of the features that Freud attributed to the death drive. It is the repository of hatred, destructiveness, and rage. Its attacks are directed against both good internal objects and persons perceived in a positive light. The internal saboteur stands against whatever is seen as good and hopeful in others. Still, to some extent, bad objects can ultimately be released and the splits in the ego healed through positive relationships, in particular in therapy, that substitute for the earlier failures.

While a number of critics express reservations about Fairbairn's particular description of endopsychic processes and inner objects, he is helpful to our discussion in bringing forward a consistent relational view. Humans are motivated, first and foremost, to seek significant contact with other persons. Illness and violence arise when these quests are left unsatisfied. Discouragement can be so deep and harmful, that all hope for meaningful engagements with others is undermined. Finally, just as illness and destructiveness were attributed to relational experience, so was health. New encounters can transform the individual, reintegrating the ego and leading to new life and hope. Thus, although death and the fear of death are not directly considered within this context, other themes often tied to these clearly are represented in Fairbairn's narrative.

For Winnicott aggression and destructiveness, as well as the erotic and love, were innate expressions of life. Still, he rejected entirely the notion of a death instinct. In his view, if "*an anti-life factor*" existed in the infant, in opposition to its natural liveliness, this was to be attributed to the mother's depression (1965a, 192). However, the topic of death meant more for him than the issue of constitutional destructiveness. Winnicott believed that when supported by others and in touch with one's true self, a sense of meaning and creativity arose that did not pale in the face of death. He wrote: "the wholeness of personal integration brings with it the *possibility* and indeed the *certainty* of death—and with the acceptance of death there can come a great relief, relief from fear of the alternatives, such as disintegration . . ." (cited in Davis and Wallbridge 1981, 180). Thus, it appears that for Winnicott, a major constituent of a healthy and meaningful life was the ability to accept death. Meaning was also understood by him in a wider context. Through contact with cultural life, each person has a sense of his or her unique role as a bridge from one generation to the next.

In Irigaray's distinctive narrative of the interhuman, the topic of death and the death drives is juxtaposed against health. Humans have both a life-affirming drive for contact, exchange, and fertility and a drive for destruction, stasis, and immobility. Health is not a matter of rejecting death or ignoring its expressions, but of the acceptance and integration of its forces. For Irigaray, it is primarily through the exchanges between the sexes that persons arrive at a realistic understanding of themselves and are able to live creatively. However, this is not the nature of the present situation, as we have seen. At the present time, men only have relations with themselves, and with this all difference and otherness, as well as death, have been banished from their horizon. Women are denied the status of being fully human, of having their own autonomy and thus standing as true partners. They have come to represent death, and through mastering women, men sustain the illusion of overcoming its threat.

Irigaray describes this as an economy of the death drives (1985, 102). This corrupting economy now governs the unconscious (the imaginary) and linguistic (the symbolic) domains, as well as the social, political, and cultural realms. The respect for human life has been overwhelmed by the omnipresent desire for possession and control of things, nature, and other persons. There is social stasis, interrupted only by despairing outbreaks of violence. Once again, for her, the remedy begins by acknowledging sexual difference, and continues through to those relationships that she describes in terms of the amorous exchange. This path allows both men and women to rediscover their fullness and their limits. A precis of her overall position is well expressed by one of her major commentators: "The argument her work sets forth is that the symbolic division in which woman represents nature, the body, sexuality, the unthought, the unthinkable, castration, and death, cut off from the transcendental, in fact prevents life, mobility, and fertility *on both sides*" (Whitford 1991, 157).

Many of the narratives of the Jewish philosophers and the psychoanalysts draw a relationship between inauthentic ways of facing death and destructive forms of communal life. This insight is probably most explicit in Rosenzweig's work. In his view, modern nations seek to prevent their inevitable disappearance from history through violence and law. However, death cannot be cheated either by individuals or groups, for, in the end, only God is All and All. Eternity can be experienced, momentarily, when communities of diversity and inclusion seek to extend the divine love for the neighbor to everyone. Buber believed that in the modern period many groups claim a unique role in history, and have an unlimited view of their own power and right. In some ways this is an extension of individual and communal lives expressing the I-It direction. However, true meaning only arises when, abandoning a one-sided obsession with power and success, individuals and groups listen to a call of judgment and responsibility directed to them. As with Buber, Levinas does not explicitly tie together the failure to acknowledge death and false community. He does see a connection between inauthentic individual life—devoted to the self's desires and violent toward others—and the egoism of states that suppress or destroy those who cannot be homogenized into the same. While fundamentally suspicious about communal life, he does believe that the individual's ethical experience can be used to present a different model and to judge the state's discourse of rights, "justice," and the necessity of war.

Erikson's discussion of the "pseudo-species" articulately incorporates many of these elements. In an effort to escape the inevitability of death, persons hope to live on in communities that they believe will continue forever. Erikson, in harmony with his overall presentation of the stages, does not see the remedy to this emerging from the interhuman. Consciousness of human nothingness comes from the individual honestly facing death—although this is partially dependent upon receiving a sense of trust, identity, and purpose from others. Klein's descriptions of the paranoid-schizoid and depressive positions are helpful here. The first constellation, which directly expresses the death instinct, seeks to control and manipulate what cannot in paranoid fashion be identified with the good self. This attitude seems to conform quite well with the "real-politique" vision of relationships between countries and also with the racism often endemic within them. The depressive position represents an integration of death and life drives, which follows upon a concern and appreciation (gratitude) for the other. With Fairbairn and Winnicott, one can say, more generally, that hate-filled individual and communal attitudes toward the other result from unsatisfactory experiences with one's earliest caregivers. The remedy for this requires that new interpersonal relationships draw upon and reinforce the lost positive aspects of these earlier experiences. Irigaray is quite clear about the destructive consequences for the patriarchal societies of the West, which reject the reality of death through projecting their unconscious fears and unaccepted features upon women. The path to reorganize this economy is through the acceptance and welcoming of women's otherness. In all, sometimes explicitly and sometimes through pastiche, a perspicacious narrative about community, authenticity, and death can be identified in these streams of philosophers and psychoanalysts of the interhuman. They find that in establishing fulfilling relationships between persons, death can be acknowledged and the foundation for genuine lives as individuals and in community can commence.

The narratives of the Jewish philosophers and the psychoanalysts combine elements of tragedy and hope in their considerations of life, history, and death. Rosenzweig, Buber, and Levinas all present versions of that inner tension of homo duplex (fear of death/love of the neighbor; I-It/I-Thou; egoism/responsibility), and believe that to a large extent inner conflict is resolved through redemptive relations with others. However, for these philosophers the fundamental tension is between the individual, on one side, and society and history, on the other. They are, to say the least, very apprehensive about history. They recount similar narratives about the nature of history—oppression, violence, and war—and hold little possibility for this account to ever drastically change. The good only infrequently appears on this stage and, certainly, it does not last. However, persons also live in another dimension. Events of authentically interhuman and communal encounter that spring up in history are at the same time messianic or eschatological moments. These units of redemption endure; they are not lost in the ebbs and tides of history. Such moments accumulate and point, but, once again, this is not recorded in history as some evolution toward a final totality. Thus, the Jewish philosophers see a fundamental tension between these redemptive moments, created through being with others, and history. This vision of the interhuman, communal, and history is also tied to an understanding of death. Death cannot be escaped, but there is meaning despite death, and this meaning, and the hope that it nourishes, is what allows persons to fully live life.

Unsurprisingly the psychoanalysts have a different vocabulary and recognize a different tension. They are suspicious about society, usually finding that the individual with others is able to arrive at a level of authenticity beyond the possibilities of larger groups or society overall. The fundamental tensions they see in life occur within the individual and between intimate persons (dependence/limited autonomy). Life and death are drives. Correspondingly, whether living in society or in acknowledging death, the term health usually takes that place that the word meaning had in the discussions of the Jewish philosophers. Despite the tensions within and between persons that the psychoanalysts delineate, they speak about the possibilities of and paths toward health; and, in the end, they probably agree with Freud's definition of health in terms of creative working and loving. There is hope that some peace or integration can be realized despite the perennial threats of death drives and disintegration. Most significantly, they insist that the self's integration and creativity can only be achieved through relationships with other persons.

In seeming to go further, utilizing terms such as "God," "messianism" and "the kingdom," do the Jewish philosophical narratives not promise more than this: perhaps, even, too much? Many critics maintain that such terms with their corresponding illusory "hope for redemption," exemplify all religious perspectives. This view is well represented by Jane Flax. Flax believes that the term "God" or its equivalents is used to provide "transcendental guarantees or illusions of innocence" (1993, 146) along with hope in "a linear, progressive, or teleological view of history in which all suffering has a purpose and time only moves in one direction, toward the redemption of us all" (1993, 31). Is this the meaning of the "messianism" that hovers within the Jewish philosophical narratives? The omnipresence of the term "responsibility" in their narratives certainly counters the first claim. In fact, they hold that the goal of religious language is precisely to silence "natural" protestations about innocence, and to generate that responsibility for the other that is both discovered each moment and infinite. The philosophers also explicitly reject "linear, progressive, or teleological" views of history. They speak of a future, but one which "has no relationship at all to time" (Rosenzweig 1972, 224); this "awaiting, where nothing is awaited" (cited in Derrida 1999, 122). Equally, there is no accumulation or progression: "no content that could be preserved" (Buber

1970, 82). Finally, messianism does not represent some victory of the individual or group, for there is neither "mine" nor "ours" in this "future without-me" (Levinas 1998, 228).

Messianism is one of the names that these Jewish philosophers attach to a belief that the meaning of the interhuman is not erased, not aborted, by death. It stands for a divine promise that thus reinforces the significance of the life between persons and in communities. Whenever the neighbor is loved, life's excess is given witness. Wherever the stranger is upheld, God's glory is made present. More cannot be promised, but that much is not an illusion. Unrecorded by history, "beyond [both] being and death" (Levinas 1998, 147), those moments belong to that other register—that alternative narrative.

Notes

1. Alexander Altmann has a famous treatment of Rosenzweig's view of history, "Franz Rosenzweig on History" (Mendes-Flohr, ed., 1998, 124–37).

2. See Robert Gibbs' discussion of religious community in his *Why Ethics?* (178–209).

3. In addition to Buber's writings explored in this chapter, see Paul Mendes-Flohr's discussion of Buber's view of community in the context of Zionism in *A Land of Two Peoples* (3–33).

4. Levinas places this quote from the *Pensées* at the beginning of *Otherwise Than Being* (vii).

5. Levinas continually argues, as we will see, that the messianic does not refer to the self's permanence, to my "resurrection" (1998, 227).

6. Much of my treatment is dependent on C. Fred Alford's book *Melanie Klein and Critical Social Theory.*

7. See the introduction to Fairbairn's *Psychoanalytic Studies of the Personality*, and its reference to some relevant texts (xvi).

8. Greenberg and Mitchell use Isaiah Berlin's *Two Concepts of Liberty* as a major resource for their analysis. Charles Taylor's book *The Sources of the Self* provides an excellent historical account of the elements that contribute to the modern Western notion of the self.

9. Irigaray's interview with Helene Rouch in *Je, Tu, Nous*, allows her to focus on another paradigm, beyond the "amorous exchange," in exploring relationships. Irigaray finds that an actual relation between self and other, which exhibits both sameness and the respect for difference, can be located in the intra-uterine period. She writes of the "almost ethical character of the fetal relation," and that; "The placental economy is therefore an organized economy, one not in a state of fusion, which respects the one and the other" (1993, 41). For me, this is not a biological essentialism, but an attempt to plumb women's experience and imagination in order to offer a different view of the human—relational from the onset of life—and of later social relations.

10. The theme of "undeadness" is a major element in Eric Santner's discussion of Rosenzweig, in *On the Psychotheology of Everyday Life.*

11. This "future *without-me*" is how I read that famous quotation from Kafka that so fascinated Walter Benjamin, "Plenty of hope, but not for us."

12. For Erikson, this particular manner of acceptance "has an affinity to the experience of women" (1969, 400).

13. John Phillips, "The Fissure of Authority," in *Reading Melanie Klein* (Phillips and Stonebridge, eds., 1988, 163).

Bibliography

Alford, C. Fred. 1989. *Melanie Klein and Critical Social Theory: An Account of Politics, Art, and Reason Based on Her Psychoanalytic Theory.* New Haven, Conn.: Yale University Press.

Altmann, Alexander. 1973. *Moses Mendelssohn: A Biographical Study.* Philadelphia: Jewish Publication Society of America.

Benjamin, Jessica. 1998. *Shadow of the Other: Intersubjectivity and Gender in Psychoanalysis.* New York: Routledge.

Berlin, Isaiah. 1958. *Two Concepts of Liberty.* Oxford: Oxford University Press.

Bernasconi, Robert, and Simon Critchley, eds. 1991. *Re-Reading Levinas.* Bloomington: Indiana University Press.

Bernasconi, Robert, and David Wood, eds. 1988. *The Provocation of Levinas.* New York: Routledge.

Bowlby, John. 1986. "The Nature of the Child's Tie to His Mother." In *Essential Papers on Object Relations*, edited by Peter Buckley. New York: New York University Press.

Buber, Martin. 1958. *Paths in Utopia.* Boston: Macmillian.

———. 1961. *Two Types of Faith.* New York: Harper and Row.

———. 1965. *Between Man and Man.* New York: Macmillian.

———. 1965a. *The Knowledge of Man.* New York: Harper and Row.

———. 1970. *I and Thou.* Translated by Walter Kaufmann. New York: Charles Scribner's Sons.

———. 1973. "Hebrew Humanism." In *The Zionist Idea: A Historical Analysis and Reader*, edited by Arthur Hertzberg. New York: Atheneum.

———. 1991. *The Letters of Martin Buber: A Life of Dialogue.* Edited by Nahum Glatzer and Paul Mendes-Flohr. New York: Schocken Books.

Byrnes, Joseph. 1984. *The Psychology of Religion.* New York: Free Press.

Capps, Donald. 1997. *Men, Religion, and Melancholia: James, Otto, Jung, and Erikson.* New Haven, Conn.: Yale University Press.

Caputo, John D., and Michael Scanlon, eds. 1999. *God, the Gift and Postmodernism.* Bloomington: Indiana University Press.

Carrithers, Michael, Steven Collins, and Steven Lukes, eds. 1985. *The Category of the Person: Anthropology, Philosophy, History.* Cambridge: Cambridge University Press.

Casper, Bernhard. 1984. "Franz Rosenzweig's Criticism of Buber's *I and Thou.*" In *Martin Buber: A Centenary Volume,* edited by Haim Gordon and Jochanan Bloch. New York: Ktav.

Chalier, Catherine. 1991. "Ethics and the Feminine." In *Re-Reading Levinas,* edited by Robert Bernasconi and Simon Critchley. Bloomington: Indiana University Press.

Chanter, Tina. 1988. "Feminism and the Other." In *The Provocation of Levinas: Rethinking the Other,* edited by Robert Bernasconi and David Wood. London: Routledge.

———. 1991. "Antigone's Dilemma." In *Re-Reading Levinas,* edited by Robert Bernasconi and Simon Critchley. Bloomington: Indiana University Press.

———. 1995. *Ethics of Eros: Irigaray's Rewriting of the Philosophers.* New York: Routledge.

Chanter, Tina, ed. 2001. *Feminist Interpretations of Levinas.* University Park: Pennsylvania State University Press.

Cohen, Richard. 1992. "God in Levinas." *Journal of Jewish Thought and Philosophy,* vol. 1.

———. 1994. *Elevations: The Height of the Good in Rosenzweig and Levinas.* Chicago: University of Chicago Press.

Cohen, Richard, ed. 1987. *Face to Face with Levinas.* Albany: State University of New York Press.

Dallery, Arleen B., and Charles E. Scott, eds. 1989. *The Question of the Other: Essays in Contemporary Continental Philosophy.* Albany: State University of New York Press.

Davis, Madeleine, and David Wallbridge. 1981. *Boundary and Space: An Introduction to the Work of D. W. Winnicott.* New York: Brunner/Mazel Publishers.

Derrida, Jacques. 1978. *Writing and Difference.* Chicago: University of Chicago Press.

———. 1995. *The Gift of Death.* Chicago: University of Chicago Press.

———. 1999. *Adieu: To Emmanuel Levinas.* Stanford, Calif.: Stanford University Press.

DiCenso, James J. 1999. *The Other Freud: Religion, Culture, and Psychoanalysis.* London: Routledge.

Eagle, Morris N. 1987. *Recent Developments in Psychoanalysis: A Critical Evaluation.* Cambridge, Mass.: Harvard University Press.

Elliott, Anthony. 1994. *Psychoanalytic Theory: An Introduction.* Oxford: Blackwell Publishers.

Elliott, Anthony, ed. 1999. *Freud 2000.* New York: Routledge.

Erikson, Erik H. 1962. *Young Man Luther: A Study in Psychoanalysis and History.* New York: W. W. Norton.

———. 1963. *Childhood and Society.* New York: W. W. Norton.

———. 1964. *Insight and Responsibility: Lectures on the Ethical Implications of Psychoanalytic Insight.* New York: W. W. Norton.

———. 1968. *Identity, Youth and Crisis.* New York: W. W. Norton.

———. 1969. *Gandhi's Truth: On the Origins of Militant Nonviolence.* New York: W. W. Norton.

———. 1975. *Life History and the Historical Moment.* New York: W. W. Norton.

Esman, Aaron H., ed. 1990. *Essential Papers on Transference.* New York: New York University Press.

Fairbairn, W. R. D. 1986. "The Repression and the Return of Bad Objects (with Special Reference to the 'War Neuroses')." In *Essential Papers on Object Relations*, edited by Peter Buckley. New York: New York University Press.

———. 1986a. "A Revised Psychopathology of the Psychoses and Psychoneuroses." In *Essential Papers on Object Relations*, edited by Peter Buckley. New York: New York University Press.

———. 1994. *Psychoanalytic Studies of the Personality.* London: Routledge.

Flax, Jane. 1990. *Thinking Fragments: Psychoanalysis, Feminism, and Postmodernism in the Contemporary West.* Berkeley: University of California Press.

———. 1993. *Disputed Subjects: Essays on Psychoanalysis, Politics and Philosophy.* New York: Routledge.

Fraser, Nancy, and Sandra Lee Bartky, eds. 1992. *Revaluing French Feminism: Critical Essays on Difference, Agency, and Culture.* Bloomington: Indiana University Press.

Freud, Sigmund. 1948. *An Autobiographical Study.* London: Hogarth Press.

———. 1949. *An Outline of Psychoanalysis.* New York: W. W. Norton.

———. 1961. *Beyond the Pleasure Principle.* New York: W. W. Norton.

———. 1964. *The Future of an Illusion.* Garden City, N.Y.: Doubleday.

———. 1965. *New Introductory Lectures on Psychoanalysis.* New York: W. W. Norton.

———. 1969. *A General Introduction to Psychoanalysis.* New York: Simon and Schuster.

———. 1986. "On Narcissism: An Introduction." In *Essential Papers on Narcissism*, edited by Andrew Morrison. New York: New York University Press.

———. 1986a. "Three Essays on the Theory of Sexuality: I: The Sexual Abberations." In *Essential Papers on Object Relations*, edited by Peter Buckley. New York: New York University Press.

———. 1990. "Observations on Transference-Love." In *Essential Papers on Transference*, edited by Aaron Esman. New York: New York University Press.

Friedlander, Judith. 1990. *Vilna on the Seine: Jewish Intellectuals in France Since 1968.* New Haven, Conn.: Yale University Press.

Friedman, Maurice. 1956. *Martin Buber: The Life of Dialogue.* Chicago: University of Chicago Press.

Friedman, Maurice, ed. 1996. *Martin Buber and the Human Sciences.* Albany: State University of New York Press.

Galli, Barbara E. 1995. *Franz Rosenzweig and Jehuda Halevi: Translating, Translations, and Translators.* Montreal and Kingston: McGill-Queen's Press.

Gallop, Jane. 1985. *Reading Lacan.* Ithaca, N.Y.: Cornell University Press.

Gibbs, Robert. 1992. *Correlations in Rosenzweig and Levinas.* Princeton, N.J.: Princeton University Press.

———. 2000. *Why Ethics?: Signs of Responsibilities.* Princeton, N.J.: Princeton University Press.

Gordon, Haim, and Jochanan Bloch, eds. 1984. *Martin Buber: A Centenary Volume*. New York: Ktav.

Greenberg, Jay R., and Stephen A. Mitchell. 1983. *Object Relations in Psychoanalytic Theory*. Cambridge, Mass.: Harvard University Press.

Grosz, Elizabeth. 1990. *Jacques Lacan: A Feminist Introduction*. London: Routledge.

Guntrip, Harry. 1986. "My Experience of Analysis with Fairbairn and Winnicott (How Complete a Result Does Psycho-Analytic Therapy Achieve?)." In *Essential Papers on Object Relations*, edited by Peter Buckley. New York: New York University Press.

Guttmann, Julius. 1964. *Philosophies of Judaism*. London: Routledge & Kegan Paul.

Harasym, Sarah, ed. 1998. *Levinas and Lacan: The Missed Encounter*. Albany: State University of New York Press.

Hughes, Judith M. 1989. *Reshaping the Psychoanalytic Domain: The Work of Melanie Klein, W. R. D. Fairbairn, and D. W. Winnicott*. Berkeley: University of California Press.

Irigaray, Luce. 1985. *This Sex Which Is Not One*. Ithaca, N.Y.: Cornell University Press.

———. 1985a. *Speculum of the Other Woman*. Ithaca, N.Y.: Cornell University Press.

———. 1986. "The Fecundity of the Caress: A Reading of Levinas, *Totality and Infinity*, section IV, B, 'The Phenomenology of Eros.'" In *Face to Face with Levinas*, edited by Richard Cohen. Albany: State University of New York Press.

———. 1991. "Questions to Emmanuel Levinas: On the Divinity of Love." In *Re-Reading Levinas*, edited by Robert Bernasconi and Simon Critchley. Bloomington: Indiana University Press.

———. 1991a. "The Three *Genres*." In *The Irigaray Reader*, edited by Margaret Whitford. Cambridge, Mass.: Basil Blackwell.

———. 1991b. "Sexual Difference." In *The Irigaray Reader*, edited by Margaret Whitford. Cambridge, Mass.: Basil Blackwell.

———. 1993. *Je, Tu, Nous: Toward a Culture of Difference*. New York: Routledge.

James, William. 1958. *The Varieties of Religious Experience*. New York: Penguin Books.

Jones, James W. 1991. *Contemporary Psychoanalysis and Religion: Transference and Transcendence*. New Haven, Conn.: Yale University Press.

Katz, Claire Elise. 2003. *Levinas, Judaism, and the Feminine: The Silent Footsteps of Rebecca*. Bloomington: Indiana University Press.

Kepnes, Steven. 1992. *The Text As Thou*. Bloomington: Indiana University Press.

Kepnes, Steven, ed. 1996. *Interpreting Judaism in a Postmodern Age*. New York: New York University Press.

Kernberg, Otto. 1986. "Structural Derivatives of Object Relationships," in *Essential Papers on Object Relations*, edited by Peter Buckley. New York: New York University Press.

Kierkegaard, Søren. 1995. *Works of Love*. Princeton, N.J.: Princeton University Press.

Kirschner, Suzanne R. 1996. *The Religious and Romantic Origins of Psychoanalysis: Individuation and Integration in Post-Freudian Theory*. Cambridge: Cambridge University Press.

Klein, Melanie. 1986. "A Contribution to the Psychogenesis of Manic-Depressive States." In *Essential Papers on Object Relations*, edited by Peter Buckley. New York: New York University Press.

———. 1990. "The Origins of Transference." In *Essential Papers on Transference*, edited by Aaron Esman. New York: New York University Press.

———. 1997. *Envy and Gratitude: And Other Works 1946–1963*. London: Random House.

Komter, Aafke. 1996. *The Gift: An Interdisciplinary Perspective*. Amsterdam: Amsterdam University Press.

Lacan, Jacques. 1981. *The Four Fundamental Concepts of Psycho-Analysis*. New York: W. W. Norton.

Leavy, Stanley. 1988. *In the Image of God: A Psychoanalyst's View*. New Haven, Conn.: Yale University Press.

Levinas, Emmanuel. 1969. *Totality and Infinity: An Essay on Exteriority*. Pittsburgh: Duquesne University Press.

———. 1981. *Otherwise Than Being Or Beyond Essence*. Boston: Martinus Nijhoff.

———. 1983. "Franz Rosenzweig." *Midstream*, vol. 19, no. 9, November.

———. 1985. *Ethics and Infinity: Conversations with Philippe Nemo*. Pittsburgh: Duquesne University Press.

———. 1986. "Dialogue with Emmanuel Levinas." In *Face to Face with Levinas*, edited by Richard Cohen. New York: State University of New York Press.

———. 1987. *Time and the Other: And Additional Essays*. Pittsburgh: Duquesne University Press.

———. 1989. *The Levinas Reader*. Edited by Sean Hand. Oxford: Basil Blackwell.

———. 1990. *Difficult Freedom: Essays on Judaism*. Baltimore: Johns Hopkins University Press.

———. 1990a. *Nine Talmudic Readings*. Bloomington: Indiana University Press.

———. 1994. *Beyond the Verse: Talmudic Readings and Lectures*. Bloomington: Indiana University Press.

———. 1994a. *In the Time of the Nations*. Bloomington: Indiana University Press.

———. 1994b. *Outside the Subject*. Stanford, Calif.: Stanford University Press.

———. 1998. *Entre Nous: On Thinking-of-the-Other*. New York: Columbia University Press.

———. 1998a. *Of God Who Comes to Mind*. Stanford, Calif.: Stanford University Press.

Llewelyn, John. 1995. *Emmanuel Levinas: The Genealogy of Ethics*. London: Routledge.

Loewald, Hans W. 1986. "On the Therapeutic Action of Psycho-Analysis." In *Essential Papers on Object Relations*, edited by Peter Buckley. New York: New York University Press.

———. 2000. *The Essential Loewald: Collected Papers and Monographs*. Hagerstown, Md.: University Publishing Group.

Mahler, Margaret S. 1986. "On the First Three Subphases of the Separation-Individuation Process." In *Essential Papers on Object Relations*, edited by Peter Buckley. New York: New York University Press.

Mauss, Marcel. 1970. *The Gift: Forms and Functions of Exchange*. London: Routledge & Kegan Paul.

Mendes-Flohr, Paul, ed. 1983. *A Land of Two Peoples: Martin Buber on Jews and Arabs*. New York: Oxford University Press.

———. 1988. *The Philosophy of Franz Rosenzweig*. Hanover, N.H.: University Press of New England.

Mitchell, Stephen A. 1988. *Relational Concepts in Psychoanalysis: An Integration.* Cambridge, Mass.: Harvard University Press.
———. 1993. *Hope and Dread in Psychoanalysis.* New York: Basic Books.
———. 2000. *Relationality: From Attachment to Intersubjectivity.* Hillsdale, N.J.: The Analytic Press.
———. 2003. *Can Love Last? The Fate of Romance Over Time.* New York: W. W. Norton.
Mitchell, Stephen A., and Margaret J. Black. 1995. *Freud and Beyond: A History of Modern Psychoanalytic Thought.* New York: HarperCollins Publishers.
Mitchell, Stephen A., and Lewis Aron, eds. 1999. *Relational Psychoanalysis: The Emergence of a Tradition.* Hillsdale, N.J.: The Analytic Press.
Moi, Toril. 1987. *French Feminist Thought: A Reader.* Oxford: Basil Blackwall.
Morrison, Andrew P., ed. 1986. *Essential Papers on Narcissism.* New York: New York University Press.
Mosès, Stéphane. 1992. *System and Revelation: The Philosophy of Franz Rosenzweig.* Detroit: Wayne State University Press.
Ogden, Thomas H. 1994. *Subjects of Analysis.* Northvale, N.J.: Jason Aronson.
———. 1997. *The Matrix of the Mind: Object Relations and the Psychoanalytic Dialogue.* Northvale, N.J.: Jason Aronson.
Oppenheim, Michael. 1978. "Death and Man's Fear of Death in Franz Rosenzweig's *The Star of Redemption.*" *Judaism,* vol. 27, no. 4.
———. 1981. "The Meaning of Hasidut: Martin Buber and Gershom Scholem." *The Journal of the American Academy of Religion,* vol. 44, no. 3.
———. 1985. *What Does Revelation Mean for the Modern Jew? Rosenzweig, Buber, Fackenheim.* Lewiston, N.Y.: Edwin Mellen.
———. 1992. *Mutual Upholding: Fashioning Jewish Philosophy Through Letters.* New York: Peter Lang.
———. 1996. "Feminism, Jewish Philosophy, and Religious Pluralism." *Modern Judaism,* vol. 16, no. 2.
———. 1997. *Speaking/Writing of God: Jewish Philosophical Reflections on the Life with Others.* Albany: State University of New York Press.
———. 1999. "Four Narratives of the Interhuman: Kierkegaard, Buber, Rosenzweig, and Levinas." In *International Kierkegaard Commentary: Works of Love,* edited by Robert L. Perkins. Macon, Georgia: Mercer University Press.
Phillips, John, and Lyndsey Stonebridge, eds. 1988. *Reading Melanie Klein.* London: Routledge.
Ricoeur, Paul. 1970. *Freud and Philosophy.* New Haven, Conn.: Yale University Press.
Rieff, Philip. 1979. *Freud: The Mind of the Moralist.* Chicago: Chicago University Press.
Rorty, Richard. 1979. *Philosophy and the Mirror of Nature.* Princeton, N.J.: Princeton University Press.
———. 1987. "Pragmatism and Philosophy." In *After Philosophy: End or Transformation?,* edited by Kenneth Baynes, James Bohman, and Thomas McCarthy. Cambridge, Mass.: MIT Press.
———. 1999. *Philosophy and Social Hope.* London: Penguin Books.

Rosenzweig, Franz. 1937. "Zur Encyclopaedia Judaica: Zum Zweiten Band, Mit einer Anmerkung über Anthropomorphismus." In *Kleinere Schriften.* Berlin: Schocken Verlag.
———. 1965. *On Jewish Learning.* Edited by N. N. Glatzer. New York: Schocken Books.
———. 1970. *Franz Rosenzweig: His Life and Thought.* Edited by Nahum N. Glatzer. New York: Schocken Books.
———. 1972. *The Star of Redemption.* Boston: Beacon Press.
———. 1976–1984. *Franz Rosenzweig: Der Mensch und sein Werk: Gesammelte Schriften.* The Hague: Martinus Nijhoff.
———. 1995. *Jehuda Halevi.* In *Franz Rosenzweig and Jehuda Halevi: Translating, Translations, and Translators,* by Barbara E. Galli. Montreal and Kingston: McGill-Queen's Press.
———. 1998. *God, Man, and the World: Lectures and Essays.* Edited by Barbara E. Galli. Syracuse: Syracuse University Press.
———. 1999. *Franz Rosenzweig's "The New Thinking."* Edited by Alan Udoff and Barbara E. Galli. Syracuse, N.Y.: Syracuse University Press.
———. 1999a. *Understanding the Sick and the Healthy: A View of World, Man, and God.* Cambridge, Mass.: Harvard University Press.
Rustin, Michael. 1991. *The Good Society and the Inner World: Psychoanalysis, Politics and Culture.* London: Verso.
Santner, Eric L. 2001. *On the Psychotheology of Everyday Life: Reflections on Freud and Rosenzweig.* Chicago: The University of Chicago Press.
Schafer, Roy. 1976. *A New Language for Psychoanalysis.* New Haven, Conn.: Yale University Press.
———. 1992. *Retelling a Life: Narration and Dialogue in Psychoanalysis.* New York: HarperCollins Publishers.
———. 1997. *Tradition and Change in Psychoanalysis.* Madison, Conn.: International University Press.
Schilpp, Paul, and Maurice Friedman, eds. 1967. *The Philosophy of Martin Buber.* La Salle, Ill.: Open Court.
Scholem, Gershom. 1971. *The Messianic Idea in Judaism: And Other Essays on Jewish Spirituality.* New York: Schocken Books.
Shapiro, Susan E. 2003. "'And God Created Woman': Reading the Bible Otherwise." In *Levinas and Biblical Studies,* edited by Tamara Cohn Eskenazi, Gary Allen Phillips, and David Jobling. Atlanta: Society of Biblical Literature.
Skolnick, Neil J., and David E. Scharff, eds. 1998. *Fairbairn: Then and Now.* Hillsdale, N.J.: The Analytic Press.
Spence, Donald P. 1982. *Narrative Truth and Historical Truth: Meaning and Interpretation in Psychoanalysis.* New York: W. W. Norton.
Spilka, Bernard, and Daniel McIntosh, eds. 1997. *The Psychology of Religion: Theoretical Approaches.* Boulder, Colo.: Westview Press.
Stahmer, Harold. 1968. *"Speak that I may see Thee!"* New York: Macmillan.
Stern, Daniel N. 2000. *The Interpersonal World of the Infant: A View from Psychoanalysis and Developmental Psychology.* New York: Basic Books.

Taylor, Charles. 1989. *Sources of the Self: The Making of Modern Identity.* Cambridge, Mass.: Harvard University Press.

Taylor, Mark C. 1987. *Altarity.* Chicago: University of Chicago Press.

Tirosh-Rothschild, Hava. 1994. "'Dare to Know': Feminism and the Discipline of Jewish Philosophy." In *Feminist Perspectives on Jewish Studies*, edited by Lynn Davidman and Shelly Tenenbaum. New Haven, Conn.: Yale University Press.

Tracy, David. 1994. *Plurality and Ambiguity: Hermeneutics, Religion, Hope.* Chicago: University of Chicago Press.

Whitford, Margaret. 1991. *Luce Irigaray: Philosophy in the Feminine.* London: Routledge.

Whitford, Margaret, ed. 1991. *The Irigaray Reader.* Cambridge, Mass.: Basil Blackwell.

Winnicott, D. W. 1965. *The Family and Individual Development.* London: Tavistock Publications.

———. 1965a. *The Maturational Process and the Facilitating Environment: Studies in the Theory of Emotional Development.* London: Hogarth Press.

———. 1971. *Playing and Reality.* New York: Tavistock Publications.

———. 1986. "The Theory of the Parent-Infant Relationship." In *Essential Papers on Object Relations*, edited by Peter Buckley. New York: New York University Press.

———. 1986a. "Transitional Objects and Transitional Phenomena." In *Essential Papers on Object Relations*, edited by Peter Buckley. New York: New York University Press.

———. 1990. "On Transference." In *Essential Papers on Transference*, edited by Aaron Esman. New York: New York University Press.

Wyschogrod, Edith. 1972. "Emmanuel Levinas and the Problem of Religious Language." *The Thomist*, vol. 36, no. 1, January.

———. 1974. *Emmanuel Levinas: The Problem of Ethical Metaphysics.* The Hague: Martinus Nijhoff.

Index

About the Author

Michael Oppenheim is a professor in the Department of Religion at Concordia University in Montreal. His areas of teaching and research include modern Jewish philosophy, philosophy of religion, psychology of religion, feminism, and Judaism in the modern period. The present work extends his treatment of Jewish philosophy in *Speaking/Writing of God: Jewish Philosophical Reflections on the Life with Others* (1997) by examining post-Freudian psychoanalytic narratives about the self and others.